THE CIVIL RIGHTS MOVEMENT

OPPOSING VIEWPOINTS®

Other Books of Related Interest:

American History Series

The American Frontier
The American Revolution
The Bill of Rights
The Civil War
The Cold War
The Creation of the Constitution
The Great Depression
Immigration
Isolationism
Puritanism
Reconstruction
Slavery
The Women's Rights Movement

Opposing Viewpoints in American History

Volume I: From Colonial Times to Reconstruction
Volume II: From Reconstruction to the Present

Opposing Viewpoints Series

Race Relations
Interracial America

THE CIVIL RIGHTS MOVEMENT
OPPOSING VIEWPOINTS®

David L. Bender, *Publisher*
Bruno Leone, *Executive Editor*

William Dudley, *Series Editor*
John C. Chalberg, Ph.D., professor of history,
  Normandale Community College, *Consulting
  Editor*

William Dudley, *Book Editor*

Greenhaven Press, Inc.
San Diego, California

Cover photographs, clockwise from top: 1) Sign at bus station in Jackson, Mississippi, 1961 (Archive Photos); 2) Martin Luther King Jr. at the March on Washington, August 28, 1963 (Archive Photos); 3) W.E.B. Du Bois (Archive Photos); 4) Cesar Chavez (The George Meany Memorial Archives)

Library of Congress Cataloging-in-Publication Data

The civil rights movement : opposing viewpoints / William Dudley, book editor.
        p.   cm. — (American history series)
    Includes bibliographical references and index.
    ISBN 1-56510-369-6 (lib. bdg. : alk. paper) —
  ISBN 1-56510-368-8 (pbk. : alk. paper)
        1. Afro-Americans—Civil rights—History—20th century. 2. Civil rights movements—United States—History—20th century. I. Series: American history series (San Diego, Calif.).
    E185.61.C615   1996
    323.1'196073—dc20   95-48244
                                                                                              CIP

Contents

Chapter 1: Precursors of the Civil Rights Movement

Chapter 2: Desegregating the Schools

Chapter 3: Means and Goals of the Civil Rights Movement

Chapter 4: Debates on National Civil Rights Acts

Chapter 5: From Civil Rights to Black Power

Chapter 6: Two Historians Examine the Civil Rights Movement

Foreword

Aboard the *Arbella* as it lurched across the cold, gray Atlantic, John Winthrop was as calm as the waters surrounding him were wild. With the confidence of a leader, Winthrop gathered his Puritan companions around him. It was time to offer a sermon. England lay behind them, and years of strife and persecution for their religious beliefs were over, he said. But the Puritan abandonment of England, he reminded his followers, did not mean that England was beyond redemption. Winthrop wanted his followers to remember England even as they were leaving it behind. Their goal should be to create a new England, one far removed from the authority of the Anglican church and King Charles I. In Winthrop's words, their settlement in the New World ought to be "a city upon a hill," a just society for corrupt England to emulate.

A Chance to Start Over

One June 8, 1630, John Winthrop and his company of refugees had their first glimpse of what they came to call New England. High on the surrounding hills stood a welcoming band of fir trees whose fragrance drifted to the *Arbella* on a morning breeze. To Winthrop, the "smell off the shore [was] like the smell of a garden." This new world would, in fact, often be compared to the Garden of Eden. Here, John Winthrop would have his opportunity to start life over again. So would his family and his shipmates. So would all those who came after them. These victims of conflict in old England hoped to find peace in New England.

Winthrop, for one, had experienced much conflict in his life. As a Puritan, he was opposed to Catholicism and Anglicanism, both of which, he believed, were burdened by distracting rituals and distant hierarchies. A parliamentarian by conviction, he despised Charles I, who had spurned Parliament and created a private army to do his bidding. Winthrop believed in individual responsibility and fought against the loss of religious and political freedom. A gentleman landowner, he feared the rising economic power of a merchant class that seemed to value only money. Once Winthrop stepped aboard the *Arbella*, he hoped, these conflicts would not be a part of his American future.

Yet his Puritan religion told Winthrop that human beings are fallen creatures and that perfection, whether communal or individual, is unachievable on this earth. Therefore, he faced a paradox: On the one hand, his religion demanded that he attempt to live a perfect life in an imperfect world. On the other hand, it told him that he was destined to fail.

Soon after Winthrop disembarked from the *Arbella*, he came face-to-face with this maddening dilemma. He found himself presiding not over a utopia but over a colony caught up in disputes as troubling as any he had confronted in his English past. John Winthrop, it seems, was not the only Puritan with a dream of a heaven on earth. But others in the community saw the dream differently. They wanted greater political and religious freedom than their leader was prepared to grant. Often, Winthrop was able to handle this conflict diplomatically. For example, he expanded, participation in elections and allowed the voters of Massachusetts Bay greater power.

But religious conflict was another matter because it was grounded in competing visions of the Puritan utopia. In Roger Williams and Anne Hutchinson, two of his fellow colonists, John Winthrop faced rivals unprepared to accept his definition of the perfect community. To Williams, perfection demanded that he separate himself from the Puritan institutions in his community and create an even "purer" church. Winthrop, however, disagreed and exiled Williams to Rhode Island. Hutchinson presumed that she could interpret God's will without a minister. Again, Winthrop did not agree. Hutchinson was tried on charges of heresy, convicted, and banished from Massachusetts.

John Winthrop's Massachusetts colony was the first but far from the last American attempt to build a unified, peaceful community that, in the end, only provoked a discord. This glimpse at its history reveals what Winthrop confronted: the unavoidable presence of conflict in American life.

American Assumptions

From America's origins in the early seventeenth century, Americans have often held several interrelated assumptions about their country. First, people believe that to be American is to be free. Second, because Americans did not have to free themselves from feudal lords or an entrenched aristocracy, America has been seen as a perpetual haven from the troubles and disputes that are found in the Old World.

John Winthrop lived his life as though these assumptions were true. But the opposing viewpoints presented in the American History Series should reveal that for many Americans, these assumptions were and are myths. Indeed, for numerous Americans, liberty has not always been guaranteed, and disputes have been an integral, sometimes welcome part of their life.

The American landscape has been torn apart again and again by a great variety of clashes—theological, ideological, political, economic, geographical, and social. But such a landscape is not necessarily a hopelessly divided country. If the editors hope to prove anything during the course of this series, it is not that the United States has been destroyed by conflict but rather that it has been enlivened, enriched, and even strengthened by Americans who have disagreed with one another.

Thomas Jefferson was one of the least confrontational of Americans, but he boldly and irrevocably enriched American life with his individualistic views. Like John Winthrop before him, he had a notion of an American Eden. Like Winthrop, he offered a vision of a harmonious society. And like Winthrop, he not only became enmeshed in conflict but eventually presided over a people beset by it. But unlike Winthrop, Jefferson believed this Eden was not located in a specific community but in each individual American. His Declaration of Independence from Great Britain could also be read as a declaration of independence for each individual in American society.

Jefferson's Ideal

Jefferson's ideal world was composed of "yeoman farmers," each of whom was roughly equal to the others in society's eyes, each of whom was free from the restrictions of both government and fellow citizens. Throughout his life, Jefferson offered a continuing challenge to Americans: Advance individualism and equality or see the death of the American experiment. Jefferson believed that the strength of this experiment depended upon a society of autonomous individuals and a society without great gaps between rich and poor. His challenge to his fellow Americans to create—and sustain—such a society has itself produced both economic and political conflict.

A society whose guiding document is the Declaration of Independence is a society assured of the freedom to dream—and to disagree. We know that Jefferson hated conflict, both personal and political. His tendency was to avoid confrontations of any sort, to squirrel himself away and write rather than to stand up and speak his mind. It is only through his written words that we can grasp Jefferson's utopian dream of a society of independent farmers, all pursuing their private dreams and all leading lives of middling prosperity.

Jefferson, this man of wealth and intellect, lived an essentially happy private life. But his public life was much more troublesome. From the first rumblings of the American Revolution in the 1760s to the North-South skirmishes of the 1820s that ultimately produced the Civil War, Jefferson was at or near the center of American political history. The issues were almost too many—and too crucial—for one lifetime: Jefferson had to choose between supporting or rejecting the path of revolution. During and after the ensuing war, he was at the forefront of the battle for religious liberty. After endorsing the Constitution, he opposed the economic plans of Alexander Hamilton. At the end of the century, he fought the infamous Alien and Sedition Acts, which limited civil liberties. As president, he opposed the Federalist court, conspiracies to divide the union, and calls for a new war against England. Throughout his life, Thomas Jefferson, slaveholder, pondered the conflict between American freedom and American slavery. And from retirement at his Monticello retreat, he frowned at the rising spirit of commercialism he feared was dividing Americans and destroying his dream of American harmony.

No matter the issue, however, Thomas Jefferson invariably supported the rights of the individual. Worried as he was about the excesses of commercialism, he accepted them because his main concern was to live in a society where liberty and individualism could flourish. To Jefferson, Americans had to be free to worship as they desired. They also deserved to be free from an over-reaching government. To Jefferson, Americans should also be free to possess slaves.

Harmony, an Elusive Goal

Before reading the articles in this anthology, the editors ask readers to ponder the lives of John Winthrop and Thomas Jefferson. Each held a utopian vision, one based upon the demands of community and the other on the autonomy of the individual. Each dreamed of a country of perpetual new beginnings. Each found himself thrust into a position of leadership and found that conflict could not be avoided. Harmony, whether communal or individual, was a forever elusive goal.

The opposing visions of Winthrop and Jefferson have been at the heart of many differences among Americans from many backgrounds through the whole of American history. Moreover, their visions have provoked important responses that have helped shape American society, the American character, and many an American battle.

The editors of the American History Series have done extensive research to find representative opinions on the issues included in these volumes. They have found numerous outstanding opposing viewpoints from people of all times, classes, and genders in American history. From those, they have selected commentaries that best fit the nature and flavor of the period and topic under consideration. Every attempt was made to include the most important and relevant viewpoints in each chapter. Obviously, not every notable viewpoint could be included. Therefore, a selective, annotated bibliography has been provided at the end of each book to aid readers in seeking additional information.

The editors are confident that as this series reveals past conflicts, it will help revitalize the reader's views of the American present. In that spirit, the American History Series is dedicated to the proposition that American history is more complicated, more fascinating, and more troubling than John Winthrop or Thomas Jefferson ever dared to imagine.

John C. Chalberg
Consulting Editor

Introduction

"The civil rights movement brought America face to face with the gap between its egalitarian ideals and its racial realities."

On February 1, 1960, four black college students entered the Woolworth's store in downtown Greensboro, North Carolina. After purchasing a few items, they sat at the lunch counter to buy coffee. "I'm sorry," the white waitress told Ezell Blair Jr., Franklin McCain, Joseph McNeil, and David Richmond, "we don't serve coloreds in here." Blair replied politely that they had just been served when buying items at the store counters. The students remained seated until the store closed; meanwhile, the waitress ignored them, a black dishwasher scolded them for being "troublemakers," a white policeman stood stiffly behind them, unsure of what to do, and white customers reacted in various ways, some cursing, some praising the students' presence at the "white" lunch counter.

The next day they returned with twenty other students. The day after that the students filled sixty of the Woolworth's sixty-three seats. The "sit-in" attracted national news coverage. Within two months similar protests had spread to fifty-four cities in nine states, involving thousands of students and others. Reactions to the sit-in movement varied. Some students were expelled from college. Demonstrators were often cursed and abused by surrounding groups of whites; some protesters were arrested, and in some cases brutalized, by police. However, the movement also attracted the attention and sympathy of many. "It is in the American tradition to stand up for one's rights," stated Democratic presidential candidate John F. Kennedy, "even if the new way is to sit down." Ella Baker, a civil rights worker who helped organize a student conference in April 1960 to coordinate the growing sit-in movement, wrote in the *Southern Patriot*:

> The Student Leadership Conference made it crystal clear that current sit-ins and other demonstrations are concerned with some thing much bigger than a hamburger or even a giant-sized coke.

> Whatever may be the difference in approach to their goal, the Negro and white students, North and South, are seeking to rid America of the scourge of racial segregation and discrimination—not only at lunch counters, but in every aspect of life.

In reports, casual conversations, discussion groups, and speeches, the sense and the spirit of the following statement that appeared in the initial newsletter of the Students at Barber-Scotia College, Concord, N.C., were re-echoed time and again: "We want the world to know that we no longer accept the inferior position of second-class citizenship. We are willing to go to jail, be ridiculed, spat upon and even suffer physical violence to obtain First Class Citizenship."

By July 25, 1960, all Greensboro lunch counters had been desegregated. But the nonviolent protests the sit-in movement had helped to inspire were far from over. The years preceding and following the February 1960 Woolworth's confrontation span what is now known as the civil rights movement—the interracial campaign led by various organizations and individuals intent on achieving "First Class Citizenship" for African Americans. To understand both the causes and consequences of the seemingly simple request for coffee by the four college students in North Carolina, it is necessary to know something of the situation facing blacks in America at that time, almost a century after the abolition of slavery.

Blacks in America

In 1857 the Supreme Court ruled in *Dred Scott v. Sanford* that blacks (most of whom were then slaves) were not citizens of the United States and that neither the civil rights of citizenship as prescribed in the U.S. Constitution nor the Declaration of Independence's assertion that "all men are created equal" applied to them. Following the Civil War and the abolition of slavery in the United States, the Thirteenth, Fourteenth, and Fifteenth Amendments to the Constitution were adopted. These amendments, in theory, reversed the *Dred Scott* decision and made blacks free and equal citizens, with rights to due process of law and equal protection under the law. The Fifteenth Amendment specifically granted all black males the right to vote. Congress also passed in the 1860s and 1870s a series of legislative acts that granted blacks various civil rights, including the right to sue, to hold property, and to have equal access to public conveyances and accommodations. With federal troops on hand to enforce the voting rights of blacks, many African Americans in the South were elected to local and national government offices.

The gains of the Reconstruction Era proved temporary. By 1877 all federal troops had been withdrawn from the South. White politicians in the former slave states (where three out of four African Americans then lived) effectively circumvented the constitutional guarantees of civil rights for blacks, including the right to vote. In these endeavors the politicians were assisted by the

Supreme Court. In 1883 the high court ruled that the 1875 federal civil rights act guaranteeing equal access to hotels and other facilities that served the public was unconstitutional, arguing that such social rights were not within the proper jurisdiction of the federal government. In 1896, the Supreme Court ruled in *Plessy v. Ferguson* that a Louisiana law separating railroad passengers by race was constitutional, establishing the "separate but equal" doctrine that became the legal basis of southern race relations.

Between the end of Reconstruction and World War I whites in southern states enacted numerous state and local "Jim Crow" laws and customs that defined the place of "colored" people in southern life until the civil rights movement in the 1950s. Blacks were segregated in separate educational, medical, and recreational facilities that were seldom, by any measure, equal in quality to those available to whites. Blacks and whites swore on separate Bibles in southern courts and used separate elevators, drinking fountains, and toilets. In their social encounters blacks were expected to be deferential to all whites; "uppity" blacks were beaten and in some cases lynched. Between 1882 and 1920 more then three thousand black men and women were killed by lynch mobs, for reasons ranging from suspected sexual crimes against whites to being too successful in business or farming. Lynchings persisted into the civil rights era, as the 1955 Mississippi murders of Emmett Till (for whistling at a white woman) and George Lee (for registering to vote) attest.

Changing Conditions

By the middle of the twentieth century certain developments had begun to change the lot of blacks and to lay the foundation for the civil rights movement. Among those developments were the fruition of the work of the National Association for the Advancement of Colored People (NAACP), the migration of many blacks to northern cities, and World War II and its aftermath.

For five decades after its founding by blacks and whites in 1909, the NAACP was the foremost organization working for the civil rights of black Americans. It concentrated on working within America's legal system to attain civil rights for black people and on publicizing and lobbying for such legislative reforms as a federal anti-lynching law (which twice passed the House of Representatives in the 1930s only to die in the Senate). Its efforts helped lay the groundwork for a legal assault on Jim Crow.

While the NAACP was pursuing its work, many blacks tried to improve their lives by migrating north. Between 1910 and 1940 more than 1.75 million black Americans left the South, doubling the black population outside the region. Most escaped tenant farm situations to seek better-paying factory jobs. While still facing racial discrimination in many areas, including schools and housing, blacks who left the South did acquire rights of citizenship that they were previously denied, including suffrage. Armed with the vote, blacks in several northern cities, such as New York and Chicago, began to exercise a measure of political clout with both major parties, especially the Democratic Party.

World War II brought additional changes. Many blacks served in the military, although they did so in segregated units. In addition, after the threat of a massive black march on Washington compelled President Franklin D. Roosevelt to issue an executive order against racial discrimination in hiring defense workers, many African Americans found new employment in wartime industries. Their substantial contributions to the war effort lent moral justification to their claims to equality. In addition, Adolf Hitler's racist ideologies and the Holocaust that sprang from them caused many Americans to reexamine and reflect on the presence—and dangers—of racism in their own country.

Despite these developments, blacks, especially in the South, remained second-class citizens. At the middle of the twentieth century, blacks averaged only half the annual income and twice the poverty and unemployment rates of whites. And blacks in the South still lived under oppressive and segregated conditions.

Beginnings of the Civil Rights Movement

In the 1950s two important events captured the nation's attention and started a movement. They were the *Brown v. Board of Education* Supreme Court decision on May 17, 1954, and the Montgomery bus boycott, which began with the arrest of Rosa Parks on December 1, 1955.

In *Brown v. Board of Education* the U.S. Supreme Court directly reversed the *Plessy v. Ferguson* precedent, declaring that segregated schools were "inherently unequal." The decision suddenly removed the legal underpinning of racial segregation in the South. The NAACP lawyers who had argued on behalf of the black students seeking school integration were confident that they had struck a crippling blow against segregation. However, the immediate effect of the decision in many parts of the South was the growth of white resistance to school integration and civil rights progress. Historian Robert Weisbrot writes:

> Although some officials pledged to implement the law, headlines and thumping electoral victories went to those who vowed to defend segregation. District attorneys sought injunctions to prohibit NAACP branches from operating, and in Alabama they were entirely successful by 1957. The Ku Klux Klan, the White Citizens Council, and other fringe vehicles of racial hate experienced overnight revivals after the Court decision.

One of the most noteworthy instances of white resistance to school integration happened in Little Rock, Arkansas, on September 4, 1957. The state's governor, Orval Faubus, dispatched a unit of the National Guard to prevent nine black students from enrolling in a previously all-white high school. After a standoff of almost three weeks, President Dwight D. Eisenhower federalized the National Guard and ordered army units to escort the students to school.

Although the events at Little Rock were discouraging to many, both the *Brown* decision and white resistance to the ruling helped embolden the civil rights movement. Weisbrot writes:

> The clash at Little Rock sobered many blacks and whites who hoped that a purely legalistic approach might quickly and neatly dismantle Jim Crow patterns. Still, the *Brown* case exerted an impact on race relations far beyond the scant immediate changes in Southern schools. It provided a yardstick of color-blind justice against which Americans could measure their progress toward the ideal of equal opportunity. It also conferred a symbol of legitimacy on black activists, who prepared bolder assaults on segregation in the South.

One of the most significant and widely publicized of these assaults was the Montgomery bus boycott. On December 1, 1955, Rosa Parks of Montgomery, Alabama, refused to relinquish her seat to a white bus passenger. Her arrest for this action, which violated local segregation laws, inspired the black residents of that city to boycott the city bus service for a year. The boycott not only succeeded in crippling Montgomery's bus service, but it also demonstrated the unity and potential strength of the local black community. In conjunction with a legal appeal to the Supreme Court, the boycott ended racial segregation on the city's buses. It also thrust a young black minister, Martin Luther King Jr., into national prominence.

The Montgomery bus boycott marked the beginning of a new phase in the civil rights movement—the widespread emergence of nonviolent direct action. King, who in 1957 founded the Southern Christian Leadership Conference (SCLC) to work for civil rights, defended nonviolent civil disobedience as a way of generating "creative tension" within a community by forcing black and white citizens to "confront the issue" of racial injustice. His powerful words, as well as the peaceful behavior of the black boycotters of Montgomery, helped inspire the four college students to make their fateful request for coffee at Woolworth's a few years later.

The Student Nonviolent Coordinating Committee grew directly out of the sit-in movement. SNCC (pronounced "snick") coordinated sit-ins and other demonstrations and carefully trained its participants to endure abuse without resorting to violence. Later

SNCC programs concentrated on voter registration and education.

Notable nonviolent direct actions included the "Freedom Rides," sponsored by the Congress of Racial Equality (CORE), in which interracial groups traveled on interstate buses in defiance of local customs and laws. Other milestones included protest marches and demonstrations in Albany, Georgia, in 1961 and 1962, and the gathering of more than 200,000 people in Washington, D.C., in August 1963 to demand civil rights. Perhaps the most dramatic demonstrations took place in April 1963 in the highly segregated city of Birmingham, Alabama, when dogs and fire hoses were directed at the civil rights demonstrators, including children.

The civil rights movement operated on several levels between 1960 and 1965. One was the continuing legal and lobbying work aimed at the federal government. The lobbying of the NAACP helped gain the passage of civil rights acts in 1957, 1960, 1964, and 1965. These laws, of which the latter two were the most important, outlawed discrimination in public accommodations and employment and strengthened the federal government's authority to investigate and enforce civil rights laws and to protect the rights of minorities to vote.

Related to the lobbying work was the civil rights movement's success in focusing national attention on conditions in the South. For this effort television coverage was essential. Much of the campaign for civil rights took place within American homes as people watched on their television sets the brutal treatment of nonviolent protesters by police in places such as Birmingham and Selma, Alabama. The television images shocked the nation and galvanized public sympathy for the cause. Many Americans gravitated toward supporting the civil rights demonstrators because their stated demands usually involved something as basic as the right to buy coffee at Woolworth's, to ride integrated buses, to vote, or to peaceably assemble.

The debate on civil rights had an international dimension as well. In the early 1960s, many African nations won independence from colonial rule, inspiring large numbers of African Americans in their own struggle for freedom. In addition, the Cold War between the United States and the Soviet Union played an important role in the developing civil rights movement. Although some opponents attempted to discredit the civil rights movement by linking it with communism, many American leaders came to support the civil rights cause in order to compete with the Soviet Union for the favor of emerging nonwhite nations and to defend the United States against Soviet accusations that America was not truly a land of freedom and equality.

At the same time, many of the actions of the civil rights movement were local in nature. The civil rights movement, in fact, consisted of many movements and campaigns in different communities: a wade-in for integrated swimming pools, a class for teaching blacks how to fill out registration forms, a "Freedom School" to teach black youngsters about their heritage. In several instances tensions arose between local civil rights activists and national leaders such as King, who often had different goals: Local leaders wanted immediate and concrete results, while national leaders sought publicity for the cause and federal government action.

As important formal gains for civil rights were won, civil rights activists after 1965 increasingly focused on larger issues of social and economic equality for blacks. Some observers argued that the lives of many poorer blacks, especially ghetto residents outside the South, had been little affected by the civil rights movement's legislative achievements. As the movement turned to these broader goals, "villains" comparable to the abusive southern policeman or the Woolworth's waitress who refused to serve blacks were harder to identify and confront. In fighting against poverty, residential segregation, and de facto school segregation, civil rights activists found that expansive interracial support was harder to obtain, especially after urban riots broke out in Watts, Los Angeles, in August 1965, and other American cities over the next three summers.

Divisions within the civil rights movement's organizations, always present, became more evident in the mid-1960s. A growing number of blacks, including Malcolm X and Stokely Carmichael, questioned whether nonviolence could truly lead America to reform, repudiated integration, and spoke of leading the masses of the black ghettos through a "black revolution." Responding to criticisms from some black leaders and the possibilities of renewed urban violence, Martin Luther King Jr. made plans to rejuvenate and redefine the movement by stressing economic issues and uniting poor people of all races in new protests; his assassination on April 4, 1968, cut short his vision and, for many, marked the symbolic end of the civil rights movement.

While perhaps unfinished in its ultimate goal of racial equality, the civil rights movement did accomplish much. It essentially ended the Jim Crow system of official white supremacy—and black deference—in the South. It brought thousands of previously excluded blacks into the political process (the number of black elected officials increased from one hundred in 1965 to almost eight thousand in 1993). Finally, the civil rights movement brought America face to face with the gap between its egalitarian ideals and its racial realities—a gap that, many argue, still needs addressing today.

CHAPTER 1

Precursors of the Civil Rights Movement

Chapter Preface

The civil rights movement that captured America's attention in the 1950s and 1960s had roots in the experiences and protest activities of blacks in America in prior decades. Many of the most famous actions of the civil rights movement were anticipated by previous events. For example, the first organized "sit-ins," in which multiracial groups peacefully occupied and requested service in white-only sections of restaurants, were held in Chicago in 1943, seventeen years before similar actions by black students in the South gained national attention. Rosa Parks's famous refusal to relinquish a seat for a white bus passenger in 1955 was prefigured by the individual actions of others, including Ida Bell Wells-Barnett, who in 1887 was thrown off a train for sitting in a section reserved for whites (she successfully sued the railroad company for damages, but lost on appeal). The noted bus boycott staged by the black residents of Montgomery, Alabama, following Park's arrest was preceded by a similar protest boycott of the city's streetcars in the years 1900 to 1902.

In addition to specific protest activities, the debates within the black community during the civil rights movement can also be found in prior African American history. During the first half of the twentieth century numerous and varied organizations were formed by those concerned with the civil rights and general welfare of blacks. These organizations included the National Association for the Advancement of Colored People (NAACP), the Universal Negro Improvement Association (UNIA), and the Association of Southern Women for the Prevention of Lynching. The goals of these organizations were divergent and in some cases opposing. W.E.B. Du Bois and other members of the multiracial NAACP, for example, supported racial integration and sought full constitutional rights as citizens for African Americans. Other black leaders and organizations, such as Booker T. Washington of the Tuskegee Institute and Marcus Garvey of the UNIA, sought to improve the place of blacks in American society through education and economic self-sufficiency rather than through political action for civil rights. These differing ideas within the black community, a small sampling of which is found in this chapter, foreshadowed many of the debates about and within the civil rights movement in the 1950s and 1960s.

"The wisest among my race understand that the agitation of questions of social equality is the extremest folly."

The American Negro Should Not Agitate for Civil Rights

Booker T. Washington (1856–1915)

Booker T. Washington was the preeminent leader of black Americans from 1895 to 1915—years marked by the growth of "Jim Crow" laws and other measures that disfranchised blacks and legalized racial segregation. A former slave who founded the Tuskegee Institute in Alabama, a vocational institute for blacks, Washington eventually became a leader of a network of black newspapers, schools, and organizations, and an unofficial adviser on race issues to Presidents Theodore Roosevelt and William H. Taft. Washington's rise to national prominence began with his address at the 1895 Atlanta Exposition, reprinted here. Washington advocates a policy of accommodation on civil rights issues, arguing that blacks can assure a better future for themselves by concentrating on self-improvement through vocational education and work in agriculture and industry, than by trying to change discriminatory laws and customs through legal and political action.

Other black leaders, including W.E.B. Du Bois, criticized Washington's "Atlanta Compromise" as being too amenable to the deprivation of political and civil rights of blacks. Disputes over the relative importance of political action to secure civil rights and economic self-reliance continued to be a divisive issue within the black community as the twentieth century unfolded.

From Booker T. Washington's speech at the Atlanta Exposition, September 18, 1895.

Mr. President and Gentlemen of the Board of Directors and Citizens:

One-third of the population of the South is of the Negro race. No enterprise seeking the material, civil, or moral welfare of this section can disregard this element of our population and reach the highest success. I but convey to you, Mr. President and Directors, the sentiment of the masses of my race when I say that in no way have the value and manhood of the American Negro been more fittingly and generously recognized than by the managers of this magnificent exposition at every stage of its progress. It is a recognition that will do more to cement the friendship of the two races than any occurrence since the dawn of our freedom.

Not only this, but the opportunity here afforded will awaken among us a new era of industrial progress. Ignorant and inexperienced, it is not strange that in the first years of our new life we began at the top instead of at the bottom; that a seat in Congress or the state legislature was more sought than real estate or industrial skill; that the political convention or stump speaking had more attractions than starting a dairy farm or truck garden.

A ship lost at sea for many days suddenly sighted a friendly vessel. From the mast of the unfortunate vessel was seen a signal: "Water, water; we die of thirst!" The answer from the friendly vessel at once came back: "Cast down your bucket where you are." A second time the signal, "Water, water, send us water!" ran up from the distressed vessel, and was answered: "Cast down your bucket where you are." And a third and fourth signal for water was answered: "Cast down your bucket where you are." The captain of the distressed vessel, at last heeding the injunction, cast down his bucket, and it came up full of fresh, sparkling water from the mouth of the Amazon River.

To those of my race who depend on bettering their condition in a foreign land or who underestimate the importance of cultivating friendly relations with the Southern white man, who is their next-door neighbor, I would say: Cast down your bucket where you are; cast it down in making friends, in every manly way, of the people of all races by whom we are surrounded. Cast it down in agriculture, mechanics, in commerce, in domestic service, and in the professions. And in this connection it is well to bear in mind that whatever other sins the South may be called to bear, when it comes to business, pure and simple, it is in the South that the Negro is given a man's chance in the commercial world, and in nothing is this exposition more eloquent than in emphasizing this chance.

Our greatest danger is that, in the great leap from slavery to freedom, we may overlook the fact that the masses of us are to live by the productions of our hands and fail to keep in mind that we shall prosper in proportion as we learn to dignify and glorify common labor, and put brains and skill into the common occupations of life; shall prosper in proportion as we learn to draw the line between the superficial and the substantial, the ornamental gewgaws of life and the useful. No race can prosper till it learns that there is as much dignity in tilling a field as in writing a poem. It is at the bottom of life we must begin, and not at the top. Nor should we permit our grievances to overshadow our opportunities.

A Question for the Future

In his 1899 book The Future of the American Negro, *Booker T. Washington reiterates his beliefs in black education and self-improvement, and argues that political rights will eventually follow.*

To state in detail just what place the black man will occupy in the South as a citizen . . . is beyond the wisdom of any one. Much will depend upon the sense of justice which can be kept alive in the breast of the American people. Almost as much will depend upon the good sense of the Negro himself. That question, I confess, does not give me the most concern just now. The important and pressing question is, Will the Negro with his own help and that of his friends take advantage of the opportunities that now surround him? When he has done this, I believe that, speaking of his future in general terms, he will be treated with justice, will be given the protection of the law, and will be given the recognition in a large measure which his usefulness and ability warrant. If, fifty years ago, any one had predicted that the Negro would have received the recognition and honour which individuals have already received, he would have been laughed at as an idle dreamer. Time, patience, and constant achievement are great factors in the rise of a race. . . .

My own feeling is that the South will gradually reach the point where it will see the wisdom and the justice of enacting an educational or property qualification, or both, for voting, that shall be made to apply honestly to both races. The industrial development of the Negro in connection with education and Christian character will help to hasten this end. When this is done, we shall have a foundation, in my opinion, upon which to build a government that is honest and that will be in a high degree satisfactory to both races.

To those of the white race who look to the incoming of those of foreign birth and strange tongue and habits for the prosperity of the South, were I permitted I would repeat what I say to my own race, "Cast down your bucket where you are." Cast it down among the 8 million Negroes whose habits you know, whose fidelity and love you have tested in days when to have proved treacherous meant the ruin of your firesides. Cast down your bucket among these people who have, without strikes and labor wars, tilled your fields, cleared your forests, builded your railroads and cities, and brought forth treasures from the bowels of the earth and helped make possible this magnificent representation of the progress of the South. Casting down your bucket among my people, helping and encouraging them as you are doing on these grounds, and, with education of head, hand, and heart, you will find that they will buy your surplus land, make blossom the waste places in your fields, and run your factories.

While doing this, you can be sure in the future, as in the past, that you and your families will be surrounded by the most patient, faithful, law-abiding, and unresentful people that the world has seen. As we have proved our loyalty to you in the past, in nursing your children, watching by the sickbed of your mothers and fathers, and often following them with tear-dimmed eyes to their graves, so in the future, in our humble way, we shall stand by you with a devotion that no foreigner can approach, ready to lay down our lives, if need be, in defense of yours; interlacing our industrial, commercial, civil, and religious life with yours in a way that shall make the interests of both races one. In all things that are purely social we can be as separate as the fingers, yet one as the hand in all things essential to mutual progress.

Development for All

There is no defense or security for any of us except in the highest intelligence and development of all. If anywhere there are efforts tending to curtail the fullest growth of the Negro, let these efforts be turned into stimulating, encouraging, and making him the most useful and intelligent citizen. Effort or means so invested will pay a thousand percent interest. These efforts will be twice blessed—"blessing him that gives and him that takes."

There is no escape, through law of man or God, from the inevitable:

The laws of changeless justice bind
Oppressor with oppressed;
And close as sin and suffering joined
We march to fate abreast

Nearly 16 millions of hands will aid you in pulling the load upward, or they will pull against you the load downward. We shall constitute one-third and more of the ignorance and crime of the South, or one-third its intelligence and progress; we shall contribute one-third to the business and industrial prosperity of the South, or we shall prove a veritable body of death, stagnating, depressing, retarding every effort to advance the body politic.

Gentlemen of the exposition, as we present to you our humble effort at an exhibition of our progress, you must not expect overmuch. Starting thirty years ago with ownership here and there in a few quilts and pumpkins and chickens (gathered from miscellaneous sources), remember: the path that has led from these to the invention and production of agricultural implements, buggies, steam engines, newspapers, books, statuary, carving, paintings, the management of drugstores and banks, has not been trodden without contact with thorns and thistles. While we take pride in what we exhibit as a result of our independent efforts, we do not for a moment forget that our part in this exhibition would fall far short of your expectations but for the constant help that has come to our educational life, not only from the Southern states but especially from Northern philanthropists who have made their gifts a constant stream of blessing and encouragement.

Archive Photos

For two decades, Booker T. Washington was the most influential black voice in the United States.

The wisest among my race understand that the agitation of questions of social equality is the extremest folly, and that progress in the enjoyment of all the privileges that will come to us must be the result of severe and constant struggle rather than of artificial forcing. No race that has anything to contribute to the markets of the world is long in any degree ostracized. It is important and right that all privileges of the law be ours, but it is vastly more important that we be prepared for the exercise of these privileges. The opportunity to earn a dollar in a factory just now is worth infinitely more than the opportunity to spend a dollar in an opera house.

A Pledge to Cooperate

In conclusion, may I repeat that nothing in thirty years has given us more hope and encouragement and drawn us so near to you of the white race as this opportunity offered by the exposition; and here bending, as it were, over the altar that represents the results of the struggles of your race and mine, both starting practically empty-handed three decades ago, I pledge that, in your effort to work out the great and intricate problem which God has laid at the doors of the South, you shall have at all times the patient, sympathetic help of my race; only let this be constantly in mind that, while from representations in these buildings of the product of field, of forest, of mine, of factory, letters, and art, much good will come—yet far above and beyond material benefits will be that higher good, that let us pray God will come, in a blotting out of sectional differences and racial animosities and suspicions, in a determination to administer absolute justice, in a willing obedience among all classes to the mandates of law. This, coupled with our material prosperity, will bring into our beloved South a new heaven and a new earth.

VIEWPOINT 2

"By every civilized and peaceful method we must strive for the rights which the world accords to men."

The American Negro Should Strive for Civil Rights

W.E.B. Du Bois (1868–1963)

The long public career of writer, scholar, and civil rights activist W.E.B. Du Bois spanned from the end of the nineteenth century to the height of the civil rights movement in the early 1960s. The first African American to receive a doctorate from Harvard (in 1895), Du Bois gained acclaim for his book *The Souls of Black Folk*, published in 1903. In the part of the book excerpted here, Du Bois criticizes black leader Booker T. Washington for abandoning the political struggle against racial segregation. Du Bois was the most prominent black public figure of his time to question Washington's ideas.

Du Bois and other blacks who shared his opinions met at Niagara Falls in 1905 and drafted a list of demands for black rights, including an end to segregation in courts and public accommodations. The Niagara Movement disbanded after a few years due to lack of financial support, but its work was continued by the National Association for the Advancement of Colored People (NAACP), an interracial organization founded by Du Bois and others in 1909 that strove to realize some of the political goals described in this viewpoint.

Excerpted from W.E.B. Du Bois, *The Souls of Black Folk*. (Chicago: A.C. McClurg, 1903).

Easily the most striking thing in the history of the American Negro since 1876 is the ascendancy of Mr. Booker T. Washington. It began at the time when war memories and ideals were rapidly passing; a day of astonishing commercial development was dawning; a sense of doubt and hesitation overtook the freedmen's sons,—then it was that his leading began. Mr. Washington came, with a single definite programme, at the psychological moment when the nation was a little ashamed of having bestowed so much sentiment on Negroes, and was concentrating its energies on Dollars. His programme of industrial education, conciliation of the South, and submission and silence as to civil and political rights, was not wholly original; the Free Negroes from 1830 up to wartime had striven to build industrial schools, and the American Missionary Association had from the first taught various trades; and [Joseph C.] Price and others had sought a way of honorable alliance with the best of the Southerners. But Mr. Washington first indissolubly linked these things; he put enthusiasm, unlimited energy, and perfect faith into this programme, and changed it from a by-path into a veritable Way of Life. And the tale of the methods by which he did this is a fascinating study of human life.

It startled the nation to hear a Negro advocating such a programme after many decades of bitter complaint: it startled and won the applause of the South, it interested and won the admiration of the North; and after a confused murmur of protest, it silenced if it did not convert the Negroes themselves.

Washington's Achievements

To gain the sympathy and coöperation of the various elements comprising the white South was Mr. Washington's first task; and this, at the time Tuskegee was founded, seemed, for a black man, well-nigh impossible. And yet ten years later it was done in the word spoken at Atlanta: "In all things purely social we can be as separate as the five fingers, and yet one as the hand in all things essential to mutual progress." This "Atlanta Compromise" is by all odds the most notable thing in Mr. Washington's career. The South interpreted it in different ways: the radicals received it as a complete surrender of the demand for civil and political equality; the conservatives, as a generously conceived working basis for mutual understanding. So both approved it, and to-day its author is certainly the most distinguished Southerner since Jefferson Davis, and the one with the largest personal following.

Next to this achievement comes Mr. Washington's work in gaining place and consideration in the North. Others less shrewd and tactful had formerly essayed to sit on these two stools and had fallen between them; but as Mr. Washington knew the heart of the South from birth and training, so by singular insight he intuitively grasped the spirit of the age which was dominating the North. And so thoroughly did he learn the speech and thought of triumphant commercialism, and the ideals of material prosperity, that the picture of a lone black boy poring over a French grammar amid the weeds and dirt of a neglected home soon seemed to him the acme of absurdities. One wonders what Socrates and St. Francis of Assisi would say to this.

And yet this very singleness of vision and thorough oneness with his age is a mark of the successful man. It is as though Nature must needs make men narrow in order to give them force. So Mr. Washington's cult has gained unquestioning followers, his work has wonderfully prospered, his friends are legion, and his enemies are confounded. To-day he stands as the one recognized spokesman of his ten million fellows, and one of the most notable figures in a nation of seventy millions. One hesitates, therefore, to criticise a life which, beginning with so little, has done so much. And yet the time is come when one may speak in all sincerity and utter courtesy of the mistakes and shortcomings of Mr. Washington's career, as well as of his triumphs, without being thought captious or envious, and without forgetting that it is easier to do ill than well in the world. . . .

Mr. Washington represents in Negro thought the old attitude of adjustment and submission; but adjustment at such a peculiar time as to make his programme unique. This is an age of unusual economic development, and Mr. Washington's programme naturally takes an economic cast, becoming a gospel of Work and Money to such an extent as apparently almost completely to overshadow the higher aims of life. Moreover, this is an age when the more advanced races are coming in closer contact with the less developed races, and the race-feeling is therefore intensified; and Mr. Washington's programme practically accepts the alleged inferiority of the Negro races. In our own land, the reaction from the sentiment of war time has given impetus to race-prejudice against Negroes, and Mr. Washington withdraws many of the high demands of Negroes as men and American citizens. In other periods of intensified prejudice all the Negro's tendency to self-assertion has been called forth; at this period a policy of submission is advocated. In the history of nearly all other races and peoples the doctrine preached at such crises has been that manly self-respect is worth more than lands and houses, and that a people who voluntarily surrender such respect, or cease striving for it, are not worth civilizing.

In answer to this, it has been claimed that the Negro can survive only through submission. Mr. Washington distinctly asks that black people give up, at least for the present, three things,—

First, political power,

Second, insistence on civil rights,

Third, higher education of Negro youth,—

and concentrate all their energies on industrial education, the accumulation of wealth, and the conciliation of the South. This policy has been courageously and insistently advocated for over fifteen years, and has been triumphant for perhaps ten years. As a result of this tender of the palm-branch, what has been the return? In these years there have occurred:

1. The disfranchisement of the Negro
2. The legal creation of a distinct status of civil inferiority for the Negro
3. The steady withdrawal of aid from institutions for the higher training of the Negro

These movements are not, to be sure, direct results of Mr. Washington's teachings; but his propaganda has, without a shadow of doubt, helped their speedier accomplishment. The question then comes: Is it possible, and probable, that nine millions of men can make effective progress in economic lines if they are deprived of political rights, made a servile caste, and allowed only the most meager chance for developing their exceptional men? If history and reason give any distinct answer to these questions, it is an emphatic *No.* And Mr. Washington thus faces the triple paradox of his career:

1. He is striving nobly to make Negro artisans business men and property-owners; but it is utterly impossible, under modern competitive methods, for workingmen and property-owners to defend their rights and exist without the right of suffrage.
2. He insists on thrift and self-respect, but at the same time counsels a silent submission to civic inferiority such as is bound to sap the manhood of any race in the long run.
3. He advocates common-school and industrial training, and depreciates institutions of higher learning; but neither the Negro common-schools, nor Tuskegee itself, could remain open a day were it not for teachers trained in Negro colleges, or trained by their graduates.

This triple paradox in Mr. Washington's position is the object of criticism by two classes of colored Americans. One class is spiritually descended from Toussaint the Savior [Haitian rebellion leader Toussaint L'Ouverture], through Gabriel, Vesey, and Turner [Gabriel Prosser, Denmark Vesey, Nat Turner], and they represent the attitude of revolt and revenge; they hate the white South blindly and distrust the white race generally, and so far as they agree on definite action, think that the Negro's only hope lies in emigration beyond the borders of the United States. And yet, by the irony of fate, nothing has more effectually made this programme seem hopeless than the recent course of the United States toward weaker and darker peoples in the West Indies, Hawaii, and the Philippines,—for where in the world may we go and be safe from lying and brute force?

The other class of Negroes who cannot agree with Mr. Washington has hitherto said little aloud. They deprecate the sight of scattered counsels, of internal disagreement; and especially they dislike making their just criticism of a useful and earnest man an excuse for a general discharge of venom from small-minded opponents. Nevertheless, the questions involved are so fundamental and serious that it is difficult to see how men like . . . Kelly Miller, J.W.E. Bowen, and other representatives of this group, can much longer be silent. Such men feel in conscience bound to ask of this nation three things:

1. The right to vote
2. Civic equality
3. The education of youth according to ability

They acknowledge Mr. Washington's invaluable service in counselling patience and courtesy in such demands; they do not ask that ignorant black men vote when ignorant whites are debarred, or that any reasonable restrictions in the suffrage should not be applied; they know that the low social level of the mass of the race is responsible for much discrimination against it, but they also know, and the nation knows, that relentless color-prejudice is more often a cause than a result of the Negro's degradation; they seek the abatement of this relic of barbarism, and not its systematic encouragement and pampering by all agencies of social power from the Associated Press to the Church of Christ. They advocate, with Mr. Washington, a broad system of Negro common schools supplemented by thorough industrial training; but they are surprised that a man of Mr. Washington's insight cannot see that no such educational system ever has rested or can rest on any other basis than that of the well-equipped college and university, and they insist that there is a demand for a few such institutions throughout the South to train the best of the Negro youth as teachers, professional men, and leaders.

This group of men honor Mr. Washington for his attitude of conciliation toward the white South; they accept the "Atlanta Compromise" in its broadest interpretation; they recognize, with him, many signs of promise, many men of high purpose and fair judgment, in this section; they know that no easy task has been laid upon a region already tottering under heavy burdens. But, nevertheless, they insist that the way to truth and right lies in

The Niagara Movement

The Niagara Movement grew out of a July 1905 meeting between W.E.B. Du Bois and other blacks dissatisfied with the leadership and ideas of Booker T. Washington. Excerpts from their "Declaration of Principles" are reprinted here.

The members of the conference, known as the Niagara Movement, . . . congratulate the Negro-Americans on certain undoubted evidences of progress in the last decade, particularly the increase of intelligence, the buying of property, the checking of crime, and uplift in home life, the advance in literature and art, and the demonstration of constructive and executive ability in the conduct of great religious, economic and educational institutions.

At the same time, we believe that this class of American citizens should protest emphatically and continually against the curtailment of their political rights. We believe in manhood suffrage; we believe that no man is so good, intelligent or wealthy as to be entrusted wholly with the welfare of his neighbor.

We believe also in protest against the curtailment of our civil rights. All American citizens have the right to equal treatment in places of public accommodation according to their behavior and deserts.

We especially complain against the denial of equal opportunities to us in economic life; in the rural districts of the South this amounts to peonage and virtual slavery; all over the South it tends to crush labor and small business enterprises; and everywhere American prejudice, helped often by iniquitous laws, is making it more difficult for Negro-Americans to earn a decent living. . . .

We protest against the "Jim Crow" car, since its effect is and must be, to make us pay first-class fare for third-class accommodations, render us open to insults and discomfort and to crucify wantonly our manhood, womanhood and self-respect. . . .

Of the above grievances we do not hesitate to complain, and to complain loudly and insistently. To ignore, overlook, or apologize for these wrongs is to prove ourselves unworthy of freedom. Persistent manly agitation is the way to liberty, and toward this goal the Niagara Movement has started and asks the co-operation of all men of all races.

straightforward honesty, not in indiscriminate flattery; in praising those of the South who do well and criticising uncompromisingly those who do ill; in taking advantage of the opportunities at hand and urging their fellows to do the same, but at the same time in remembering that only a firm adherence to their higher ideals and aspirations will ever keep those ideals within the realm of possibility. They do not expect that the free right to vote, to enjoy civic rights, and to be educated, will come in a moment; they do not expect to see the bias and prejudices of years disappear at the blast of a trumpet; but they are absolutely certain that the way for a people to gain their reasonable rights is not by voluntarily throwing them away and insisting that they do not want them; that the way for a people to gain respect is not by continually belittling and ridiculing themselves; that, on the contrary, Negroes must insist continually, in season and out of season, that voting is necessary to modern manhood, that color discrimination is barbarism, and that black boys need education as well as white boys.

Legitimate Demands

In failing thus to state plainly and unequivocally the legitimate demands of their people, even at the cost of opposing an honored leader, the thinking classes of American Negroes would shirk a heavy responsibility,—a responsibility to themselves, a responsibility to the struggling masses, a responsibility to the darker races of men whose future depends so largely on this American experiment, but especially a responsibility to this nation,—this common Fatherland. It is wrong to encourage a man or a people in evildoing; it is wrong to aid and abet a national crime simply because it is unpopular not to do so. The growing spirit of kindliness and reconciliation between the North and South after the frightful difference of a generation ago ought to be a source of deep congratulation to all, and especially to those whose mistreatment caused the war; but if that reconciliation is to be marked by the industrial slavery and civic death of those same black men, with permanent legislation into a position of inferiority, then those black men, if they are really men, are called upon by every consideration of patriotism and loyalty to oppose such a course by all civilized methods, even though such opposition involves disagreement with Mr. Booker T. Washington. We have no right to sit silently by while the inevitable seeds are sown for a harvest of disaster to our children, black and white.

First, it is the duty of black men to judge the South discriminatingly. The present generation of Southerners are not responsible for the past, and they should not be blindly hated or blamed for it. Furthermore, to no class is the indiscriminate endorsement of the recent course of the South toward Negroes more nauseating than to the best thought of the South. The South is not "solid"; it is a land in the ferment of social change, wherein forces of all kinds are fighting for supremacy; and to praise the ill the South is to-day perpetrating is just as wrong as to condemn the good. Discriminating and broad-minded criticism is what the South needs,—needs it for the sake of her own white sons and daughters, and for the insurance of robust, healthy mental and moral development.

To-day even the attitude of the Southern whites toward the

34

blacks is not, as so many assume, in all cases the same; the ignorant Southerner hates the Negro, the workingmen fear his competition, the money-makers wish to use him as a laborer, some of the educated see a menace in his upward development, while others—usually the sons of the masters—wish to help him to rise. National opinion has enabled this last class to maintain the Negro common schools, and to protect the Negro partially in property, life, and limb. Through the pressure of the money-makers, the Negro is in danger of being reduced to semi-slavery, especially in the country districts; the workingmen, and those of the educated who fear the Negro, have united to disfranchise him, and some have urged his deportation; while the passions of the ignorant are easily aroused to lynch and abuse any black man. To praise this intricate whirl of thought and prejudice is nonsense; to inveigh indiscriminately against "the South" is unjust; but to use the same breath in praising Governor [Charles B.] Aycock, exposing Senator [John T.] Morgan, arguing with Mr. Thomas Nelson Page, and denouncing Senator Ben Tillman, is not only sane, but the imperative duty of thinking black men.

Half-Truths

It would be unjust to Mr. Washington not to acknowledge that in several instances he has opposed movements in the South which were unjust to the Negro; he sent memorials to the Louisiana and Alabama constitutional conventions, he has spoken against lynching, and in other ways has openly or silently set his influence against sinister schemes and unfortunate happenings. Notwithstanding this, it is equally true to assert that on the whole the distinct impression left by Mr. Washington's propaganda is, first, that the South is justified in its present attitude toward the Negro because of the Negro's degradation; secondly, that the prime cause of the Negro's failure to rise more quickly is his wrong education in the past; and, thirdly, that his future rise depends primarily on his own efforts. Each of these propositions is a dangerous half-truth. The supplementary truths must never be lost sight of first, slavery and race-prejudice are potent if not sufficient causes of the Negro's position; second, industrial and common-school training were necessarily slow in planting because they had to await the black teachers trained by higher institutions,—it being extremely doubtful if any essentially different development was possible, and certainly a Tuskegee was unthinkable before 1880; and, third, while it is a great truth to say that the Negro must strive and strive mightily to help himself, it is equally true that unless his striving be not simply seconded, but rather aroused and encouraged, by the initiative of the richer and wiser environing group, he cannot hope for great success.

In his failure to realize and impress this last point, Mr. Washington is especially to be criticised. His doctrine has tended to make the whites, North and South, shift the burden of the Negro problem to the Negro's shoulders and stand aside as critical and rather pessimistic spectators; when in fact the burden belongs to the nation, and the hands of none of us are clean if we bend not our energies to righting these great wrongs.

The South ought to be led, by candid and honest criticism, to assert her better self and do her full duty to the race she has cruelly wronged and is still wronging. The North—her co-partner in guilt—cannot salve her conscience by plastering it with gold. We cannot settle this problem by diplomacy and suaveness, by "policy" alone. If worse comes to worst, can the moral fibre of this country survive the slow throttling and murder of nine millions of men?

The black men of America have a duty to perform, a duty stern and delicate,—a forward movement to oppose a part of the work of their greatest leader. So far as Mr. Washington preaches Thrift, Patience, and Industrial Training for the masses, we must hold up his hands and strive with him, rejoicing in his honors and glorying in the strength of this Joshua called of God and of man to lead the headless host. But so far as Mr. Washington apologizes for injustice, North or South, does not rightly value the privilege and duty of voting, belittles the emasculating effects of caste distinctions, and opposes the higher training and ambition of our brighter minds,—so far as he, the South, or the Nation, does this,—we must unceasingly and firmly oppose them. By every civilized and peaceful method we must strive for the rights which the world accords to men, clinging unwaveringly to those great words which the sons of the Fathers would fain forget: "We hold these truths to be self-evident: That all men are created equal; that they are endowed by their Creator with certain unalienable rights; that among these are life, liberty, and the pursuit of happiness."

VIEWPOINT 3

"At the mere words 'social equality' some white people froth at the mouth and some colored people grow panic stricken. There is no necessity for either action."

Blacks Should Press for Social Equality

James Weldon Johnson (1871–1938)

Disagreements within the black community over how to respond to inequality in America continued in the years immediately following Booker T. Washington's death in 1915. Two of the most influential organizations at that time were the National Association for the Advancement of Colored People (NAACP), founded in 1909 by a group of blacks and whites that included W.E.B. Du Bois, and the Universal Negro Improvement Association (UNIA), founded in 1914 in Jamaica by Marcus Garvey (the organization moved with Garvey to New York in 1916). The two organizations differed greatly in their organization and approach to race and civil rights issues and ultimately became bitter rivals. The NAACP, itself integrated in its membership, sought to advance racial integration and fight abuses against blacks in the American criminal justice and political systems by political lobbying, publicity, and litigation. The UNIA, based on the personal charisma of the Jamaican-born Garvey, preached black nationalism and the separate destiny of the black and white races. It was more successful than the NAACP in gaining a mass following of blacks.

The following viewpoint consists of a critique of Marcus Garvey by one of the leading civil rights activists of the period, James Weldon Johnson. Johnson, also a poet, diplomat, songwriter, and novelist, was an NAACP field secretary from 1916 to 1921 (during which time he expanded the organization's membership in the South) and the organization's first black executive secretary

James Weldon Johnson, "A Crime Against Nature," *Negro World*, October 1, 1921.

from 1921 to 1930. Johnson begins his article by quoting a statement Garvey made attacking NAACP member W.E.B. Du Bois (Garvey specifically mentioned the 1921 Pan-African Congress, a meeting of black leaders from America, Africa, Europe, and the West Indies that Du Bois helped to organize) and accusing Du Bois and his followers of promoting racial "amalgamation." Johnson decries the ideas of racial purity expressed in Garvey's statement and stresses the imperative for blacks to strive for social equality, which he defines as the free exercise of the rights of American citizenship, including the freedom of association.

Recently Mr. Marcus Garvey, president-general of the Universal Negro Improvement Association, was quoted in one of the daily papers as making the following statement:

> The Universal Negro Improvement Association stands in opposition to the Pan-African Congress and to the leadership of Dr. DuBois because they seek to bring about a destruction of the black and white races by the social amalgamation of both. The Dr. DuBois group believe that Negroes should settle down in communities of whites and by social contact and miscegenation bring about a new type. The Universal Negro Improvement Association believes that both races have separate and distinct social destinies; that each and every race should develop on its own social lines, and that any attempt to bring about the amalgamation of any two opposite races is a crime against nature.

This is a statement in which Mr. Garvey consciously or unconsciously plays to the most deep-seated prejudices of the white man in America. It is the very sort of thing that [Mississippi senator James K.] Vardaman, [South Carolina governor] Cole Blease and the rest of that ilk say and wish to have accepted. Does Mr. Garvey realize the full implication of his statement when he says that any attempt to bring about the amalgamation of any two opposite races is "a crime against nature"? Does he not see that a statement of this kind places the Negro in a position outside of the pale of the human race, somewhere between brute and man?

These are the exact words that have been used by men like Vardaman, who wish to infer that in any such relationship between the white and black races the white is guilty of something akin to bestiality. Furthermore, if such a relation between white and black were a crime against nature, the result of such relationship would be a monstrosity of sin. Is Mr. Garvey willing to say that Frederick Douglass and Booker T. Washington were such monstrosities?

If Mr. Garvey has the idea that the Negro, situated as he is in the United States, can fully duplicate the whole machinery of civilization, it is a sign of sheer simplicity.

Social Equality

When Mr. Garvey talks about social equality he should not do so in the loose manner in which Southern white people talk. He should say what he means by "social equality." If by "social equality" is meant the forcing of one's self into social intercourse with others, no self-respecting Negro wants it. But if by "social equality" is meant the right of the Negro to participate fully in all of the common rights of American citizenship and to arrange his own personal associations, wherever those associations are mutually agreeable, without being prohibited by any ban either of law or mob opinion, then no Negro can be self-respecting who does

A Lunatic or a Traitor

The dispute between W.E.B. Du Bois and Marcus Garvey included personal attacks. Excerpted below are passages from an editorial Du Bois wrote for Crisis *in May 1924.*

Marcus Garvey is, without doubt, the most dangerous enemy of the Negro race in America and in the world. He is either a lunatic or a traitor. He is sending all over this country tons of letters and pamphlets appealing to Congressmen, business men, philanthropists and educators to join him on a platform whose half concealed planks may be interpreted as follows:

That no person of Negro descent can ever hope to become an American citizen.

That forcible separation of the races and the banishment of Negroes to Africa is the only solution of the Negro problem.

That race war is sure to follow any attempt to realize the program of the N.A.A.C.P.

We would have refused to believe that any man of Negro descent could have fathered such a propaganda if the evidence did not lie before us in black and white signed by this man. . . .

From one of Garvey's articles we abstract one phrase:

"THE WHITE RACE CAN BEST HELP THE NEGRO BY TELLING HIM THE TRUTH, AND NOT BY FLATTERING HIM INTO BELIEVING THAT HE IS AS GOOD AS ANY WHITE MAN."

Not even Tom Dixon or Ben Tillman or the hatefulest enemies of the Negro have ever stooped to a more vicious campaign than Marcus Garvey, sane or insane, is carrying on. He is not attacking white prejudice, he is grovelling before it and applauding it; his only attack is on men of his own race who are striving for freedom; his only contempt is for Negroes; his only threats are for black blood.

not stand for it.

It is on the cry of "social equality" in the loose sense that Negroes are refused in public places, driven out of Pullman cars, herded in "jim crow" pens, stuck up in the front end of street cars, given inferior schools and subjected to a hundred other humiliations and injustices. The only sensible definition of social equality is: The right of any person to associate with any other person when the wish to do so is mutual.

Social equality in its strict sense should be a matter left entirely to individuals; but it is not. It is regulated by law and mob opinion. The Negro must either protest against such caste regulation or accept the position of self-acknowledged inferiority. At the mere words "social equality" some white people froth at the mouth and some colored people grow panic stricken. There is no necessity for either action. To the rabid whites we would say that there is no one in these United States so weak that he can be forced against his will to accept anybody's society. To the dissembling Negroes we would say that absolutely nothing is gained by letting the white man feel that we consider ourselves unfit for human association with the other groups in this country.

We assume that Mr. Garvey is working for equality of opportunity for the Negro (we are discussing the Negro in the United States), and we assume also that he has too much sense to think it can be achieved by attempting to substitute black domination for white domination. By what feasible plan does Mr. Garvey propose to secure it?

Cooperation Between White and Black

The only possible end of the race problem in the United States to which we can now look without despair is one which embraces the fullest co-operation between white and black in all the phases of national activity. If that end can be reached save through the recognition of all kinds of equalities, we should be glad to have Mr. Garvey tell us.

Of course, there may some day arise one or two or three great empires in Africa that will compel the recognition of the full rights of men of African blood everywhere. Or there may come sooner than expected the ultimate downfall of the white race. But, as Kipling would say, that is another story—in fact, a couple.

VIEWPOINT 4

"There is quite a difference between fighting for social equality and fighting for social justice."

Blacks Should Not Press for Social Equality

Marcus Garvey (1887–1940)

Marcus Garvey was the founder and leader of the Universal Negro Improvement Association (UNIA), which was for a time in the 1920s the largest black secular organization in the United States. The goals of the UNIA, whose membership included black residents in the Caribbean and Africa, were the promotion of race pride, independence for colonies in Africa, support for black business, economic and political self-determination (rather than integration) of black communities, and economic and political cooperation among blacks throughout the world. Garvey in his speeches also attacked black leaders such as W.E.B. Du Bois of the NAACP for advocating a "mixing" of the white and black races and called for the creation of a black nation in Africa, rather than an integrated America, as the ultimate destiny of America's blacks.

Garvey attracted many followers in America despite being criticized by Du Bois and other black leaders for advocating the separation of the black and white races in terms often similar to those used by whites arguing for racial "purity." The following viewpoint is taken from a newspaper essay in which Garvey responds to a printed attack by James Weldon Johnson, executive secretary

Marcus Garvey, "I Demand Social Justice," *Negro World*, October 1, 1921.

of the NAACP, for failing to work for social equality for blacks. Garvey argues that social justice and political power, rather than social equality and racial integration, should be the goals of blacks.

Garvey continued to be a major force in black America until 1925, when he was imprisoned on charges of mail fraud stemming from a failed shipping line the UNIA had established. He was deported to his native Jamaica in 1927.

It is for me to inform James Weldon Johnson that I mean every word stated in the paragraph quoted . . . .

In making this statement Johnson will therefore realize that I am conscious of the import of the paragraph. Mr. Johnson states that in my statement I am supporting "every sort of thing that Vardaman and Cole Blease and the rest of that ilk say and wish to have accepted." It is for me to inform Mr. Johnson that I do not give two rows of pins for Vardaman and Cole Blease; I am concerned with the destiny of the Negro. If Vardaman and Cole Blease happen to say things that can be interpreted to mean the same things I say in the interest of my race, then Mr. Johnson is welcome to the comparison.

Social Equality and Social Justice

I will not question Mr. Johnson's intelligence to ask him if he realizes the full import of what he states, because I am forced to accept Mr. Johnson as a leader of the Negro race, and therefore, must give him credit for the intelligence of his own statement. Mr. Johnson and I differ in that Mr. Johnson and his associates and probably co-workers hanker after social equality with white people. I demand social justice. There is quite a difference between fighting for social equality and fighting for social justice. I would like to see the man who would be able to compel me by law or otherwise to accept him as my companion if I did not care to do so. This is forcing the issue of social equality; but I demand from every man in the name of and by the law my constitutional right to go anywhere in the country of which I am a citizen. This is the difference between the Pan-African Congress, Dr. DuBois, Mr. Johnson and their followers, and the Universal Negro Improvement Association, the movement I represent.

Build Up the Race

If Negroes will stop making all this noise about social equality, giving the white people the idea that we are hankering after their company, and get down to business and build up a strong race, industrially, commercially, educationally and politically, everything social will come afterwards.

Social Equality a False Goal

In this excerpt from a speech reprinted in Philosophy and Opinions of Marcus Garvey *(published in 1925), Garvey contrasts his goals for American blacks with those of the NAACP and claims the support of black people.*

The time is opportune to regulate the relationship between both races. Let the Negro have a country of his own. Help him to return to his original home, Africa, and there give him the opportunity to climb from the lowest to the highest positions in a state of his own. If not, then the nation will have to hearken to the demand of the aggressive, "social equality" organization, known as the National Association for the Advancement of Colored People, of which W.E.B. Du Bois is leader, which declares vehemently for social and political equality, viz.: Negroes and whites in the same hotels, homes, residential districts, public and private places, a Negro as president, members of the Cabinet, Governors of States, Mayors of cities, and leaders of society in the United States. In this agitation, Du Bois is ably supported by the "Chicago Defender," a colored newspaper published in Chicago. This paper advocates Negroes in the Cabinet and Senate. All these, as everybody knows, are the Negroes' constitutional rights, but reason dictates that the masses of the white race will never stand by the ascendency of an opposite minority group to the favored positions in a government, society and industry that exist by the will of the majority, hence the demand of the Du Bois group of colored leaders will only lead, ultimately, to further disturbances in riots, lynching and mob rule. The only logical solution therefore, is to supply the Negro with opportunities and environments of his own, and there[by] point him to the fullness of his ambition. . . .

The masses of Negroes think differently from the self-appointed leaders of the race. The majority of Negro leaders are selfish, self-appointed and not elected by the people. The people desire freedom in a land of their own, while the colored politician desires office and social equality for himself in America, and that is why we are asking white America to help the masses to realize their objective.

It is human to be prejudiced, it has been so since creation, and it will be so until Gabriel blows his horn; and where you have a race of slave masters admitting into citizenship a race of slaves, you are not going to expect the race of slave masters to yield up to the race of slaves, equality in everything, until the race of slaves has brought itself up to the standard of the race of slave masters.

It is all tomfoolery talking about a better time is coming when the white man's heart will be softened toward the Negro and will accept him as a social equal. You are crazy if you think that time will ever come on this side of Jordan until the Negro, either in America or elsewhere builds himself up as a great power to force the recognition of the world.

Mr. Johnson well knows that I have no imputation against great men like Frederick Douglass and Booker T. Washington, but these men were brought into the world under unfortunate circumstances; they were brought into the world through bastardy, the rape of the one race upon the other, and the abuse and advantage of the mothers of the one race by the men of the other. Does Mr. Johnson want us to perpetuate that order of society by which we must bring in a race of illegitimates to be called in the future a race of bastards rather than for us to get among ourselves now and regulate the social order under which we should live? The difference between Mr. Johnson's policy and the Universal Negro Improvement Association's is that he believes that the only society for the Negro is that of the white man's. We believe to the contrary. We think that the black man's society is as good as that of any other race, and we are determined to build up a Negro society even superior to that of the whites. Therefore, we are not going to make any noise about social equality among white folks; we are going to use our time in building up a social standard among ourselves, and if Mr. Johnson and his followers will get off the subsidized pinnacle of looking to the white people for everything social and financial and depend upon the brawn, sinew, sweat and ability of the Negro, it will be better for him and those who follow.

Agitation Does Harm

Mr. Johnson defeats his own argument when he says that "it is on the cry of social equality that Negroes are refused in public places, driven out of Pullman cars, herded in Jim Crow pens, stuck up in the front end of street cars, given inferior schools, and subjected to a hundred other humiliations and injustices." This is just what we want to prove, and that is why we are demonstrating to the white race that we do not give a row of pins about social equality with them, because we believe in our own good company; whilst on the contrary Mr. Johnson is aggravating this question of social equality by always wanting to be with the white folks. Now, who is doing more harm to the Negro race, Mr. Johnson or I? Johnson will agitate between now and eternity and he will never get social equality with white people, until he gets down and by a hard day's work builds up a race independently and then demands justice through the strength of the race.

I am not going to waste time with Mr. Johnson and his associates waiting for white people to recognize me. I am going to put in all my time with my race and help to bring them to a standard where they will demand things and get them, and not beg and be refused.

I am glad Mr. Johnson admits that one day two or three great empires in Africa will arise. The Universal Negro Improvement Association has traveled a long way to get Mr. Johnson and his followers to admit this. Thank God, the hour is drawing near.

Viewpoint 5

"Negroes can build a mammoth machine of mass action . . . that can shatter and crush the evil fortress of race prejudice and hate."

Civil Rights Can Be Secured by Mass Action

A. Philip Randolph (1889–1979)

World War II brought great changes to blacks and to race relations in the United States. During the war nearly a million African Americans served in the military, and an additional 700,000 left the South to seek jobs in the defense industry. However, blacks faced much racial discrimination in both the armed forces and private industry. In 1941 A. Philip Randolph, a black labor organizer and president of the Brotherhood of Sleeping Car Porters, conceived of the idea to organize thousands of black demonstrators for a march on Washington, D.C., to demand equal opportunities for blacks in the military and in defense industries. The following viewpoint is taken from an article in the *Black Worker*, the official publication of the Brotherhood of Sleeping Car Porters, calling for African Americans to gather and march on Washington on July 1, 1941. Randolph argues that such a mass demonstration would build unity within the black community and would compel the federal government to act against racial discrimination.

The threat of such a march did persuade President Franklin D. Roosevelt to issue an executive order desegregating the defense industries and creating the Fair Employment Practices Commission to enforce this new policy, and Randolph agreed to call off the July 1 march. Randolph's ideas on mass demonstrations prefigured much of the thinking behind the later civil rights movement. He was one of the organizers of, and a speaker at, the 1963 March on Washington.

From A. Philip Randolph, "Call to Negro America to March on Washington for Jobs and Equal Participation in National Defense on July 1, 1941," *The Black Worker*, May 1941.

We call upon you to fight for jobs in National Defense.

We call upon you to struggle for the integration of Negroes in the armed forces, such as the Air Corps, Navy, Army and Marine Corps of the Nation.

We call upon you to demonstrate for the abolition of Jim-Crowism in all Government departments and defense employment.

An Hour of Crisis

This is an hour of crisis. It is a crisis of democracy. It is a crisis of minority groups. It is a crisis of Negro Americans.

What is this crisis?

To American Negroes, it is the denial of jobs in Government defense projects. It is racial discrimination in Government departments. It is widespread Jim-Crowism in the armed forces of the Nation.

While billions of the taxpayers' money are being spent for war weapons, Negro workers are being turned away from the gates of factories, mines and mills—being flatly told, "NOTHING DOING." Some employers refuse to give Negroes jobs when they are without "union cards," and some unions refuse Negro workers union cards when they are "without jobs."

What shall we do?

What a dilemma!

What a runaround!

What a disgrace!

What a blow below the belt!

'Though dark, doubtful and discouraging, all is not lost, all is not hopeless. 'Though battered and bruised, we are not beaten, broken or bewildered.

Verily, the Negroes' deepest disappointments and direst defeats, their tragic trials and outrageous oppressions in these dreadful days of destruction and disaster to democracy and freedom, and the rights of minority peoples, and the dignity and independence of the human spirit, is the Negroes' greatest opportunity to rise to the highest heights of struggle for freedom and justice in Government, in industry, in labor unions, education, social service, religion and culture.

Self-Liberation

With faith and confidence of the Negro people in their own power for self-liberation, Negroes can break down the barriers of discrimination against employment in National Defense. Negroes can kill the deadly serpent of race hatred in the Army, Navy, Air and Marine Corps, and smash through and blast the Government, business and labor-union red tape to win the right to equal opportunity in vocational training and re-training in defense employment.

Most important and vital to all, Negroes, by the mobilization and coordination of their mass power, can cause PRESIDENT ROOSEVELT TO ISSUE AN EXECUTIVE ORDER ABOLISHING DISCRIMINATIONS IN ALL GOVERNMENT DEPARTMENTS, ARMY, NAVY, AIR CORPS AND NATIONAL DEFENSE JOBS.

Of course, the task is not easy. In very truth, it is big, tremendous and difficult.

It will cost money.

It will require sacrifice.

It will tax the Negroes' courage, determination and will to struggle. But we can, must and will triumph.

The Negroes' stake in national defense is big. It consists of jobs, thousands of jobs. It may represent millions, yes, hundreds of millions of dollars in wages. It consists of new industrial opportunities and hope. This is worth fighting for.

But to win our stakes, it will require an "all-out," bold and total effort and demonstration of colossal proportions.

Negroes can build a mammoth machine of mass action with a terrific and tremendous driving and striking power that can shatter and crush the evil fortress of race prejudice and hate, if they will only resolve to do so and never stop, until victory comes.

Dear fellow Negro Americans, be not dismayed in these terrible times. You possess power, great power. Our problem is to harness and hitch it up for action on the broadest, daring and most gigantic scale.

Aggressive Mass Action

In this period of power politics, nothing counts but pressure, more pressure, and still more pressure, through the tactic and strategy of broad, organized, aggressive mass action behind the vital and important issues of the Negro. To this end, we propose that ten thousand Negroes MARCH ON WASHINGTON FOR JOBS IN NATIONAL DEFENSE AND EQUAL INTEGRATION IN THE FIGHTING FORCES OF THE UNITED STATES.

An "all-out" thundering march on Washington, ending in a monster and huge demonstration at Lincoln's Monument will shake up white America.

It will shake up official Washington.

It will give encouragement to our white friends to fight all the harder by our side, with us, for our righteous cause.

It will gain respect for the Negro people.

It will create a new sense of self-respect among Negroes.

But what of national unity?

We believe in national unity which recognizes equal opportunity of black and white citizens to jobs in national defense and the armed forces, and in all other institutions and endeavors in America. We condemn all dictatorships, Fascist, Nazi and Communist. We are loyal, patriotic Americans, all.

An All-Negro Movement

A. Philip Randolph was criticized by some for excluding whites from his proposed march on Washington. In a September 1942 speech he explains why he believes the march should be an all-black affair.

While the March on Washington Movement may find it advisable to form a citizens committee of friendly white citizens to give moral support to a fight against the Poll tax or white primaries, it does not imply that these white citizens or citizens of any racial group should be taken into the March on Washington Movement as members. The essential value of an all-Negro movement such as the March on Washington is that it helps to create faith by Negroes in Negroes. It develops a sense of self-reliance with Negroes depending on Negroes in vital matters. It helps to break down the slave psychology and inferiority-complex in Negroes which comes and is nourished with Negroes relying on white people for direction and support. This inevitably happens in mixed organizations that are supposed to be in the interest of the Negro.

But, if American democracy will not defend its defenders; if American democracy will not protect its protectors; if American democracy will not give jobs to its toilers because of race or color; if American democracy will not insure equality of opportunity, freedom and justice to its citizens, black and white, it is a hollow mockery and belies the principles for which it is supposed to stand.

To the hard, difficult and trying problem of securing equal participation in national defense, we summon all Negro Americans to march on Washington. We summon Negro Americans to form committees in various cities to recruit and register marchers and raise funds through the sale of buttons and other legitimate means for the expenses of marchers to Washington by buses, train, private automobiles, trucks, and on foot.

We summon Negro Americans to stage marches on their City Halls and Councils in their respective cities and urge them to memorialize the President to issue an executive order to abolish discrimination in the Government and national defense.

However, we sternly counsel against violence and ill-considered and intemperate action and the abuse of power. Mass power, like physical power, when misdirected is more harmful than helpful.

We summon you to mass action that is orderly and lawful, but aggressive and militant, for justice, equality and freedom.

Crispus Attucks marched and died as a martyr for American independence. Nat Turner, Denmark Vesey, Gabriel Prosser, Harriet Tubman and Frederick Douglass fought, bled and died for the emancipation of Negro slaves and the preservation of American democracy.

Abraham Lincoln, in times of the grave emergency of the Civil War, issued the Proclamation of Emancipation for the freedom of Negro slaves and the preservation of American democracy.

Freedom from Stigma

Today, we call upon President Roosevelt, a great humanitarian and idealist, to follow in the footsteps of his noble and illustrious predecessor and take the second decisive step in this world and national emergency and free American Negro citizens of the stigma, humiliation and insult of discrimination and Jim-Crowism in Government departments and national defense.

The Federal Government cannot with clear conscience call upon private industry and labor unions to abolish discrimination based upon race and color as long as it practices discrimination itself against Negro Americans.

VIEWPOINT 6

"The attack on discrimination by use of legal machinery has only scratched the surface."

Civil Rights Can Be Secured by Legal Action

Thurgood Marshall (1908–1993)

During World War II, while black leaders such as A. Philip Randolph were advocating mass protest demonstrations of blacks, the National Association for the Advancement of Colored People (NAACP) was continuing its work against racial discrimination through legal channels. A key figure of this campaign was Thurgood Marshall. As chief counsel for the NAACP from 1938 to 1961, he argued thirty-two cases before the Supreme Court, and won twenty-nine of them. Among these cases were *Smith v. Allwright* in 1944, which won for blacks the right to vote in primary elections in Texas, and *Brown v. Board of Education* in 1954, which invalidated state-enforced racial segregation in public schools. Marshall later was appointed to the Supreme Court as its first black justice.

In the following viewpoint, taken from a 1944 address before a special wartime conference of the NAACP, Marshall explains the legal strategies of the NAACP and the philosophy behind them. He describes the legal basis of the civil rights of Americans, including blacks (which rested on a far smaller body of law in 1944 than in the present), and he calls for action to ensure that existing civil rights laws be enforced and that new laws be passed.

From Thurgood Marshall, "The Legal Attack to Secure Civil Rights," speech delivered July 13, 1944, at the NAACP Wartime Conference. Reprinted by permission of the Estate of Thurgood Marshall.

The struggle for full citizenship rights can be speeded by enforcement of existing statutory provisions protecting our civil rights. The attack on discrimination by use of legal machinery has only scratched the surface. An understanding of the existing statutes protecting our civil rights is necessary if we are to work toward enforcement of these statutes.

Defining Civil Rights

The titles "civil rights" and "civil liberties" have grown to include large numbers of subjects, some of which are properly included under these titles and others which should not be included. One legal treatise has defined the subject of civil rights as follows: "In its broadest sense, the term civil rights includes those rights which are the outgrowth of civilization, the existence and exercise of which necessarily follow from the rights that repose in the subjects of a country exercising self-government."

The Fourteenth and Fifteenth Amendments to the Constitution are prohibitions against action by the states and state officers violating civil rights. In addition to these provisions of the United States Constitution and a few others, there are several statutes of the United States which also attempt to protect the rights of individual citizens against private persons as well as public officers. Whether these provisions are included under the title of "civil rights" or "civil liberties" or any other subject is more or less unimportant as long as we bear in mind the provisions themselves.

All of the statutes, both federal and state, which protect the individual rights of Americans are important to Negroes as well as other citizens. Many of these provisions, however, are of peculiar significance to Negroes because of the fact that in many instances these statutes are the only protection to which Negroes can look for redress. It should also be pointed out that many officials of both state and federal governments are reluctant to protect the rights of Negroes. It is often difficult to enforce our rights when they are perfectly clear. It is practically impossible to secure enforcement of any of our rights if there is any doubt whatsoever as to whether or not a particular statute applies to the particular state of facts.

As to law enforcement itself, the rule as to most American citizens is that if there is any way possible to prosecute individuals who have willfully interfered with the rights of other individuals such prosecution is attempted. However, when the complaining party is a Negro, the rule is usually to look for any possible grounds for *not* prosecuting. It is therefore imperative that Negroes be thoroughly familiar with the rights guaranteed them by law in order that they may be in a position to insist that all of their fundamental rights as American citizens be protected.

The Thirteenth Amendment to the Constitution, abolishing slavery, the Fourteenth Amendment, prohibiting any action of state officials denying due process or the equal protection of its laws, and the Fifteenth Amendment, prohibiting discrimination by the states in voting are well-known to all of us. In addition to these provisions of the Constitution, there are the so-called Federal "Civil Rights Statutes" which include several Acts of Congress such as the Civil Rights Act and other statutes which have been amended from time to time and are now grouped together in several sections of the United States Code. The original Civil Rights Act was passed in Congress in 1866, but was vetoed by President Andrew Johnson the same year. It was, however, passed over the veto. It was reintroduced and passed in 1870 because there was some doubt as to its constitutionality, having been passed before the Fourteenth Amendment was ratified. The second bill has been construed several times and has been held constitutional by the United States Supreme Court, which in one case stated that "the plain objects of these statutes, as of the Constitution which authorized them, was to place the colored race, in respect to civil rights, upon a level with the whites. They made the rights and responsibilities, civil and criminal, of the two races exactly the same." (Virginia v. Rives, 100 U.S. 313 [1879])

The Thirteenth and Fourteenth and Fifteenth Amendments, along with the civil rights statutes, protect the following rights:

1. Slavery is abolished and peonage is punishable as a federal crime. (13th amendment)

2. All persons born or naturalized in the U.S. are citizens and no state shall make or enforce any law abridging their privileges or immunities, or deny them equal protection of the law. (14th amendment)

3. The right of citizens to vote cannot be abridged by the United States or by any state on account of race or color. (15th amendment)

4. All persons within the jurisdiction of the United States shall have the same right to enforce contracts, or sue, be parties, give evidence, and to the full and equal benefit of all laws and proceedings as is enjoyed by white citizens.

5. All persons shall be subject to like punishment, pains, penalties, taxes, licenses, and extractions of every kind, and to no other.

6. All citizens shall have the same right in every state and territory, as is enjoyed by white citizens to inherit, purchase, lease, sell, hold and convey property.

7. Every person who, under color of statutes, custom or usage,

subjects any citizen of the United States or person within the jurisdiction thereof to the deprivation of any rights, privileges, or immunities secured by the Constitution and laws is liable in an action at law, suit in equity, or other proper proceedings for redress.

8. Citizens possessing all other qualifications may not be disqualified from jury service in federal or state courts on account of race or color; any officer charged with the duty of selection or summoning of jurors who shall exclude citizens for reasons of race or color shall be guilty of a misdemeanor.

9. A conspiracy of two or more persons to deprive any person or class of persons of any rights guaranteed by constitution and laws is punishable as a crime and the conspirators are also liable in damages.

Most of these provisions only protect the citizen against wrongdoing by public officials, although the peonage statutes and one or two others protect against wrongs by private persons.

Despite the purposes of these Acts which the United States Supreme Court insisted in 1879 "made the rights and responsibilities, civil and criminal, of the two races exactly the same," the experience of all of us points to the fact that this purpose has not as yet been accomplished. There are several reasons for this. In the first place, in certain sections of this country, especially in the deep south, judges, prosecutors and members of grand and petit juries, have simply refused to follow the letter or spirit of these provisions. Very often it happens that although the judge and prosecutor are anxious to enforce the laws, members of the jury are reluctant to protect the rights of Negroes. A third reason is that many Negroes themselves for one reason or another hesitate to avail themselves of the protection afforded by the United States Constitution and statutes.

These statutes protecting our civil rights in several instances provide for both criminal and civil redress. Some are criminal only and others are for civil action only. Criminal prosecution for violation of the federal statutes can be obtained only through the United States Department of Justice.

Up through and including the administration of Attorney General Homer S. Cummings, Negroes were unable to persuade the U.S. Department of Justice to enforce any of the civil rights statutes where Negroes were the complaining parties. The NAACP and its staff made repeated requests and in many instances filed detailed statements and briefs requesting prosecution for lynch mobs, persons guilty of peonage and other apparent violations of the federal statutes. It was not until the [1939–1940] administration of Attorney General Frank Murphy that any substantial efforts were made to enforce the civil rights statutes as they apply to Negroes. Attorney General Murphy established a Civil Rights Section in the Department of Justice.

During the present [1944] administration of Attorney General Francis Biddle there have been several instances of prosecution of members of lynch mobs for the first time in the history of the United States Department of Justice. There have also been numerous successful prosecutions of persons guilty of peonage and slavery. However, other cases involving the question of the beating and killing of Negro soldiers by local police officers, the case involving the action of Sheriff Tip Hunter, of Brownsville, Tennessee, who killed at least one Negro citizen and forced several others to leave town, the several cases of refusal to permit qualified Negroes to vote, as well as other cases, have received the attention of the Department of Justice only to the extent of "investigating." Our civil rights as guaranteed by the federal statutes will never become a reality until the U.S. Department of Justice decides that it represents the entire United States and is not required to fear offending any section of the country which believes that it has the God-given right to be above the laws of the United States and the United States Supreme Court. . . .

There are, however, certain bright spots in the enforcement of the federal statutes. In addition to the lynching and peonage cases handled by the Washington office of the Department of Justice, there have been a few instances of courageous United States Attorneys in such places as Georgia who have vigorously prosecuted police officers who have used the power of their office as a cloak for beating up Negro citizens.

An Example of Civil Rights Enforcement

As a result of the recent decision in the Texas Primary Case [*Smith v. Allwright*], it is possible to use an example of criminal prosecution under the civil rights statutes by taking a typical case of the refusal to permit the Negroes to vote in the Democratic Primary elections. Let us see how a prosecution is started: In Waycross, Georgia, for example, we will suppose a Negro elector on July 4, 1944, went to the polls with his tax receipt and demanded to vote in the Democratic Primary. He should, of course, have witnesses with him. Let us also assume that the election officials refused to let him vote solely because of his race or color.

As a matter of law, the election officials violated a federal criminal law and are subject to fine and imprisonment. But how should the voter or the organized Negro citizens, or the local NAACP Branch go about trying to get the machinery of criminal justice in motion? Of course, the details of what happens must be put in writing and sworn to by the person who tried to vote and also by his witnesses. Then the matter must be placed before the

United States Attorney. This is the *federal* district attorney.

I wonder how many of the delegates here know who is the United States Attorney for their district, or even where his office is. Every Branch should know the United States Attorney for that area, even if a delegation goes in just to get acquainted and let him know that we expect him to enforce the civil rights laws with the same vigor as used in enforcing other criminal statutes.

But back to the voting case. The affidavits must be presented to the United States Attorney with a demand that he investigate and place the evidence before the Federal Grand Jury. At the same time copies of the affidavits and statements in the case should be sent to the National Office. We will see that they get to the Attorney General in Washington. I wish that I could guarantee you that the Attorney General would put pressure on local United States Attorneys who seem reluctant to prosecute. At least we can assure you that we will give the Attorney General no rest unless he gets behind these reluctant United States attorneys throughout the south.

There is no reason why a hundred clear cases of this sort should not be placed before the United States Attorneys and the Attorney General every year until the election officials discover that it is both wiser and safer to follow the United States laws than to violate them. It is up to us to see that these officials of the Department of Justice are called upon to act again and again wherever there are violations of the civil rights statutes. Unfortunately, there are plenty of such cases. It is equally unfortunate that there are not enough individuals and groups presenting these cases and demanding action.

Neglected Civil Rights Statutes

The responsibility for enforcement of the civil provisions of the civil rights statutes rests solely with the individual. In the past we have neglected to make full use of these statutes. Although they have been on the books since 1870, there were very few cases under these statutes until recent years. Whereas in the field of general law there are many, many precedents for all other types of action, there are very few precedents for the protection of civil liberties.

The most important of the civil rights provisions is the one which provides that "every person who, under color of any statute, ordinance, regulation, custom or usage of any state or territory, subjects or causes to be subjected any citizen of the United States or person within the jurisdiction thereof to the deprivation of any rights, privileges or immunities secured by the Constitution and laws shall be liable to the party injured in an action at law, suit in equity or other proper proceeding for redress." Under this statute any officer of a state, county or municipality who while acting in an official capacity, denies to any citizen or person within the state any of the rights guaranteed by the Constitution or laws is subject to a civil action. This statute has been used to equalize teachers' salaries and to obtain bus transportation for Negro schoolchildren. It can be used to attack *every* form of discrimination against Negroes by public school systems. . . .

The Federal Government's Duty

In a special message to Congress on February 2, 1948, President Harry S. Truman called for the passage of new civil rights legislation. Few of his proposals were approved by Congress.

Today, the American people enjoy more freedom and opportunity than ever before. Never in our history has there been better reason to hope for the complete realization of the ideals of liberty and equality. . . .

The Federal Government has a clear duty to see that Constitutional guarantees of individual liberties and of equal protection under the laws are not denied or abridged anywhere in our Union. That duty is shared by all three branches of the Government, but it can be fulfilled only if the Congress enacts modern, comprehensive civil rights laws, adequate to the needs of the day, and demonstrating our continuing faith in the free way of life.

This statute, along with other of the civil rights statutes, can be used to enforce the right to register and vote throughout the country. The threats of many of the bigots in the south to disregard the ruling of the Supreme Court of the United States in the recent Texas Primary decision has not intimidated a single person. The United States Supreme Court remains the highest court in this land. Election officials in states affected by this decision will either let Negroes vote in the Democratic Primaries, or they will be subjected to both criminal and civil prosecution under the civil rights statutes. In every state in the deep south Negroes have this year attempted to vote in the primary elections. Affidavits concerning the refusal to permit them to vote in Alabama, Florida and Georgia have already been sent to the United States Department of Justice. We will insist that these election officials be prosecuted and will also file civil suits against the guilty officials.

It can be seen from these examples that we have just begun to scratch the surface in the fight for full enforcement of these statutes. The NAACP can move no faster than the individuals who have been discriminated against. We only take up cases where we are requested to do so by persons who have been discriminated against.

Another crucial problem is the ever-present problem of segregation. Whereas the principle has been established by cases handled by the NAACP that neither states nor municipalities can pass ordinances segregating residences by race, the growing problem today is the problem of segregation by means of restrictive covenants, whereby private owners band together to prevent Negro occupancy of particular neighborhoods. Although this problem is particularly acute in Chicago, it is at the same time growing in intensity throughout the country. It has the full support of the real estate boards in the several cities, as well as most of the banks and other leading agencies. The legal attack on this problem has met with spotty success. In several instances restrictive covenants have been declared invalid because the neighborhood has changed, or for other reasons. Other cases have been lost. However, the NAACP is in the process of preparing a detailed memorandum and will establish procedure which will lead to an all-out legal attack on restrictive covenants. Whether or not this attack will be successful cannot be determined at this time. [Editor's note: In 1948 the Supreme Court in *Shelley v. Kraemer* ruled that racially restrictive covenants could not be legally enforced under the Constitution.]

The National Housing Agency and the Federal Public Housing Authority have established a policy of segregation in federal public housing projects. A test case has been filed in Detroit, Mich., and is still pending in the local federal courts. The Detroit situation is the same as in other sections of the country. Despite the fact that the Housing Authority and other agencies insist that they will maintain separate but equal facilities, it never develops that the separate facilities are equal in all respects. In Detroit separate projects were built and it developed that by the first of this year every single white family in the area eligible for public housing had been accommodated and there were still some 800 "white" units vacant with "no takers." At the same time there were some 45,000 Negroes inadequately housed and with no units open to them. This is the inevitable result of "separate but equal" treatment. . . .

State Laws

We should also be mindful of the several so-called civil rights statutes in the several states. There are civil rights acts in at least 18 states, all of which are in the north and middle west. These statutes are in California, Colorado, Connecticut, Illinois, Indiana, Iowa, Kansas, Massachusetts, Michigan, Minnesota, Nebraska, New Jersey, New York, Ohio, Pennsylvania, Rhode Island and Washington. California provides only for civil action. Illinois,

Kansas, Minnesota, New York and Ohio have both civil and criminal provisions. In New Jersey the only action is a criminal action, or an action for penalty in the name of the state, the amount of the penalty going to the state.

In those states not having civil rights statutes it is necessary that every effort be made to secure passage of one. In states having weak civil rights statutes efforts should be made to have them strengthened. In states with reasonably strong civil rights statutes, like Illinois and New York, it is necessary that every effort be made to enforce them. . . .

Outside of New York City there are very few successful cases against the civil rights statutes because of the fact that members of the jury are usually reluctant to enforce the statutes. I understand the same is true for Illinois. The only method of counteracting this vicious practice is by means of educating the general public, from which juries are chosen, to the plight of the Negro.

It should also be pointed out that many of our friends of other races are not as loud and vociferous as the enemies of our race. In northern and mid-western cities it repeatedly happens that a prejudiced southerner on entering a hotel or restaurant, seeing Negroes present makes an immediate and loud protest to the manager. It is very seldom that any of our friends go to the managers of places where Negroes are excluded and complain to them of this fact. Quite a job can be done if our friends of other races will only realize the importance of this problem and get up from their comfortable chairs and actually go to work on the problem.

Bring Civil Rights Violators to Justice

Thus it seems clear that although it is necessary and vital to all of us that we continue our program for additional legislation to guarantee and enforce certain of our rights, at the same time we must continue with ever-increasing vigor to enforce those few statutes, both federal and state, which are now on the statute books. We must not be delayed by people who say "the time is not ripe," nor should we proceed with caution for fear of destroying the "status quo." Persons who deny to us our civil rights should be brought to justice now. Many people believe the time is always "ripe" to discriminate against Negroes. All right then— the time is always "ripe" to bring them to justice. The responsibility for the enforcement of these statutes rests with every American citizen regardless of race or color. However, the real job has to be done by the Negro population with whatever friends of the other races are willing to join in.

Chapter 2

Desegregating the Schools

Chapter Preface

On May 17, 1954, the United States Supreme Court announced its unanimous ruling in *Brown v. Board of Education:* racial segregation in public schools was unconstitutional. The decision reversed the 1896 Supreme Court precedent of *Plessy v. Ferguson*, in which "separate but equal" public facilities were deemed acceptable, and invalidated the compulsory segregation laws found in seventeen states. In subsequent decisions the Supreme Court extended its invalidation of the "separate but equal" doctrine to strike down segregation in parks, buses, and other public areas.

The *Brown* decision was the culmination of a carefully planned campaign by the National Association for the Advancement of Colored People (NAACP) to attack the legal foundations of racial segregation through the courts. Conceived in the 1930s by Charles Hamilton Houston, the plan called for a gradual attack on the "separate but equal" doctrine. Beginning in 1938, NAACP efforts resulted in several Supreme Court rulings that forbade graduate schools from refusing admission to qualified black applicants. The Supreme Court based these decisions on the grounds that "separate but equal" graduate institutions for blacks did not exist. In 1950 the NAACP decided to challenge segregated schools on the basis that segregation itself was inherently unequal. Five separate cases against segregated public school districts were consolidated and argued before the Supreme Court. The result was the *Brown* decision, which seemed to many observers to be vindication of the NAACP's legal strategy for securing civil rights.

The ruling in favor of integration was celebrated by most black Americans, as well as by many whites. However, many white southern residents and political leaders criticized the decision as an illegitimate usurpation of local authority by the federal government. Behind many such legal and constitutional arguments was the fear among southern whites, sometimes expressed and sometimes not, of "race mixing." Communities in the South resorted to various methods to circumvent the *Brown* ruling, including legal appeals seeking delays in implementing school desegregation, and in some cases shutting down their public schools altogether. Many whites joined local White Citizens' Councils to preserve racial segregation by harassing and intimidating those who sought to implement the *Brown* decision or agitate for black civil rights. In several instances, such as in Little Rock, Arkansas, in 1957, and at the University of Mississippi in 1962, state governors ordered police and national guard units to prevent school integration in defiance of federal court orders.

White resistance to school desegregation eventually resulted in black civil rights activists' going beyond the NAACP's legal approach by including sit-ins, demonstrations, marches, and boycotts in their efforts to implement the *Brown* decision and secure their civil rights. Thus the civil rights movement of the late 1950s and early 1960s was in a sense a direct response both to the invalidation of racial segregation decreed in *Brown* and to white resistance to school integration and racial equality.

VIEWPOINT 1

"We conclude that in the field of public education the doctrine of 'separate but equal' has no place."

Racial Segregation in Public Schools Is Unconstitutional

Earl Warren (1891–1974)

Earl Warren, a moderate Republican governor of California who unsuccessfully sought the Republican Party's nomination for president in 1948 and 1952, was appointed Supreme Court chief justice in 1953 by President Dwight D. Eisenhower. Warren went on to become one of the most influential chief justices in the nation's history, presiding over many landmark decisions on social and civil rights issues. Perhaps the most important of these rulings was the first: the 1954 unanimous decision in *Brown v. Board of Education* declaring that racially segregated public schools were unconstitutional. The ruling reversed the "separate but equal" doctrine affirmed by the 1896 Supreme Court decision in *Plessy v. Ferguson*. Warren wrote the opinion of the Court in *Brown*, reprinted below, making significant use of the arguments advanced by Thurgood Marshall of the National Association for the Advancement of Colored People (NAACP), the organization that represented the black plaintiffs challenging racial segregation in public schools.

Earl Warren, from the decision of the U.S. Supreme Court in *Brown v. Board of Education*, 347 U.S. 483 (1954).

These cases come to us from the States of Kansas, South Carolina, Virginia, and Delaware. They are premised on different facts and different local conditions, but a common legal question justifies their consideration together in this consolidated opinion.

In each of the cases, minors of the Negro race, through their legal representatives, seek the aid of the courts in obtaining admission to the public schools of their community on a nonsegregated basis. In each instance, they had been denied admission to schools attended by white children under laws requiring or permitting segregation according to race. This segregation was alleged to deprive the plaintiffs of the equal protection of the laws under the Fourteenth Amendment. In each of the cases other than the Delaware case, a three-judge federal district court denied relief to the plaintiffs on the so-called "separate but equal" doctrine announced by this Court in *Plessy v. Ferguson.* . . . Under that doctrine, equality of treatment is accorded when the races are provided substantially equal facilities, even though these facilities be separate. In the Delaware case, the Supreme Court of Delaware adhered to that doctrine, but ordered that the plaintiffs be admitted to the white schools because of their superiority to the Negro schools.

The plaintiffs contend that segregated public schools are not "equal" and cannot be made "equal," and that hence they are deprived of the equal protection of the laws. Because of the obvious importance of the question presented, the Court took jurisdiction. Argument was heard in the 1952 Term, and reargument was heard this Term on certain questions propounded by the Court.

The Fourteenth Amendment

Reargument was largely devoted to the circumstances surrounding the adoption of the Fourteenth Amendment in 1868. It covered exhaustively consideration of the Amendment in Congress, ratification by the states, then existing practices in racial segregation, and the views of proponents and opponents of the Amendment. This discussion and our own investigation convince us that, although these sources cast some light, it is not enough to resolve the problem with which we are faced. At best, they are inconclusive. The most avid proponents of the post-War Amendments undoubtedly intended them to remove all legal distinctions among "all persons born or naturalized in the United States." Their opponents, just as certainly, were antagonistic to both the letter and the spirit of the Amendments and wished them to have the most limited effect. What others in Congress and the state legislatures had in mind cannot be determined with any degree of certainty.

An additional reason for the inconclusive nature of the Amendment's history, with respect to segregated schools, is the status of public education at that time. In the South, the movement toward free common schools, supported by general taxation, had not yet taken hold. Education of white children was largely in the hands of private groups. Education of Negroes was almost nonexistent, and practically all of the race were illiterate. In fact, any education of Negroes was forbidden by law in some states. Today, in contrast, many Negroes have achieved outstanding success in the arts and sciences as well as in the business and professional world. It is true that public school education at the time of the Amendment had advanced further in the North, but the effect of the Amendment on Northern States was generally ignored in the congressional debates. Even in the North, the conditions of public education did not approximate those existing today. The curriculum was usually rudimentary; ungraded schools were common in rural areas; the school term was but three months a year in many states; and compulsory school attendance was virtually unknown. As a consequence, it is not surprising that there should be so little in the history of the Fourteenth Amendment relating to its intended effect on public education.

In the first cases in this Court construing the Fourteenth Amendment, decided shortly after its adoption, the Court inter-

The NAACP lawyers who argued the case for school integration before the Supreme Court in Brown v. Board of Education, *George E.C. Hayes (left), Thurgood Marshall (center), and James M. Nabrit (right), pose outside the Supreme Court on May 17, 1954, the day the decision was announced.*

preted it as proscribing all state-imposed discriminations against the Negro race. The doctrine of "separate but equal" did not make its appearance in this Court until 1896 in the case of *Plessy v. Ferguson*, . . . involving not education but transportation. American courts have since labored with the doctrines for over half a century. In this Court, there have been six cases involving the "separate but equal" doctrine in the field of public education. In *Cumming v. County Board of Education* . . . and *Gong Lum v. Rice*, . . . the validity of the doctrine itself was not challenged. In more recent cases, all on the graduate school level, inequality was found in that specific benefits enjoyed by white students were denied to Negro students of the same educational qualifications. . . . In none of these cases was it necessary to re-examine the doctrine to grant relief to the Negro plaintiff. And in *Sweatt v. Painter*, . . . the Court expressly reserved decision on the question whether *Plessy v. Ferguson* should be held inapplicable to public education.

In the instant cases, that question is directly presented. Here, unlike *Sweatt v. Painter*, there are findings below that the Negro and white schools involved have been equalized, or are being equalized, with respect to buildings, curricula, qualifications and salaries of teachers, and other "tangible" factors. Our decision, therefore, cannot turn on merely a comparison of these tangible factors in the Negro and white schools involved in each of the cases. We must look instead to the effect of segregation itself on public education.

Segregation and Education

In approaching this problem, we cannot turn the clock back to 1868 when the Amendment was adopted, or even to 1896 when *Plessy v. Ferguson* was written. We must consider public education in the light of its full development and its present place in American life throughout the Nation. Only in this way can it be determined if segregation in public schools deprives these plaintiffs of the equal protection of the laws.

Today, education is perhaps the most important function of state and local governments. Compulsory school attendance laws and the great expenditures for education both demonstrate our recognition of the importance of education to our democratic society. It is required in the performance of our most basic public responsibilities, even service in the armed forces. It is the very foundation of good citizenship. Today it is a principal instrument in awakening the child to cultural values, in preparing him for later professional training, and in helping him to adjust normally to his environment. In these days, it is doubtful that any child may reasonably be expected to succeed in life if he is denied the opportunity of an education. Such an opportunity, where the state has undertaken to provide it, is a right which must be made available to all on equal terms.

We come then to the question presented: Does segregation of children in public schools solely on the basis of race, even though the physical facilities and other "tangible" factors may be equal, deprive the children of the minority group of equal educational opportunities? We believe that it does.

Segregation and Children's Attitudes

As part of their legal brief against school segregation submitted in the Brown v. Board of Education *case, the NAACP submitted an appendix written collectively by thirty-one experts (including noted child psychologist Kenneth B. Clark) that argued that segregation in and of itself harmed black children.*

At the recent Mid-century White House Conference on Children and Youth, a fact-finding report on the effect of prejudice, discrimination and segregation on the personality of children was prepared as a basis for some of the deliberations. This report brought together the available social science and psychological studies which were related to the problem of how racial and religious prejudices influenced the development of a healthy personality. It highlighted the fact that segregation, prejudices and discriminations, and their social concomitants potentially damage the personality of all children—the children of the majority group in a somewhat different way than the more obviously damaged children of the minority group.

The report indicates that as minority group children learn the inferior status to which they are assigned—as they observe the fact that they are almost always segregated and kept apart from others who are treated with more respect by the society as a whole—they often react with feelings of inferiority and a sense of personal humiliation. Many of them become confused about their own personal worth. On the one hand, like all other human beings they require a sense of personal dignity; on the other hand, almost nowhere in the larger society do they find their own dignity as human beings respected by others. Under these conditions, the minority group child is thrown into a conflict with regard to his feelings about himself and his group. He wonders whether his group and he himself are worthy of no more respect than they receive. This conflict leads to self-hatred and rejection of his own group. . . .

The report indicates that minority group children of all social and economic classes often react with a generally defeatist attitude and a lowering of personal ambitions. This, for example, is reflected in lower pupil morale and a depression of the educational aspiration level among minority group children in segregated schools. In producing such effects, segregated schools impair the ability of the child to profit from the educational opportunities provided him.

In *Sweatt v. Painter*, . . . in finding that a segregated law school for Negroes could not provide them equal educational opportunities, this Court relied in large part on "those qualities which are incapable of objective measurement but which make for greatness in a law school." In *McLaurin v. Oklahoma State Regents*, . . . the Court, in requiring that a Negro admitted to a white graduate school be treated like all other students, again resorted to intangible considerations: ". . . his ability to study, to engage in discussions and exchange views with other students, and, in general, to learn his profession." Such considerations apply with added force to children in grade and high schools. To separate them from others of similar age and qualifications solely because of their race generates a feeling of inferiority as to their status in the community that may affect their hearts and minds in a way unlikely ever to be undone. The effect of this separation on their educational opportunities was well stated by a finding in the Kansas case by a court which nevertheless felt compelled to rule against the Negro plaintiffs:

> Segregation of white and colored children in public schools has a detrimental effect upon the colored children. The impact is greater when it has the sanction of the law; for the policy of separating the races is usually interpreted as denoting the inferiority of the negro group. A sense of inferiority affects the motivation of a child to learn. Segregation with the sanction of law, therefore, has a tendency to [retard] the education and mental development of negro children and to deprive them of some of the benefits they would receive in a racial[ly] integrated school system.

Whatever may have been the extent of psychological knowledge at the time of *Plessy v. Ferguson*, this finding is amply supported by modern authority. Any language in *Plessy v. Ferguson* contrary to this finding is rejected.

Separate and Unequal

We conclude that in the field of public education the doctrine of "separate but equal" has no place. Separate educational facilities are inherently unequal. Therefore, we hold that the plaintiffs and others similarly situated for whom the actions have been brought are, by reason of the segregation complained of, deprived of the equal protection of the laws guaranteed by the Fourteenth Amendment. This disposition makes unnecessary any discussion whether such segregation also violates the Due Process Clause of the Fourteenth Amendment.

Because these are class actions, because of the wide applicability of this decision, and because of the great variety of local conditions, the formulation of decrees in these cases presents problems of considerable complexity. On reargument, the consideration of appropriate relief was necessarily subordinated to the primary question—the constitutionality of segregation on public education. We have now announced that such segregation is a denial of the equal protection of the laws. In order that we may have the full assistance of the parties in formulating decrees, the cases will be restored to the docket, and the parties are requested to present further argument on Questions 4 and 5 previously propounded by the Court for the reargument this Term. The Attorney General of the United States is again invited to participate. The Attorneys General of the states requiring or permitting segregation in public education will also be permitted to appear as *Amici Curiae* upon request, to do so by September 15, 1954, and submission of briefs by October 1, 1954.

VIEWPOINT 2

"This unwarranted exercise of power by the Court, contrary to the Constitution, is creating chaos and confusion in the States principally affected."

The Supreme Court Should Not Interfere in Southern Racial Practices

The Southern Manifesto

The U.S. Supreme Court in the landmark case *Brown v. Board of Education* ruled that racially segregated public schools were unconstitutional. The Court made no direct statement on how this ruling was to be implemented; one year later the Court issued an "Enforcement Decree" calling for states to desegregate their schools "with all deliberate speed." Despite these pronouncements, many southern states actively resisted school desegregation, passing within the next four years 196 laws designed to delay or circumvent school integration. In 1956 one hundred senators and congressional representatives from eleven southern states signed a declaration of opposition to *Brown*, entitled the "Southern Manifesto." Most of the writing of the Southern Manifesto was the work of North Carolina senator Sam J. Ervin Jr. Among its signers were Senators Strom Thurmond, J. William Fulbright, and Richard B. Russell. The declaration, reprinted here, argues that the Supreme Court went beyond its proper authority in its ruling. The signing members of Congress go on to support all efforts to "resist forced integration by any lawful means."

From the "Southern Manifesto: Declaration of Constitutional Principles," *Cong. Rec.*, 84th Cong., 2nd sess. (March 12, 1956).

The unwarranted decision of the Supreme Court in the public school cases is now bearing the fruit always produced when men substitute naked power for established law.

The Founding Fathers gave us a Constitution of checks and balances because they realized the inescapable lesson of history that no man or group of men can be safely entrusted with unlimited power. They framed this Constitution with its provisions for change by amendment in order to secure the fundamentals of government against the dangers of temporary popular passion or the personal predilections of public office-holders.

An Abuse of Power

We regard the decision of the Supreme Court in the school cases as a clear abuse of judicial power. It climaxes a trend in the Federal Judiciary undertaking to legislate, in derogation of the authority of Congress, and to encroach upon the reserved rights of the States and the people.

The original Constitution does not mention education. Neither does the 14th amendment nor any other amendment. The debates preceding the submission of the 14th amendment clearly show that there was no intent that it should affect the system of education maintained by the States.

The very Congress which proposed the amendment subsequently provided for segregated schools in the District of Columbia.

When the amendment was adopted in 1868, there were 37 States of the Union. Every one of the 26 States that had any substantial racial differences among its people, either approved the operation of segregated schools already in existence or subsequently established such schools by action of the same lawmaking body which considered the 14th amendment.

As admitted by the Supreme Court in the public school case (*Brown v. Board of Education*), the doctrine of separate but equal schools "apparently originated in *Roberts v. City of Boston* (1849), upholding school segregation against attack as being violative of a State constitutional guarantee of equality." This constitutional doctrine began in the North, not in the South, and it was followed not only in Massachusetts, but in Connecticut, New York, Illinois, Indiana, Michigan, Minnesota, New Jersey, Ohio, Pennsylvania and other northern States until they, exercising their rights as States through the constitutional processes of local self-government, changed their school systems.

In the case of *Plessy v. Ferguson* in 1896 the Supreme Court expressly declared that under the 14th amendment no person was denied any of his rights if the States provided separate but equal public facilities. This decision has been followed in many other cases. It is notable that the Supreme Court, speaking through Chief Justice [William H.] Taft, a former President of the United States, unanimously declared in 1927 in *Lum v. Rice* that the "separate but equal" principle is "within the discretion of the State in regulating its public schools and does not conflict with the 14th amendment."

Black Monday

Tom P. Brady was one of the leaders of the movement creating Citizens' Councils in many southern communities, organizations formed in direct response to the Brown v. Board of Education *desegregation ruling. A speech of his, from which the following passage is excerpted, was published in pamphlet form in 1955 and was widely disseminated throughout the South.*

"Black Monday" is the name coined by Representative John Bell Williams of Mississippi to designate Monday, May 17th, 1954, a date long to be remembered throughout this nation. This is the date upon which the Supreme Court of the United States handed down its socialistic decision in the Segregation cases on appeal from the States of Kansas, South Carolina, Virginia and Delaware [*Brown v. Board of Education*]. "Black Monday" is indeed symbolic of the date. Black denoting darkness and terror. Black signifying the absence of light and wisdom. Black embodying grief, destruction and death. Should Representative Williams accomplish nothing more during his membership in Congress he has more than justified his years in office by the creating of this epithet, the originating of this watchword, the shouting of this battle cry.

Black Monday ranks in importance with July 4th, 1776, the date upon which our Declaration of Independence was signed. May 17th, 1954, is the date upon which the declaration of socialistic doctrine was officially proclaimed throughout this nation. It was on Black Monday that the judicial branch of our government usurped the sacred privilege and right of the respective states of this union to educate their youth. This usurpation constitutes the greatest travesty of the American Constitution and jurisprudence in the history of this nation.

This interpretation, restated time and again, became a part of the life of the people of many of the States and confirmed their habits, customs, traditions, and way of life. It is founded on elemental humanity and commonsense, for parents should not be deprived by Government of the right to direct the lives and education of their own children.

Though there has been no constitutional amendment or act of Congress changing this established legal principle almost a century old, the Supreme Court of the United States, with no legal basis for such action, undertook to exercise their naked judicial power and substituted their personal political and social ideas for the established law of the land.

This unwarranted exercise of power by the Court, contrary to the Constitution, is creating chaos and confusion in the States principally affected. It is destroying the amicable relations between the white and Negro races that have been created through 90 years of patient effort by the good people of both races. It has planted hatred and suspicion where there has been heretofore friendship and understanding.

Without regard to the consent of the governed, outside agitators are threatening immediate and revolutionary changes in our public-school systems. If done, this is certain to destroy the system of public education in some of the States.

Responding to Outside Meddlers

With the gravest concern for the explosive and dangerous condition created by this decision and inflamed by outside meddlers:

We reaffirm our reliance on the Constitution as the fundamental law of the land.

We decry the Supreme Court's encroachments on rights reserved to the States and to the people, contrary to established law, and to the Constitution.

We commend the motives of those States which have declared the intention to resist forced integration by any lawful means.

We appeal to the States and people who are not directly affected by these decisions to consider the constitutional principles involved against the time when they too, on issues vital to them, may be the victims of judicial encroachment.

Even though we constitute a minority in the present Congress, we have full faith that a majority of the American people believe in the dual system of government which has enabled us to achieve our greatness and will in time demand that the reserved rights of the States and of the people be made secure against judicial usurpation.

We pledge ourselves to use all lawful means to bring about a reversal of this decision which is contrary to the Constitution and to prevent the use of force in its implementation.

In this trying period, as we all seek to right this wrong, we appeal to our people not to be provoked by the agitators and trouble-makers invading our States and to scrupulously refrain from disorder and lawless acts.

VIEWPOINT 3

"The mingling or integration of white and Negro children in the South's primary schools would open the gates to miscegenation and widespread racial amalgamation."

Racial Segregation Is Necessary

Herbert Ravenel Sass (1884–1958)

The 1954 Supreme Court decision in *Brown v. Board of Education* declaring racial segregation in schools unconstitutional caused a storm of opposition from many white southerners, who objected both on constitutional and racial grounds. An example of the latter argument can be seen in the following excerpts from a 1956 article by Herbert Ravenel Sass, a naturalist and author of several books on the history of South Carolina. The beliefs expressed by Sass on American history and on the differences between the white and black races were shared by many whites, and help to explain why by 1962, eight years after *Brown*, less than one-half of one percent of blacks in the South were attending previously all-white schools.

What may well be the most important physical fact in the story of the United States is one which is seldom emphasized in our history books. It is the fact that throughout the three and a half centuries of our existence we have kept our several races biologically distinct and separate. Though we have encouraged the mixing of many different strains in what has been called the

From Herbert Ravenel Sass's, "Mixed Schools and Mixed Blood," *Atlantic Monthly*, November 1956.

American "melting pot," we have confined this mixing to the white peoples of European ancestry, excluding from our "melting pot" all other races. The result is that the United States today is overwhelmingly a pure white nation, with a smaller but considerable Negro population in which there is some white blood, and a much smaller American Indian population.

The fact that the United States is overwhelmingly pure white is not only important; it is also the most distinctive fact about this country when considered in relation to the rest of the New World. Except Canada, Argentina, and Uruguay, none of the approximately twenty-five other countries of this hemisphere has kept its races pure. Instead (though each contains some pure-blooded individuals) all these countries are products of an amalgamation of races—American Indian and white or American Indian, Negro, and white. In general the pure-blooded white nations have outstripped the far more numerous American mixed-blood nations in most of the achievements which constitute progress as commonly defined.

These facts are well known. But now there lurks in ambush, as it were, another fact: we have suddenly begun to move toward abandonment of our 350-year-old system of keeping our races pure and are preparing to adopt instead a method of racial amalgamation similar to that which has created the mixed-blood nations of this hemisphere; except that the amalgamation being prepared for this country is not Indian and white but Negro and white. It is the deep conviction of nearly all white Southerners in the states which have large Negro populations that the mingling or integration of white and Negro children in the South's primary schools would open the gates to miscegenation and widespread racial amalgamation.

This belief is at the heart of our race problem, and until it is realized that this is the South's basic and compelling motive, there can be no understanding of the South's attitude.

America Has Helped Negroes

It must be realized too that the Negroes of the U.S.A. are today by far the most fortunate members of their race to be found anywhere on earth. Instead of being the hapless victim of unprecedented oppression, it is nearer the truth that the Negro in the United States is by and large the product of friendliness and helpfulness unequaled in any comparable instance in all history. Nowhere else in the world, at any time of which there is record, has a helpless, backward people of another color been so swiftly uplifted and so greatly benefited by a dominant race.

What America, including the South, has done for the Negro is the truth which should be trumpeted abroad in rebuttal of the

Communist propaganda. In failing to utilize this truth we have deliberately put aside a powerful affirmative weapon of enormous potential value to the free world and have allowed ourselves to be thrown on the defensive and placed in an attitude of apologizing for our conduct in a matter where actually our record is one of which we can be very proud.

We have permitted the subject of race relations in the United States to be used not as it should be used, as a weapon for America, but as a weapon for the narrow designs of the new aggressive Negro leadership in the United States. It cannot be so used without damage to this country, and that damage is beyond computation. Instead of winning for America the plaudits and trust of the colored peoples of Asia and Africa in recognition of what we have done for our colored people, our pro-Negro propagandists have seen to it that the United States appears as an international Simon Legree—or rather a Dr. Jekyll and Mr. Hyde with the South in the villainous role.

The South has had a bad time with words. Nearly a century ago the word "slavery," even more than the thing itself, did the South irreparable damage. In a strange but real way the misused word "democracy" has injured the South; its most distinctive—and surely its greatest—period has been called undemocratic, meaning illiberal and reactionary, because it resisted the onward sweep of a centralizing governmental trend alien to our federal republic and destructive of the very "cornerstone of liberty," local self-government. Today the word "segregation" and, perhaps even more harmful, the word "prejudice" blacken the South's character before the world and make doubly difficult our effort to preserve not merely our own way of life but certain basic principles upon which our country was founded.

Words are of such transcendent importance today that the South should long ago have protested against these two. They are now too firmly imbedded in the dialectic of our race problem to be got rid of. But that very fact renders all the more necessary a careful scrutiny of them. Let us first consider the word "segregation."

Segregation and Separation

Segregation is sometimes carelessly listed as a synonym of separation, but it is not a true synonym and the difference between the two words is important.

Segregation, from the Latin *segregatus* (set apart from the flock), implies isolation; separation carries no such implication. Segregation is what we have done to the American Indian—whose grievous wrongs few reformers and still fewer politicians ever bother their heads about. By use of force and against his will we have segregated him, isolated him, on certain small reservations

76

which had and still have somewhat the character of concentration camps.

The South has not done that to the Negro. On the contrary, it has shared its countryside and its cities with him in amity and understanding, not perfect by any means, and careful of established folk custom, but far exceeding in human friendliness anything of the kind to be found in the North. Not segregation of the Negro race as the Indian is segregated on his reservations—and as the Negro is segregated in the urban Harlems of the North—but simply *separation* of the white and Negro races in certain phases of activity is what the South has always had and feels that it must somehow preserve even though the time-honored, successful, and completely moral "separate but equal" principle no longer has legal sanction.

Until the Supreme Court decision forbidding compulsory racial separation in the public schools, the South was moving steadily toward abandonment or relaxation of the compulsory separation rule in several important fields. This is no longer true. Progress in racial relations has been stopped short by the ill-advised insistence of the Northern-directed Negro leadership upon the one concession which above all the white South will not and cannot make—public school integration.

Prejudice and Preference

Another word which is doing grave damage to the South today is "prejudice" meaning race prejudice—a causeless hostility often amounting to hatred which white Southerners are alleged to feel in regard to the Negro. Here again the South, forgetful of the lessons of its past, has failed to challenge effectively an inaccurate and injurious word. Not prejudice but preference is the word that truth requires.

Between prejudice and preference there is vast difference. Prejudice is a preconceived unfavorable judgment or feeling without sound basis. Preference is a natural reaction to facts and conditions observed or experienced, and through the action of heredity generation after generation it becomes instinctive. Like separateness, it exists throughout the animal kingdom. Though the difference between two races of an animal species may be so slight that only a specialist can differentiate between them, the individuals of one race prefer as a rule to associate with other individuals of that race.

One can cite numerous examples among birds and mammals. In the human species the history of our own country provides the most striking example of race preference. The white men and women, chiefly of British, German, Dutch, and Scandinavian stocks, who colonized and occupied what is now the United

States were strongly imbued with race preference. They did not follow the example of the Spanish and Portuguese (in whom for historical reasons the instinct of race preference was much weaker) who in colonizing South and Central America amalgamated with the Indians found in possession of the land and in some cases with the Negroes brought over as slaves. Instead, the founders of the future United States maintained their practice of non-amalgamation rigorously, with only slight racial blendings along the fringes of each group.

Integration Would Create Turmoil

These excerpts from Alabama governor John Patterson's speech on January 20, 1959, the day he was sworn into office, typified the reaction of many southern politicians to Brown v. Board of Education.

I will oppose with every ounce of energy I possess and will use every power at my command to prevent any mixing of the white and Negro races in the classrooms of this state. . . . The people of this state will not tolerate nor support integrated schools, and any attempt by the federal government or anyone else to integrate the schools of this state by force would cause turmoil, chaos and violence, and would result in the destruction of our public school system.

There can be no compromise in this fight. There is no such thing as a "little integration." The determined and ruthless purpose of the race agitators and such organizations as the NAACP is to bring about as fast as possible an amalgamation of our society. They seek to destroy our culture, our heritage, and our traditions. If we compromise or surrender our rights in this fight, they will be gone forever, never to be regained or restored.

Hence it is nonsense to say that racial discrimination, the necessary consequence of race preference, is "un-American." Actually it is perhaps the most distinctively American thing there is, the reason why the American people—meaning the people of the United States—are what they are. Today when racial discrimination of any kind or degree is instantly denounced as both sinful and stupid, few stop to reflect that this nation is built solidly upon it.

Defending Discrimination

The truth is, of course, that there are many different kinds and degrees of racial discrimination. Some of them are bad—outdated relics of an earlier time when conditions were unlike those of today, and these should be, and were being, abolished until the unprecedented decree of the Supreme Court in the school cases halted all progress. But not all kinds of racial discrimination are evil—unless we are prepared to affirm that our forefathers blundered in "keeping the breed pure."

Thus it is clear that discrimination too is a misused word as commonly employed in the realm of racial relations. It does not necessarily imply either stupidity or sin. It is not a synonym for injustice, and it is very far from being, as many seem to think, a synonym for hatred. The Southern white man has always exercised discrimination in regard to the Negro but—except for a tiny and untypical minority of the white population—he has never hated the Negro. I have lived a fairly long life in a part of the South—the South Carolina Low-country—where there are many thousands of Negroes, and since early boyhood I have known many of them well, in some cases for years, in town and country. I know how I feel about them and how the white people of this old plantation region, the high and the low, the rich and the poor, the large landowner and the white mechanic, feel about them.

I am sure that among white Carolinians there is, as yet, almost no hatred of the Negro, nor is there anything that can accurately be called race prejudice. What does exist, strongly and ineradicably, is race preference. In other words, we white Southerners prefer our own race and wish to keep it as it is.

This preference should not and in fact cannot be eliminated. It is much bigger than we are, a far greater thing than our racial dilemma. It is—and here is another basic fact of great significance—an essential element in Nature's huge and complex mechanism. It is one of the reasons why evolution, ever diversifying, ever discriminating, ever separating race from race, species from species, has been able to operate in an ascending course so that what began aeons ago as something resembling an amoeba has now become Man. In preferring its own race and in striving to prevent the destruction of that race by amalgamation with another race, the white South is not flouting Nature but is in harmony with her.

If the Negro also prefers his own race and wishes to preserve its identity, then he is misrepresented by his new aggressive leadership which, whether or not this is its deliberate aim, is moving toward a totally different result. Let us see why that is so.

Protecting Racial Integrity

The crux of the race problem in the South, as I have said, is the nearly universal belief of the Southern white people that only by maintaining a certain degree of separateness of the races can the racial integrity of the white South be safeguarded. Unfortunately the opinion has prevailed outside the South that only a few Southerners hold this conviction—a handful of demagogic politicians and their most ignorant followers—and that "enlightened" white Southerners recognize the alleged danger of racial amalgamation as a trumped-up thing having no real substance.

Nothing could be farther from the truth. Because the aggressive Northern-Negro leadership continues to drive onward, the white South (except perhaps that part which is now more Western than Southern and in which Negroes are few) is today as united in its conviction that its racial integrity must be protected as it was when the same conviction drove its people—the slaveholder and the nonslaveholder, the high and the low, the educated and the ignorant—to defend the outworn institution of Negro slavery because there seemed to be no other way to preserve the social and political control needed to prevent the Africanization of the South by a combination of fanatical Northern reformers and millions of enfranchised Negroes. The South escaped that fate because after a decade of disastrous experiment the intelligent people of the victorious North realized that the racial program of their social crusaders was unsound, or at least impracticable, and gave up trying to enforce it.

Now in a surging revival of that "Reconstruction" crusade—a revival which is part dedicated idealism, part understandable racial ambition, part political expediency national and international—the same social program is again to be imposed upon the South. There are new conditions which help powerfully to promote it: the Hitlerite excesses in the name of race which have brought all race distinctions into popular disrepute; the notion that the white man, by divesting himself of race consciousness, may appease the peoples of Asia and Africa and wean them away from Communism.

In addition, a fantastic perversion of scientific authority has been publicized in support of the new crusade. Though everywhere else in Nature (as well as in all our plant breeding and animal breeding) race and heredity are recognized as of primary importance, we are told that in the human species race is of no importance and racial differences are due not to heredity but to environment. Science has proved, so we are told, that all races are equal and, in essentials, identical.

Science has most certainly not proved that all races are equal, much less identical; and, as the courageous geneticist, Dr. W.C. George of the University of North Carolina, has recently pointed out, there is overwhelming likelihood that the biological consequences of white and Negro integration in the South would be harmful. It would not be long before these biological consequences became visible. But there is good hope that we shall never see them, because any attempt to force a program of racial integration upon the South would be met with stubborn, determined, and universal opposition, probably taking the form of passive resistance of a hundred kinds. Though secession is not conceivable, persistence in an attempt to compel the South to mingle its white and Negro children in its public schools would split the United States in two as disastrously as in the [1860s] and perhaps with an even more lamentable aftermath of bitterness.

School Segregation

For the elementary public school is the most critical of those areas of activity where the South must and will at all costs maintain separateness of the races. The South must do this because, although it is a nearly universal instinct, race preference is not active in the very young. Race preference (which the propagandists miscall race prejudice or hate) is one of those instincts which develop gradually as the mind develops and which, if taken in hand early enough, can be prevented from developing at all.

Hence if the small children of the two races in approximately equal numbers—as would be the case in a great many of the South's schools—were brought together intimately and constantly and grew up in close association in integrated schools under teachers necessarily committed to the gospel of racial integration, there would be many in whom race preference would not develop. This would not be, as superficial thinkers might suppose, a good thing, the happy solution of the race problem in America. It might be a solution of a sort, but not one that the American people would desire. It would inevitably result, beginning with the least desirable elements of both races, in a great increase of racial amalgamation, the very process which throughout our history we have most sternly rejected. For although to most persons today the idea of mixed mating is disagreeable or even repugnant, this would not be true of the new generations brought up in mixed schools with the desirability of racial integration as a basic premise. Among those new generations mixed matings would become commonplace, and a greatly enlarged mixed-blood population would result.

That is the compelling reason, though by no means the only reason, why the South will resist, with all its resources of mind and body, the mixing of the races in its public schools. It is a reason which, when its validity is generally recognized, will quickly enlist millions of non-Southerners in support of the South's position. The people of the North and West do not favor the transformation of the United States into a nation composed in considerable part of mixed bloods any more than the people of the South do. Northern support of school integration in the South is due to the failure to realize its inevitable biological effect in regions of large Negro population. If Northerners did realize this, their enthusiasm for mixed schools in the South would evaporate at once.

VIEWPOINT 4

"Segregation is immoral because it has inflicted a wound upon the soul of the segregated."

Racial Segregation Is Immoral

Benjamin E. Mays (1894–1984)

Benjamin E. Mays, a Baptist minister and educator, was president of Morehouse College in Atlanta, Georgia, from 1940 to 1967. He was an important influence on Martin Luther King Jr., who graduated from the black college in 1948. The following viewpoint is taken from a speech presented by Mays on November 10, 1955, during the annual meeting of the Southern Historical Association, a gathering of professors and educators from most major colleges and universities in the South. The speech, delivered more than one year after the *Brown v. Board of Education* decision, provides several arguments why racial segregation is morally indefensible.

Whenever a strong dominant group possesses all the power, political, educational, economic, and wields all the power; makes all the laws, municipal, state and federal, and administers all the laws; writes all the constitutions, municipal, state and federal, and interprets these constitutions; collects and holds all the money, municipal, state, and federal, and distributes all the money; determines all policies—governmental, business, political and educational; when that group plans and places heavy burdens, grievous to be borne, upon the backs of the weak, that act is

From Benjamin E. Mays, "The Moral Aspects of Segregation," a paper read at the Twenty-first Annual Meeting of the Southern Historical Association, November 10, 1955. Reprinted by permission. The Mays papers are located at the Moorland-Spingarn Research Center, Howard University.

immoral. If the strong group is a Christian group or a follower of Judaism both of which contend that God is creator, judge, impartial, just, universal, love and that man was created in God's image, the act is against God and man—thus immoral. If the strong group is atheistic, the act is against humanity—still immoral.

No group is wise enough, good enough, strong enough, to assume an omnipotent and omniscient role; no group is good enough, wise enough to restrict the mind, circumscribe the soul, and to limit the physical movements of another group. To do that is blasphemy. It is a usurpation of the role of God.

Separate but Not Equal

At a conference on July 30, 1954, called by Mississippi governor Hugh White to discuss the Brown v. Board of Education *decision, T.R.M. White, a physician and founder of the Regional Council of Negro Leadership, expressed his view that the decision was just and should be speedily implemented.*

The Negroes who have come here today have not come to help work out any trick or plan to circumvent the decision of the Supreme Court outlawing segregation in the public schools. We believe that the decision is a just and humane decision and our beloved South should have known that it was the only decision that could have been given in the light of America's position in the world today. . . .

Governor, we believe that the pressure for the recent Supreme Court's decision was brought about largely because of the so-called "Separate but Equal" school theory. You know, as well as we know, that we have had the *Separate* all right but in very few cases have we had the *Equal*. You have had a school equalization law here in Mississippi since 1890 but you forgot about this law until you began to feel the sharp lash of the Supreme Court of the United States of America, and today you wish to bargain with us. You will give us schools, if we give you our freedom. Fundamentally, there is no such thing as separate but equal in a matter as vital as the education of our children. The Mississippi Negro public school system has been so lacking in buildings and facilities that the Negro children have developed a complex which has caused them to want to go to the white school in their community, not for social reasons; but because the white school was the best school in the community.

If the strong handicaps the weak on the grounds of race or color, it is all the more immoral because we penalize the group for conditions over which it has no control, for being what nature or nature's God made it. And that is tantamount to saying to God, "You made a mistake, God, when you didn't make all races white." If there were a law which said that an illiterate group had to be segregated, the segregated group could go to school and become literate. If there were a law which said that all peoples with incomes below $5,000 a year had to be segregated, the people under $5,000 a year could strive to rise above the $5,000 bracket. If there were a law which said that men and women who did not bathe had to be segregated, they could develop the habit of daily baths and remove the stigma. If there were a law which said that all groups had to be Catholics, the Jews and Protestants could do something about it by joining the Catholic Church. But to segregate a man because his skin is brown or black, red or yellow, is to segregate a man for circumstances over which he has no control. And of all immoral acts, this is the most immoral.

So the May 17, 1954, Decision of the Supreme Court and all the decisions against segregation are attempts on the part of the judges involved to abolish a great wrong which the strong has deliberately placed upon the backs of the weak. It is an attempt on the part of federal and state judges to remove this stigma, this wrong through constitutional means, which is the democratic, American way.

Three Reasons for Segregation

I said a moment ago that if the strong deliberately picks out a weak racial group and places upon it heavy burdens that act is immoral. Let me try to analyze this burden, segregation, which has been imposed upon millions of Americans of color. There are at least three main reasons for legal segregation in the United States.

1. The first objective of segregation is to place a legal badge of inferiority upon the segregated, to brand him as unfit to move freely among other human beings. This badge says the segregated is mentally, morally, and socially unfit to move around as a free man.

2. The second objective of segregation is to set the segregated apart so that he can be treated as an inferior: in the courts, in recreation, in transportation, in politics, in government, in employment, in religion, in education, in hotels, in motels, restaurants and in every other area of American life. And all of this has been done without the consent of the segregated.

3. The third objective of legalized segregation follows from the first two. It is designed to make the segregated believe that he is inferior, that he is nobody and to make him accept willingly his inferior status in society. It is these conditions which the May 17, 1954, Decision of the Supreme Court and other federal decisions against segregation are designed to correct—to remove this immoral stigma that has been placed upon 16 million Negro Americans, and these are the reasons every thinking Negro wants the le-

gal badge of segregation removed so that he might be able to walk the earth with dignity, as a man, and not cringe and kow-tow as a slave. He believes that this is his God-given right on the earth.

The Disease of Inferiority

Segregation is immoral because it has inflicted a wound upon the soul of the segregated and so restricted his mind that millions of Negroes now alive will never be cured of the disease of inferiority. Many of them have come to feel and believe that they are inferior or that the cards are so stacked against them that it is useless for them to strive for the highest and the best. Segregate a race for ninety years, tell that race in books, in law, in courts, in education, in church and school, in employment, in transportation, in hotels and motels, in the government that it is inferior—it is bound to leave its damaging mark upon the souls and minds of the segregated. It is these conditions that the federal courts seek to change.

Any country that restricts the full development of any segment of society retards its own growth and development. The segregated produces less, and even the minds of the strong group are circumscribed because they are often afraid to pursue the whole truth and they spend too much time seeking ways and means of how to keep the segregated group in "its place." Segregation is immoral because it leads to injustice, brutality, and lynching on the part of the group that segregates. The segregated is somebody that can be pushed around as desired by the segregator. As a rule equal justice in the courts is almost impossible for a member of the segregated group if it involves a member of the group imposing segregation. The segregated has no rights that the segregator is bound to respect.

The chief sin of segregation is the distortion of human personality. It damages the soul of both segregator and the segregated. It gives the segregated a feeling of inherent inferiority which is not based on facts, and it gives the segregator a feeling of superiority which is not based on facts. It is difficult to know who is damaged more—the segregated or the segregator.

What Negroes Want

It is false accusation to say that Negroes hail the May 17, 1954, Decision of the Supreme Court because they want to mingle socially with white people. Negroes want segregation abolished because they want the legal stigma of inferiority removed and because they do not believe that equality of educational opportunities can be completely achieved in a society where the laws brand a group inferior. When a Negro rides in a Pullman unsegregated he does it not because he wants to ride with white people. He wants good accommodations. When he eats in an unsegregated diner on the train, he goes in because he is hungry and not because he wants to eat with white people. He goes to the diner not even to mingle with Negroes but to get something to eat. But as he eats and rides he wants no badge of inferiority pinned on his back. He wants to eat and ride with dignity. No Negro clothed in his right mind believes that his social status will be enhanced just because he associated with white people.

It is also a false accusation to say that Negroes are insisting that segregated schools must be abolished today or tomorrow, simultaneously all over the place. As far as I know, no Negro leader has ever advocated that, and they have not even said when desegregation is to be a finished job. They do say that the Supreme Court is the highest law of the land and we should respect that law. Negro leaders do say that each local community should bring together the racial groups in that community, calmly sit down and plan ways and means not how they can circumvent the decision but how they can implement it and plan together when and where they will start. They will be able to start sooner in some places than in others and move faster in some places than in others but begin the process in good faith and with good intent. To deliberately scheme, to deliberately plan through nefarious methods, through violence, boycott and threats to nullify the Decision of the highest law in the land is not only immoral but it encourages a disregard for all laws which we do not like.

CHAPTER 3

Means and Goals of the Civil Rights Movement

Chapter Preface

The five years beginning with the student sit-in movement in 1960 and ending with the passage of the Voting Rights Act in 1965 constitute the peak of the civil rights movement. This was the time of the Freedom Rides, the March on Washington, and the nationally televised confrontations between police and school-children in Birmingham, Alabama, and other southern communities. The legal strategies of the National Association for the Advancement of Colored People (NAACP) were overshadowed to some extent by the nonviolent protests and demonstrations of such organizations as the Congress of Racial Equality (CORE) and the Student Nonviolent Coordinating Committee (SNCC).

The participants of the movement at this time included people of all races, from all parts of the nation, and from differing social and economic classes. At its height in the early and mid-1960s, the civil rights movement enabled the black community in America to speak with a voice that for unity and effectiveness has been seldom equaled before or since.

This did not mean that the civil rights movement proceeded without significant internal divisions and debates, however. Leaders of the civil rights movement differed on tactics, organizational strategies, the role of whites in the movement, and other questions relating to the *means* of securing civil rights. Some black leaders, such as Nation of Islam spokesman Malcolm X, questioned the *goals* of the civil rights movement altogether, arguing that racial integration and federal laws protecting civil rights would do little good for most black people. The following viewpoints present differing opinions on both the tactics and ultimate goals of the civil rights movement.

VIEWPOINT 1

"We are working for the right of Negroes to enter all fields of activity in American life."

Integration Should Be the Goal of the Civil Rights Movement

James Farmer (b. 1920)

James Farmer, a divinity student, was one of the founders of the Congress of Racial Equality (CORE) in 1942, and was its national director from 1961 to 1966. The interracial and nonviolent group pioneered such demonstration techniques as the sit-in, which it first used in Chicago in 1943. CORE and Farmer made headlines in 1961 with the Freedom Rides, in which multiracial groups rode on interstate buses to test enforcement of desegregation laws in public areas that served interstate travelers, including bus terminals, rest rooms, and restaurants. Farmer and other CORE members were frequently beaten and jailed while participating in Freedom Rides and other activities. Farmer later left CORE after disagreeing with its growing emphasis on black separatism. His belief that integration into mainstream American society should be the goal of blacks in the United States can be seen in the following viewpoint, excerpted from remarks made at a 1962 debate between Farmer and noted Black Muslim leader Malcolm X.

From James Farmer's contribution to "Separation or Integration? A Debate at Cornell University," March 7, 1962. Reprinted from *Dialogue*, May 1962, by permission of Cornell United Religious Work.

When the Freedom Riders left from Montgomery, Alabama, to ride into the conscience of America and into Jackson, Mississippi, there were many persons who said to us, "Don't go into Mississippi, go any place you like, go to the Union of South Africa, but stay out of Mississippi." They said, "What you found in Alabama will be nothing compared to what you will meet in Mississippi." I remember being told a story by one minister who urged us not to go. He said, "Once upon a time there was a Negro who had lived in Mississippi, lived for a long time running from county to county. Finally he left the state, and left it pretty fast, as Dick Gregory would put it, not by Greyhound, but by bloodhound, and he went to Illinois to live, in Chicago. And unable to find a job there, after several weeks of walking the street unemployed, he sat down and asked God what he should do. God said, 'Go back to Mississippi.' He said, 'Lord, you surely don't mean it, you're jesting. You don't mean for me to go back to Mississippi. There is segregation there!' The Lord said, 'Go back to Mississippi.' The man looked up and said, 'Very well, Lord, if you insist, I will do it, I will go. But will you go with me?' The Lord said 'As far as Cincinnati.'"

Confronting Racism

The Freedom Riders felt that they should go all the way because there is something wrong with our nation and we wanted to try to set it right. As one of the nation's scholars wrote at the turn of the century, "The problem of the twentieth century will be the problem of the color-line, of the relations between the lighter and the darker peoples of the earth, Asia and Africa, in America, and in the islands of the sea." What prophetic words, indeed. We have seen the struggle for freedom all over the world. We have seen it in Asia; we have seen it in the islands of the sea; we have seen it in Africa; and we are seeing it in America now. I think the racist theories of Count DeGobineu, Lothrop Stoddard, and the others have set the pattern for a racism that exists within our country. There are theories that are held today, not only by those men and their followers and successors, but by Ross Barnett, John Patterson devotees and followers of the Klan and the White Citizens Councils, and Lincoln Rockwell of the American Nazi Party.

These vicious racist theories hold that Negroes are inferior and whites are superior innately. Ordained by God, so to speak. No more vicious theory has existed in the history of mankind. I would suggest to you that no theory has provided as much human misery throughout the centuries as the theory of races—the theories that say some people are innately inferior and that others are innately superior. Although we have some of those theories in our country, we also have a creed of freedom and of democracy. As Pearl Buck put it, "Many Americans suffer from a split personality. One side of that personality is believing in democracy and freedom, as much as it is possible for a man so to believe. The other side of this personality is refusing, just as doggedly, to practice that democracy and that freedom, in which he believes." That was the split personality. Gunnar Myrdal, in his book, *The American Dilemma*, indicated that this was basically a moral problem, and that we have this credo which Americans hold to, of freedom, and democracy, and equality, but still we refuse to practice it. Gunnar Myrdal indicated that this is sorely troubling the American conscience.

All of us are a part of this system, all a part of it. We have all developed certain prejudices, I have mine, you have yours. It seems to me that it is extremely dangerous when any individual claims

---

We Have Paid the Fare

Milton A. Galamison, a pastor at Siloam Presbyterian Church in Brooklyn, New York, debated Malcolm X on television on March 27, 1963, on the subject of racial integration. The excerpts below are from his opening statement from that broadcast.

Some five thousand Negroes, slave and free, fought in the War for Independence. Many thousands more fought in the War to preserve the Union. The story of our sacrifice and loyalty is written in blood tracks around the world. The soil has been fertilized by our sweat, the factories built on our backs, the machines oiled by our tears, the homes maintained by our servitude and the nation carved by our suffering. When then we speak of integration or separation as alternatives, we must consider the degree to which the Negro is already woven into the pattern of American life. We have been integrated at the level of sowing. It is in the area of reaping that we have been short changed. We have paid the fare. The question is whether we shall fight for the ride. We have planted the tree. Shall we not demand the fruit? . . .

The new nationalists are saying to the racists, "I will show you what it is to be the object of race arrogance. I will be just as you are." The integrationists are saying, on the other hand, "Nothing could make me want to be as you are." The worst harm white supremacy could inflict on me is to mold me in the image of its buffoonery. Yet white supremacy has achieved the supreme stroke of perverted genius in convincing some Negroes that the desire for racial unity is symptomatic of inferiority and pridelessness.

It follows, therefore, that I cannot see black arrogance as an antidote for or negation of white arrogance. The proposed cure so resembles the illness that it expands rather than reduces the problem.

to be without prejudice, when he really does have it. I'm prejudiced against women drivers. I think they are a menace to civilization, and the sooner they are removed from the highways, the safer we will all be, but I know that's nothing but a prejudice. I have seen women drivers who are better drivers than I am, but does that destroy my prejudice? No. What I do then is to separate her from the group of women drivers and say, "Why she is an exception." Or maybe I say she is driving very well because she feels guilty. She knows that other women in the past have had accidents, and so she drives cautiously.

I remember several years ago when I was a youth, attending a church youth conference, and a young fellow from Mississippi and I became very good friends. The last day of the conference as we walked along the road he put his arm on my shoulder and said, "Jim, I have no race prejudice." "No," said I. "Absolutely not," said he. I raised my eyebrows. "As a matter of fact," he went on, "I was thirteen years old before I knew I was any better than a Negro." Well sometimes a supposed absence of racial prejudice runs quite along those lines. Now prejudice is a damaging thing to Negroes. We have suffered under it tremendously. It damages the lives of little children. I remember when I first came into contact with segregation; it was when I was a child in Mississippi when my mother took me downtown, and on the way back this hot July day I wanted to stop and get a Coke, and she told me I couldn't get a Coke, I had to wait until I got home. "Well why can't I, there's a little boy going in," said I. "I bet he's going to get a Coke." He was. "Well why can't I go?" "Because he's white," she said, "and you're colored." It's not important what happened to me, the fact is that the same thing over and over again happens to every mother's child whose skin happens to be dark.

The Damage of Segregation

If the damage that is done to Negroes is obvious, the damage that is done to whites in America is equally obvious, for they're prejudiced. I lived in Texas a large part of my life; remember driving through the state, and after dusk had fallen being followed by cars of whites who forced me off the road and said to me, "Don't you know that your kind is not supposed to be in this town after sundown." I wondered what was happening to these people; how their minds were being twisted, as mine and others like me had had our minds twisted by this double-edged sword of prejudice. It is a disease indeed. It is an American disease. It is an American dilemma.

The damage to Negroes is psychological; it is also economic. Negroes occupy the bottom of the economic ladder, the poorest jobs, the lowest paying jobs. Last to be hired, and first to be fired, so that today the percentage of unemployed Negroes is twice as high as that of whites. There has been political damage as well. In the South we find that comparatively few Negroes are registered to vote. Many are apathetic even when they could register. The percentage who are registered in the North is almost equally as low. As a result, comparatively few Negroes are elected to political office. Thus, the damage to the Negroes, as a result of the disease of segregation, has been psychological, economic, social, and political. I would suggest to you that the same damages have occurred to whites. Psychological damages are obvious. Economic—the nation itself suffers economically, as a result of denying the right of full development to one-tenth of its population. Skills, talents, and abilities are crushed in their cradle, are not allowed to develop. Snuffed out. Thus, the nation's economy has suffered. People who could be producing are instead walking the streets. People who could be producing in better jobs and producing more are kept in the lower jobs, sweeping the floors and serving other persons. The whole nation has been damaged by segregation. Now, all of us share the guilt too. I myself am guilty. I am guilty because I spent half my life in the South. During those years I participated in segregation, cooperated with it, and supported it.

We are all intricately involved in the system of segregation. We have not yet extricated ourselves. Negroes are involved, and guilty, and share the blame to the extent they themselves have, by their deeds and their acts, allowed segregation to go on for so long. I do not believe that guilt is a part of my genes or your genes. It hinges upon the deeds that you have done. If you have supported segregation, then you are guilty. If you continue to support it, then your guilt is multiplied. But that is your guilt, that is mine. We share the guilt for the disease of segregation, and its continued existence. All too long, Negro Americans have put up with the system of segregation, North and South. Incidentally, it is not a Southern problem, it is a Northern one as well. Segregation exists in housing and in jobs and in schools. We have put up with it, have done nothing about it.

The day before the Freedom Riders left Washington, D.C., to ride into the South, I visited my father who was in the hospital on what proved to be his deathbed. I told him I was going on a Freedom Ride into the South. He wanted to know what it was and I told him. "Where are you going?" he asked, and I told him. He said, "Well, I'm glad that you're going, son, and I hope you survive. I realize you may not return, but," said he, "I'm glad you're going because when I was a child in South Carolina and Georgia, we didn't like segregation either, but we thought that's the way things always had to be and the way they always would be, so we put up with it, took part in it, decided to exist and to stay alive. I am glad," said he, "that there are lots of people today who are no longer willing to put up with the evil of segregation, but want to do something about it and know that something can be done." How right he was indeed.

The masses of Negroes are through putting up with segregation; they are tired of it. They are tired of being pushed around in a democracy which fails to practice what it preaches. The Negro students of the South who have read the Constitution, and studied it, have read the amendments to the Constitution, and know the rights that are supposed to be theirs—they are coming to the point where they themselves want to do something about achieving these rights, not [to] depend on somebody else. The time has passed when we can look for pie in the sky, when we can depend upon someone else on high to solve the problem for us. The Negro students want to solve the problem themselves. Masses of older Negroes want to join them in that. We can't wait for the law. The Supreme Court decision in 1954 banning segregated schools has had almost eight years of existence, yet less than 8 percent of the Negro kids are in integrated schools. That is far too slow. Now the people themselves want to get involved, and they are. I was talking with one of the student leaders of the South only last week; he said, "I myself desegregated a lunch counter, not somebody else, not some big man, some powerful man, but me, little me. I walked the picket line and I sat in and the walls of segregation toppled. Now all people can eat there." One young prizefighter was a cellmate of mine in the prisons of Mississippi as a Freedom Rider; he had won his last fight and had a promising career. I saw him three weeks ago and asked him, "How are you coming along?" He said, "Not very well, I lost the last fight and I am through with the prize ring. I have no more interest in it. The only fight I want now," said he, "is the freedom fight. Because I, a little man, can become involved in it, and can help to win freedom." So that's what's happening; you see, we are going to do something about freedom now, we are not waiting for other people to do it. The student sit-ins have shown it; we are winning. As a result of one year of the student sit-ins, the lunch counters were desegregated in more than 150 cities. The walls are tumbling down.

Direct Action Brings Results

Who will say that lunch counters, which are scattered all over the country, are not important? Are we not to travel? Picket lines and boycotts brought Woolworth's to its knees. In its annual report of last year, Woolworth's indicated that profits had dropped and one reason for the drop was the nationwide boycott in which many Northern students, including Cornellians, participated. The picketing and the nationwide demonstrations are the reason that

I Have a Dream

Reprinted below are excerpts from perhaps the most famous expression of the integrationist ideal, Martin Luther King Jr.'s "I Have a Dream" address delivered during the March on Washington, on August 28, 1963.

I say to you today, my friends, even though we face the difficulties of today and tomorrow, I still have a dream. It is a dream deeply rooted in the American dream. I have a dream that one day this nation will rise up and live out the true meaning of its creed: "We hold these truths to be self-evident that all men are created equal."

I have a dream that one day on the red hills of Georgia the sons of former slaves and the sons of former slaveowners will be able to sit down together at the table of brotherhood.

I have a dream that one day even the state of Mississippi, a state sweltering with the heat of injustice, sweltering with the heat of oppression, will be transformed into an oasis of freedom and justice. I have a dream that my four little children will one day live in a nation where they will not be judged by the color of their skin but by the content of their character. I have a dream today.

I have a dream that one day down in Alabama with its vicious racists, with its Governor having his lips dripping with the words of interposition and nullification—one day right there in Alabama, little black boys and black girls will be able to join hands with little white boys and white girls as sisters and brothers.

the walls came down in the South, because people were in motion with their own bodies, marching with picket signs, sitting in, boycotting, withholding their patronage. In Savannah, Georgia, there was a boycott, in which 99 percent of the Negroes participated. They stayed out of the stores. They registered to vote. The store owners then got together and said, "We want to sit down and talk; gentlemen, you have proved your point. You have proved that you can control Negroes' purchasing power and that you can control their votes. We need no more proof, we are ready to hire the people that you send." Negroes are hired in those stores now as a result of this community-wide campaign. In Lexington, Kentucky, the theaters were opened up by CORE as a result of picketing and boycotting. Some of the theaters refused to admit Negroes, others would let Negroes sit up in the balcony. They boycotted one, picketed the others. In a short period of time, the theater owners sat down to negotiate. All of the theaters there are open now. Using the same technique, they provided scores of jobs in department stores, grocery stores, and more recently as city bus drivers.

Then came the Freedom Rides. Three hundred and twenty-five people were jailed in Jackson, Mississippi, others beaten, fighting for freedom non-violently. They brought down many, many barriers. They helped to create desegregation in cities throughout the South. The ICC [Interstate Commerce Commission] order was forthcoming as a result of the Freedom Rides and a more recent Supreme Court ruling. CORE sent test teams throughout the South after the ICC order went into effect. The test teams found that in hundreds of cities throughout the South, where terminals had been previously segregated, they now were desegregated and Negroes were using them. Mississippi is an exception, except for two cities; Louisiana is an exception, except for one pocket of the state; but by and large the Rides were successful. And then on Route 40. How many Negroes and interracial groups have driven Route 40 to Washington or to New York and carried their sandwiches, knowing that they could not eat between Wilmington and Baltimore. The Freedom Rides there, and some Cornell students participated in those Freedom Rides, brought down the barriers in more than half of those restaurants and each weekend, rides are taking place aimed at the others. By Easter we will have our Easter dinner in any place we choose on Route 40. At least fifty-three out of the eighty are now desegregated. In voter registration projects, we have registered seventeen thousand Negroes in South Carolina, previously unregistered. The politicians, segregationists, it's true, now call up our leaders and say, "I would like to talk to you because I don't believe in segregation as much as my opponent," or, "We would like to sit down and talk," or, "Can you come by my house and let's talk about this thing." Because they are realizing that now they have to be responsible to the votes of Negroes as well as the handful of whites, these are the things that are being done by people themselves in motion. Not waiting for someone else to do it, not looking forward to pie in the sky at some later date, not expecting a power on high to solve the problem for them, but working to solve it themselves and winning.

A Rejection of Racist Theories

What are our objectives: segregation, separation? Absolutely not! The disease and the evils that we have pointed to in our American culture have grown out of segregation and its partner prejudice. We are for integration, which is the repudiation of the evil of segregation. It is a rejection of the racist theories of DeGobineu, Lothrop Stoddard, and all the others. It matters not whether they say that whites are superior to Negroes and Negroes are inferior, or if they reverse the coin and say that Negroes are superior and whites are inferior. The theory is just as wrong, just as much a defiance of history. We reject those theories. We are work-

96

ing for the right of Negroes to enter all fields of activity in American life. To enter business if they choose, to enter the professions, to enter the sciences, to enter the arts, to enter the academic world. To be workers, to be laborers if they choose. Our objective is to have each individual accepted on the basis of his individual merit and not on the basis of his color. On the basis of what he is worth himself.

This has given a new pride to [a] large number of people. A pride to the people in Mississippi, who themselves saw others white and Negro, joining them in the fight for freedom; forty-one local citizens went into the jails of Mississippi joining the Freedom Riders. They have come out now and they have started their own non-violent Jackson movement for freedom. They are sitting in. They are picketing, they are boycotting, and it is working. In Macomb, Mississippi, local citizens are now seeking to register to vote, some of them registering. In Huntsville, Alabama, as a result of CORE'S campaign there (and we are now under injunction), for the past six weeks local Negro citizens have been sitting in every day at lunch counters. One of the white CORE leaders there in Huntsville was taken out of his house at gunpoint, undressed, and sprayed with mustard oil. That's the kind of treatment they have faced, but they will not give up because they know they are right and they see the effects of their efforts; they see it in the crumbling walls in interstate transportation and in other public facilities.

We are seeking an open society, an open society of freedom where people will be accepted for what they are worth, will be able to contribute fully to the total culture and the total life of the nation.

Now we know the disease, we know what is wrong with America, we know now that the CORE position is in trying to right it. We must do it in interracial groups because we do not think it is possible to fight against caste in a vehicle which in itself is a representative of caste. We know that the students are still sitting in, they are still fighting for freedom. What we want Mr. X, the representative of the Black Muslims and Elijah Muhammad, to tell us today, is what his program is, what he proposes to do about killing this disease. We know the disease, physician, what is your cure? What is your program and how do you hope to bring it into effect? How will you achieve it? It is not enough to tell us that it may be a program of a black state. The Communists had such a program in the thirties and part of the forties, and they dropped it before the fifties as being impractical. So we are not only interested in the terminology. We need to have it spelled out; if we are being asked to follow it, to believe in it, what does it mean? Is it a separate Negro society in each city? As a Harlem, a South Side Chicago? Is it a separate state in one part of the country? Is it a separate nation in Africa, or elsewhere? Then we need to know how is it to be achieved. I assume that before a large part of land could be granted to Negroes or to Jews or to anybody else in the country it would have to be approved by the Senate of the United States.

You must tell us, Mr. X, if you seriously think that the Senate of the United States which has refused or failed for all these years to pass a strong Civil Rights Bill, you must tell us if you really think that this Senate is going to give us, to give you, a black state. I am sure that Senator Eastland would so vote, but the land that he would give us would probably be in the bottom of the sea. After seeing Alabama and Mississippi, if the power were mine, I would give you those states, but the power is not mine, I do not vote in the Senate. Tell us how you expect to achieve this separate black state.

Now it is not enough for us to know that you believe in black businesses, all of us believe that all Americans who wish to go into business should go into business. We must know, we need to know, if we are to appraise your program, the kind of businesses, how they are to be established; will we have a General Motors, a General Electric? Will I be able to manufacture a Farmer Special? Where am I going to get the capital from? You must tell us if we are going to have a separate interstate bus line to take the place of Greyhound and Trailways. You must tell us how this separate interstate bus line is going to operate throughout the country if all of us are confined within one separate state.

You must tell us these things, Mr. X, spell them out. You must tell us also what the relationship will be between the black businesses which you would develop and the total American economy. Will it be a competition? Will it be a rival economy, a dual economy, or will there be cooperation between these two economies?

Our program is clear. We are going to achieve our goals of integration by non-violent direct action on an interracial level with whites and Negroes jointly cooperating to wipe out a disease which has afflicted and crippled all of them, white and black alike. The proof of the pudding is the eating. We have seen barriers fall as the result of using these techniques. We ask you, Mr. X, what is your program?

VIEWPOINT 2

"We think that the Negroes who accept token integration are . . . being hypocrites, because they are the only ones who benefit from it."

Integration Is a False Goal for Blacks

Malcolm X (1925–1965)

Although not a direct participant in the civil rights movement, Malcolm X, who was born Malcolm Little, was one of the most prominent and influential black leaders of the era. His father, a Baptist preacher and follower of 1920s black leader Marcus Garvey, was killed by white supremacists when Malcolm was six. While serving a prison sentence for burglary, Malcolm became a follower of Elijah Muhammad, the leader of the Lost-Found Nation of Islam, and changed his name to Malcolm X. After his parole in 1952 he became a Black Muslim minister in Harlem, New York. He attracted many followers and nationwide attention with sermons attacking "white devils." He asserted that only blacks could solve the problems that affected them, and urged blacks in America to form a separate nation. These views were perceived by many people as a sharp contrast to the goals of the civil rights movement as articulated by Martin Luther King Jr. and others.

The following viewpoint is taken from a 1962 debate between Malcolm X and civil rights activist James Farmer. In his remarks Malcolm gives both political and religious reasons why blacks should remain separate from whites, and questions the goals and organizations of the civil rights movement.

Malcolm X later broke from Elijah Muhammad's Nation of Islam and formed the Organization of Afro-American Unity. He was turning away from some of the beliefs expressed in this viewpoint on black separatism at the time of his assassination in 1965.

From Malcolm X's contribution to "Separation or Integration? A Debate at Cornell University," March 7, 1962. Reprinted from *Dialogue*, May 1962, by permission of Cornell United Religious Work.

In the name of Allah, the Beneficent, the Merciful, to whom all praise is due, whom we forever thank for giving America's twenty million so-called Negroes the most honorable Elijah Muhammad as our leader and our teacher and our guide.

I would point out at the beginning that I wasn't born Malcolm Little. Little is the name of the slave master who owned one of my grandparents during slavery, a white man, and the name Little was handed down to my grandfather, to my father, and on to me. But after hearing the teachings of the honorable Elijah Muhammad and realizing that Little is an English name, and I'm not an Englishman, I gave the Englishman back his name; and since my own had been stripped from me, hidden from me, and I don't know it, I use X; and someday, as we are taught by the honorable Elijah Muhammad, every black man, woman, and child in America will get back the same name, the same language, and the same culture that he had before he was kidnapped and brought to this country and stripped of these things.

I would like to point out in a recent column by James Reston on the editorial page of *The New York Times*, December 15, 1961, writing from London, [that] Mr. Reston, after interviewing several leading European statesmen, pointed out that the people of Europe, or the statesmen in Europe, don't feel that America or Europe has anything to worry about in Russia; that the people in Europe foresee the time when Russia, Europe, and America will have to unite together to ward off the threat of China and the non-white world. And if this same statement was made by a Muslim, or by the honorable Elijah Muhammad, it would be classified as racist; but Reston who is one of the leading correspondents in this country and writing for one of the most respected newspapers, points out that the holocaust that the West is facing is not something from Russia, but threats of the combined forces of the dark world against the white world.

Why do I mention this? Primarily because the most crucial problem facing the white world today is the race problem. And the most crucial problem facing white America today is the race problem. Mr. Farmer pointed out beautifully and quoted one writer actually as saying that the holocaust that America is facing is primarily still based upon race. This doesn't mean that when people point these things out that they are racist; this means that they are facing the facts of life that we are confronted with today. And one need only to look at the world troubles in their international context, national context, or local context, and one will always see the race problem right there, a problem that it is almost impossible to duck around.

It so happens that you and I were born at a time of great change, when changes are taking place. And if we can't react intelligently to these changes, then we are going to be destroyed. When you look into the United Nations set-up, the way it is, we see that there is a change of power taking place, a change of position, a change of influence, a change of control. Wherein, in the past, white people used to exercise unlimited control and authority over dark mankind, today they are losing their ability to dictate unilateral terms to dark mankind. Whereas, yesterday dark nations had no voice in their own affairs, today, the voice that they exercise in their own affairs is increasing, which means in essence that the voice of the white man or the white world is becoming more quiet every day, and the voice of the nonwhite world is becoming more loud every day. These are the facts of life and these are the changes that you and I, this generation, have to face up to on an international level, a national level, or a local level before we can get a solution to the problems that confront not only the white man, but problems that confront also the black man, or the non-white man.

When we look at the United Nations and see how these dark nations get their independence—they can out-vote the Western bloc or what is known as the white world—and to the point where up until last year the United Nations was controlled by the white powers, or Western powers, mainly Christian powers, and the secretaryship used to be in the hands of a white European Christian; but now when we look at the general structure of the United Nations we see a man from Asia, from Burma, who is occupying the position of Secretary, who is a Buddhist, by the way, and we find the man who is occupying the seat of President is a Moslem from Africa, namely Tunisia. Just in recent times all of these changes are taking place, and the white man has got to be able to face up to them, and the black man has to be able to face up to them, before we can get our problem solved, on an international level, a national level, as well as on the local level.

In terms of black and white, what this means is that the unlimited power and prestige of the white world is decreasing, while the power and prestige of the non-white world is increasing. And just as our African and Asian brothers wanted to have their own land, wanted to have their own country, wanted to exercise control over themselves and govern themselves—they didn't want to be governed by whites or Europeans or outsiders, they wanted control over something among the black masses here in America. I think it would be mighty naive on the part of the white man to see dark mankind all over the world stretching out to get a country of his own, a land of his own, an industry of his own, a society of his own, even a flag of his own, it would be mighty naive on the part of the white man to think that same feeling that is sweeping through the dark world is not going to leap nine thousand miles across the ocean and come into the black people here in this country, who have been begging you for four hundred years for something that they have yet to get.

In the areas of Asia and Africa where the whites gave freedom to the non-whites a transition took place, of friendliness and hospitality. In the areas where the non-whites had to exercise violence, today there is hostility between them and the white man. In this, we learn that the only way to solve a problem that is unjust, if you are wrong, is to take immediate action to correct it. But when the people against whom these actions have been directed have to take matters in their own hands, this creates hostility, and lack of friendliness and good relations between the two.

The Goal Is Dignity

I emphasize these things to point up the fact that we are living in an era of great change, when dark mankind wants freedom, justice, and equality. It is not a case of wanting integration or separation, it is a case of wanting freedom, justice, and equality.

Now if certain groups think that through integration they are going to get freedom, justice, equality, and human dignity, then well and good, we will go along with the integrationists. But if integration is not going to return human dignity to dark mankind, then integration is not the solution to the problem. And ofttimes we make the mistake of confusing the objective with the means by which the objective is to be obtained. It is not integration that Negroes in America want, it is human dignity. They want to be recognized as human beings. And if integration is going to bring us recognition as human beings, then we will integrate. But if integration is not going to bring us recognition as human beings, then integration [is] "out the window," and we have to find another means or method and try that to get our objectives reached.

The same hand that has been writing on the wall in Africa and Asia is also writing on the wall right here in America. The same rebellion, the same impatience, the same anger that exists in the hearts of the dark people in Africa and Asia is existing in the hearts and minds of twenty million black people in this country who have been just as thoroughly colonized as the people in Africa and Asia. Only the black man in America has been colonized mentally, his mind has been destroyed. And today, even though he goes to college, he comes out and still doesn't even know he is a black man; he is ashamed of what he is, because his culture has been destroyed, his identity has been destroyed; he has been made to hate his black skin, he has been made to hate the texture of his hair, he has been made to hate the features that

God gave him. Because the honorable Elijah Muhammad is coming along today and teaching us the truth about black people to make us love ourselves instead of realizing that it is you who taught us to hate ourselves and our own kind, you accuse the honorable Elijah Muhammad of being a hate teacher and accuse him of being a racist. He is only trying to undo the white supremacy that you have indoctrinated the entire world with.

The influence of Malcolm X on American blacks extended well beyond his death by assassination in 1965.

I might point out that it makes America look ridiculous to stand up in world conferences and refer to herself as the leader of the free world. Here is a country, Uncle Sam, standing up and pointing a finger at the Portuguese, and at the French, and at other colonizers, and there are twenty million black people in this country who are still confined to second-class citizenship, twenty million black people in this country who are still segregated and Jim-Crowed, as my friend, Dr. Farmer, has already pointed out. And despite the fact that twenty million black people here yet don't have freedom, justice, and equality, Adlai Stevenson has nerve enough to stand up in the United Nations and point the finger at

South Africa, and at Portugal, and at some of these other countries. All we say is that South Africa preaches what it practices and practices what it preaches; America preaches one thing and practices another. And we don't want to integrate with hypocrites who preach one thing and practice another.

Integration Supporters a Minority

The good point in all of this is that there is an awakening going on among whites in America today, and this awakening is manifested in this way: two years ago you didn't know that there were black people in this country who didn't want to integrate with you; two years ago the white public had been brainwashed into thinking that every black man in this country wanted to force his way into your community, force his way into your schools, or force his way into your factories; two years ago you thought that all you would have to do is give us a little token integration and the race problem would be solved. Why? Because the people in the black community who didn't want integration were never given a voice, were never given a platform, were never given an opportunity to shout out the fact that integration would never solve the problem. And it has only been during the past year that the white public has begun to realize that the problem will never be solved unless a solution is devised acceptable to the black masses, as well as the black bourgeoisie—the upper-class or middle-class Negro. And when the whites began to realize that these integration-minded Negroes were in the minority, rather than in the majority, then they began to offer an open forum and give those who want separation an opportunity to speak their mind too.

We who are black in the black belt, or black community, or black neighborhood, can easily see that our people who settle for integration are usually the middle-class so-called Negroes, who are in the minority. Why? Because they have confidence in the white man; they have absolute confidence that you will change. They believe that they can change you, they believe that there is still hope in the American dream. But what to them is an American dream to us is an American nightmare, and we don't think that it is possible for the American white man in sincerity to take the action necessary to correct the unjust conditions that twenty million black people here are made to suffer morning, noon, and night. And because we don't have any hope or confidence or faith in the American white man's ability to bring about a change in the injustices that exist, instead of asking or seeking to integrate into the American society we want to face the facts of the problem the way they are, and separate ourselves. And in separating ourselves this doesn't mean that we are anti-white, or anti-

American, or anti-anything. We feel that if integration all these years hasn't solved the problem yet, then we want to try something new, something different, and something that is in accord with the conditions as they actually exist.

The honorable Elijah Muhammad teaches us that there are over 725 million Moslems or Muslims on this earth. I use both words interchangeably. I use the word Moslem for those who can't undergo the change, and I use the word Muslim for those who can. He teaches us that the world of Islam stretches from the China Seas to the shores of West Africa and that the twenty million black people in this country are the lost-found members of the nation of Islam. He teaches us that before we were kidnapped by your grandfathers and brought to this country and put in chains, our religion was Islam, our culture was Islamic, we came from the Muslim world, we were kidnapped and brought here out of the Muslim world. And after being brought here we were stripped of our language, stripped of our ability to speak our mother tongue, and it's a crime today to have to admit that there are twenty million black people in this country who not only can't speak their mother tongue, but don't even know they ever had one. This points up the crime of how thoroughly and completely the black man in America has been robbed by the white man of his culture, of his identity, of his soul, of his self. And because he has been robbed of his self, he is trying to accept your self. Because he doesn't know who he is, now he wants to be who you are. Because he doesn't know what belongs to him, he is trying to lay claim to what belongs to you. You have brain-washed him and made him a monster. He is black on the outside, but you have made him white on the inside. Now he has a white heart and a white brain, and he's breathing down your throat and down your neck because he thinks he's a white man the same as you are. He thinks that he should have your house, that he should have your factory, he thinks that he should even have your school, and most of them even think that they should have your woman, and most of them are after your woman.

Nation of Islam Beliefs

The honorable Elijah Muhammad teaches us that the black people in America, the so-called Negroes, are the people who are referred to in the Bible as the lost sheep, who are to be returned to their own in the last days. He says that we are also referred to in the Bible, symbolically, as the lost tribe. He teaches us in our religion that we are those people whom the Bible refers to who would be lost until the end of time. Lost in a house that is not theirs, lost in a land that is not theirs, lost in a country that is not theirs, and who will be found in the last days by the Messiah who will awaken them and enlighten them, and teach them that which they had been stripped of, and then this would give them the desire to come together among their own kind and go back among their own kind.

And this, basically, is why we who are followers of the honorable Elijah Muhammad don't accept integration: we feel that we are living at the end of time, by this, we feel that we are living at the end of the world. Not the end of the earth, but the end of the world. He teaches us that there are many worlds. The planet is an earth, and there is only one earth, but there are many worlds on this earth, the Eastern world and the Western world. There is a dark world and a white world. There is the world of Christianity, and the world of Islam. All of these are worlds and he teaches us that when the book speaks of the end of time, it doesn't mean the end of the earth, but it means the end of time for certain segments of people, or a certain world that is on this earth. Today, we who are here in America who have awakened to the knowledge of ourselves, we believe that there is no God but Allah, and we believe that the religion of Islam is Allah's religion, and we believe that it is Allah's intention to spread his religion throughout the entire earth. We believe that the earth will become all Muslim, all Islam, and because we are in a Christian country we believe that this Christian country will have to accept Allah as God, accept the religion of Islam as God's religion, or otherwise God will come in and wipe it out. And we don't want to be wiped out with the American white man, we don't want to integrate with him, we want to separate from him.

Separation Is the Best Solution

The method by which the honorable Elijah Muhammad is straightening out our problem is not teaching us to force ourselves into your society, or force ourselves even into your political, economic, or any phase of your society, but he teaches us that the best way to solve this problem is for complete separation. He says that since the black man here in America is actually the property that was stolen from the East by the American white man, since you have awakened today and realized that this is what we are, we should be separated from you, and your government should ship us back to where we came from, not at our expense, because we didn't pay to come here. We were brought here in chains. So the honorable Elijah Muhammad and the Muslims who follow him, we want to go back to our own people. We want to be returned to our own people.

But in teaching this among our people and the masses of black people in this country, we discover that the American government is the foremost agency in opposing any move by any large

Neither Integration Nor Separation

The evolution of Malcolm X's views on racial separation and integration can be seen in this excerpt from a 1964 address.

America's strategy is the same strategy as that which was used in the past by the colonial powers: divide and conquer. She plays one Negro leader against the other. She plays one Negro organization against the other. She makes us think we have different goals, different objectives. As soon as one Negro says something, she runs to this Negro and asks him what do you think about what he said. Why anybody can see through that today—except some of the Negro leaders.

All of our people have the same goals. The same objective. That objective is freedom, justice, equality. All of us want recognition and respect as human beings. We don't want to be integrationists. Nor do we want to be separationists. We want to be human beings. Integration is only a method that is used by some groups to obtain freedom, justice, equality, and respect as human beings. Separation is only a method that is used by other groups to obtain freedom, justice, equality, or human dignity. . . .

We have to keep in mind at all times that we are not fighting for integration, nor are we fighting for separation. We are fighting for recognition as human beings. We are fighting for the right to live as free humans in this society. In fact, we are actually fighting for rights that are even greater than civil rights and that is human rights.

We are fighting for human rights in 1964. This is a shame. The civil-rights struggle has failed to produce concrete results because it has kept us barking up the wrong tree. It has made us put the cart ahead of the horse. We must have human rights before we can secure civil rights. We must be respected as humans before we can be recognized as citizens.

---

number of black people to leave here and go back among our own kind. The honorable Elijah Muhammad's words and work are harassed daily by the FBI and every other government agency which uses various tactics to make the so-called Negroes in every community think that we are all about to be rounded up, and they will be rounded up too if they will listen to Mr. Muhammad; but what the American government has failed to realize, the best way to open up a black man's head today and make him listen to another black man is to speak against that black man. But when you begin to pat a black man on the back, no black man in his right mind will trust that black man any longer. And it is because of this hostility on the part of the government toward our leaving here that the honorable Elijah Muhammad says then, if the American white man or the American government doesn't want us to leave, and the government has proven its inability to bring about integration or give us freedom, justice, and equality on a basis, equally mixed up with white people, then what are we going to do? If the government doesn't want us to go back among our own people, or to our own people, and at the same time the government has proven its inability to give us justice, the honorable Elijah Muhammad says if you don't want us to go and we can't stay here and live in peace together, then the best solution is separation. And this is what he means when he says that some of the territory here should be set aside, and let our people go off to ourselves and try and solve our own problem.

Some of you may say, Well, why should you give us part of this country? The honorable Elijah Muhammad says that for four hundred years we contributed our slave labor to make the country what it is. If you were to take the individual salary or allowances of each person in this audience it would amount to nothing individually, but when you take it collectively all in one pot you have a heavy load. Just the weekly wage. And if you realize that from anybody who could collect all of the wages from the persons in this audience right here for one month, why they would be so wealthy they couldn't walk. And if you see that, then you can imagine the result of millions of black people working for nothing for 310 years. And that is the contribution that we made to America. Not Jackie Robinson, not Marian Anderson, not George Washington Carver, that's not our contribution; our contribution to American society is 310 years of free slave labor for which we have not been paid one dime. We who are Muslims, followers of the honorable Elijah Muhammad, don't think that an integrated cup of coffee is sufficient payment for 310 years of slave labor. . . .

What the Majority Wants

The only way you can solve the race problem as it exists is to take into consideration the feelings of the masses, not the minority; the majority, not the minority. And it is proof that the masses of white people don't want Negroes forcing their way into their neighborhood and the masses of black people don't think it's any solution for us to force ourselves into the white neighborhood, so the only ones who want integration are the Negro minority, as I say, the bourgeoisie and the white minority, the so-called white liberals. And the same white liberal who professes to want integration whenever the Negro moves to his neighborhood, he is the first one to move out. And I was talking with one today who said he was a liberal and I asked him where did he live, and he lived in an all-white neighborhood and probably might for the rest of his life. This is conjecture, but I think it stands true. The Civil War was fought one hundred years ago, supposedly to solve this problem. After the Civil War was fought, the problem still existed. Along behind that, the Thirteenth and Fourteenth Amendments were brought about in the Constitution supposedly to solve the problem; after the Amendments, the problem was still right here with us.

Most Negroes think that the Civil War was fought to make them citizens; they think that it was fought to free them from slavery because the real purpose of the Civil War is clothed in hypocrisy. The real purpose of the Amendments is clothed in hypocrisy. The real purpose behind the Supreme Court Desegregation decision was clothed in hypocrisy. And any time integrationists, NAACP, CORE, Urban League, or what have you, will stand up and tell me to spell out how we are going to bring about separation, and here they are integrationists, a philosophy which is supposed to have the support of the Senate, Congress, President, and the Supreme Court, and still with all of that support and hypocritical agreeing, eight years after the desegregation decision, you still don't have what the Court decided on.

So we think this, that when whites talk integration they are being hypocrites, and we think that the Negroes who accept token integration are also being hypocrites, because they are the only ones who benefit from it, the handful of hand-picked, high-class, middle-class Uncle Tom Negroes. They are hand-picked by whites and turned loose in a white community and they're satisfied. But if all of the black people went into the white community, overnight you would have a race war. If four or five little black students going to school in New Orleans bring about the riots that we saw down there, what do you think would happen if all of the black people tried to go to any school that they want, you would have a race war. So our approach to it, those of us who follow the honorable Elijah Muhammad, we feel that it is more sensible than running around here waiting for the whites to allow us inside their attic or inside their basement.

Civil Rights Groups

Every Negro group that we find in the Negro community that is integrated is controlled by the whites who belong to it, or it is led by the whites who belong to it. NAACP has had a white president for fifty-three years, it has been in existence for fifty-three years; Roy Wilkins is the executive secretary, but Spingarn, a white man, has been the president for the past twenty-three years, and before him, his brother, another white man, was president. They have never had a black president. Urban League, another so-called Negro organization, doesn't have a black president, it has a white president. Now this doesn't mean that that's racism, it only means that the same organizations that are accusing you of practicing discrimination, when it comes to the leadership they're practicing discrimination themselves.

The honorable Elijah Muhammad says, and points out to us that in this book (*Anti-Slavery*) written by a professor from the University of Michigan, Dwight Lowell Dumond, a person who is an authority on the race question or slave question, his findings were used by Thurgood Marshall in winning the Supreme Court Desegregation decision. And in the preface of this book, it says that second-class citizenship is only a modified form of slavery. Now I'll tell you why I'm dwelling on this; everything that you have devised yourself to solve the race problem has been hypocrisy, because the scientists who delved into it teach us or tell us that second-class citizenship is only a modified form of slavery, which means the Civil War didn't end slavery and the Amendments didn't end slavery. They didn't do it because we still have to wrestle the Supreme Court and the Congress and the Senate to correct the hypocrisy that's been practiced against us by whites for the past umteen years.

And because this was done, the American white man today subconsciously still regards that black man as something below himself. And you will never get the American white man to accept the so-called Negro as an integrated part of his society until the image of the Negro the white man has is changed, and until the image that the Negro has of himself is also changed.

"When rights are consistently denied, a cause should be pressed in the courts and in negotiations among local leaders, and not in the streets."

Civil Disobedience Should Not Be Employed

Alabama Clergymen Public Statements

Birmingham, Alabama, became the focus of national attention in the spring of 1963 as civil rights activists led by Martin Luther King Jr. and Fred L. Shuttlesworth participated in large marches, sit-ins, and other large nonviolent demonstrations. Local authorities, led by police commissioner Eugene "Bull" Connor, responded with massive arrests and the use of cattle prods, attack dogs, and high-pressure water hoses to disperse the demonstrators. King was among the thousands of people arrested and jailed. The size of the demonstrations and the response they created provoked debate on the civil disobedience practiced by King and his followers.

The following viewpoint consists of two public statements by religious leaders in Birmingham made before and during these civil rights confrontations. The first was made on January 17, 1963, and was aimed primarily at whites (including Alabama governor George Wallace) who advocated resistance to court orders instituting desegregation. The second statement was made on April 12, 1963, and was aimed at black civil rights leaders who were planning and leading the demonstrations. In both cases the religious leaders emphasize the importance of obeying the law. Their criticism of the civil disobedience of civil rights protesters inspired one of the most famous documents of the civil rights movement, King's "Letter from Birmingham City Jail."

"An Appeal for Law and Order and Common Sense" and "Letter to Dr. King," two public statements from Alabama clergymen published in the *Birmingham News*, January 17 and April 12, 1963, respectively.

I

In these times of tremendous tensions, and changes in cherished patterns of life in our beloved Southland, it is essential that men who occupy places of responsibility and leadership shall speak concerning their honest convictions.

We the undersigned clergymen have been chosen to carry heavy responsibility. . . . We speak in a spirit of humility, and we do not pretend to know all the answers, for the issues are not simple. Nevertheless, we believe our people expect and deserve leadership from us, and speak with firm conviction for we do know the ultimate spirit in which all problems of human relations must be solved.

It is clear that a series of court decisions may soon bring about the desegregation of certain schools and colleges in Alabama. Many sincere people oppose this change and are deeply troubled by it. As Southerners, we understand this. We nevertheless feel that defiance is neither the right answer nor the solution. And we feel that inflammatory and rebellious statements can lead only to violence, discord, confusion and disgrace for our beloved state.

We therefore affirm and commend to our people:

1. That hatred and violence have no sanction in our religious and political tradition.

2. That there may be disagreement concerning laws and social change without advocating defiance, anarchy and subversion.

3. That laws may be tested in courts or changed by legislation, but not ignored by whim of individuals.

4. That constitutions may be amended or judges impeached by proper action, but our American way of life depends upon obedience to the decision of courts of competent jurisdiction in the meantime.

5. That no person's freedom is safe unless every person's freedom is equally protected.

6. That freedom of speech must at all costs be preserved and exercised, without fear of recrimination or harassment.

7. That every human being is created in the image of God and is entitled to respect as a fellow human being with all basic rights, privileges and responsibilities which belong to humanity.

It is understood that those who strongly oppose desegregation may frankly and fairly pursue their convictions in the courts, and in the meantime should peacefully abide by the decisions of those same courts.

We recognize that our problems cannot be solved in our own strength nor on the basis of human wisdom alone. The situation which confronts us calls for earnest prayer, for clear thought, for

Photographs and television images of civil rights demonstrators being met with fire hoses and other violent measures drew national attention to Birmingham, Alabama, in 1963.

understanding love, and for courageous action. Thus we call on all people of goodwill to join us in seeking divine guidance for law and order and common sense.

Signed by:

Bishop Nolan B. Harmon, Bishop of the North Alabama Conference of the Methodist Church

Bishop Paul Hardin, Bishop of the Alabama-West Florida Conference of the Methodist Church

C.C.J. Carpenter, D.D., LL.D., Episcopal Bishop of Alabama

Joseph A. Durick, D.D., Auxiliary Bishop, Catholic Diocese of Mobile-Birmingham

Earl Stallings, pastor, First Baptist Church, Birmingham, Alabama

George M. Murray, D.D., LL.D., Bishop Coadjutor, Episcopal Diocese of Alabama

Rabbi Milton L. Grafman, Temple Emanu-El, Birmingham, Alabama

Edward V. Ramage, D.D., moderator, Synod of the Alabama Presbyterian Church in the United States

Rev. Soterios D. Gouvellis, priest, Holy Trinity Holy Cross Greek Orthodox Church

Rabbi Eugene Blackschleger, Temple Beth-Or, Montgomery, Alabama

J.T. Beale, secretary-director, Christian Churches of Alabama

II

We the undersigned clergymen are among those who, in January, issued "An Appeal for Law and Order and Common Sense," in dealing with racial problems in Alabama. We expressed understanding that honest convictions in racial matters could properly be pursued in the courts, but urged that decisions of those courts should in the meantime be peacefully obeyed.

Since that time there had been some evidence of increased forbearance and a willingness to face facts. Responsible citizens have undertaken to work on various problems which cause racial friction and unrest. In Birmingham, recent public events have given indication that we all have opportunity for a new constructive and realistic approach to racial problems.

Untimely Demonstrations

However, we are now confronted by a series of demonstrations by some of our Negro citizens, directed and led in part by outsiders. We recognize the natural impatience of people who feel that their hopes are slow in being realized. But we are convinced that these demonstrations are unwise and untimely.

We agree rather with certain local Negro leadership which has called for honest and open negotiation of racial issues in our area. And we believe this kind of facing of issues can best be accomplished by citizens of our own metropolitan area, white and Negro, meeting with their knowledge and experience of the local situation. All of us need to face that responsibility and find proper channels for its accomplishment.

Just as we formerly pointed out that "hatred and violence have no sanction in our religious and political traditions," we also point out that such actions as incite to hatred and violence, however technically peaceful those actions may be, have not contributed to the resolution of our local problems. We do not believe that these days of new hope are days when extreme measures are justified in Birmingham.

We commend the community as a whole, and the local news media and law enforcement officials in particular, on the calm manner in which these demonstrations have been handled. We urge the public to continue to show restraint should the demonstrations continue, and the law enforcement officials to remain calm and continue to protect our city from violence.

We further strongly urge our own Negro community to withdraw support from these demonstrations, and to unite locally in working peacefully for a better Birmingham. When rights are consistently denied, a cause should be pressed in the courts and in negotiations among local leaders, and not in the streets. We appeal to both our white and Negro citizenry to observe the principles of law and order and common sense.

Signed by:

C.C.J. Carpenter, D.D., LL.D., Episcopal Bishop of Alabama

Joseph A. Durick, D.D., Auxiliary Bishop, Catholic Diocese of Mobile-Birmingham

Rabbi Milton L. Grafman, Temple Emanu-El, Birmingham, Alabama

Bishop Paul Hardin, Bishop of the Alabama-West Florida Conference of the Methodist Church

Bishop Nolan B. Harmon, Bishop of the North Alabama Conference of the Methodist Church

George M. Murray, D.D., LL.D., Bishop Coadjutor, Episcopal Diocese of Alabama

Edward V. Ramage, Moderator, Synod of the Alabama Presbyterian Church in the United States

Earl Stallings, Pastor, First Baptist Church, Birmingham, Alabama

VIEWPOINT 4

"There are just *laws and there are* unjust *laws. . . .
One has a moral responsibility to disobey unjust laws."*

Civil Disobedience Should Be Employed

Martin Luther King Jr. (1929–1968)

In April 1963 a civil rights campaign of demonstrations and sit-ins began in Birmingham, Alabama, one of the most segregated cities of the South. The campaigns were organized by the Southern Christian Leadership Conference (SCLC), led by Martin Luther King Jr., and the Alabama Christian Movement for Human Rights (ACMHR), a local civil rights group led by Fred L. Shuttlesworth. On April 12, 1963, King defied a state court order barring further demonstrations and was arrested and placed in solitary confinement. King's actions were criticized by a group of local clergymen in an open letter that described the civil rights demonstrations as "unwise and untimely." The following viewpoint is excerpted from King's response to these criticisms written while he was in jail. King's "Letter from Birmingham City Jail" was later published as a pamphlet and reprinted in several national periodicals. In his response, King defends the practice of civil disobedience as a necessary step to force the United States to confront the issues of racism and civil rights.

My Dear Fellow Clergymen,
While confined here in the Birmingham City Jail, I came across your recent statement calling our present activities "unwise and untimely." Seldom, if ever, do I pause to answer criticism of my

From Martin Luther King Jr., "Letter from Birmingham City Jail," April 16, 1963. Reprinted by arrangement with The Heirs to the Estate of Martin Luther King Jr., c/o Joan Daves Agency as agent for the proprietor. Copyright 1963 by Martin Luther King Jr.; copyright renewed 1991 by Coretta Scott King.

work and ideas. If I sought to answer all of the criticisms that cross my desk, my secretaries would be engaged in little else in the course of the day and I would have no time for constructive work. But since I feel that you are men of genuine good will and your criticisms are sincerely set forth, I would like to answer your statement in what I hope will be patient and reasonable terms.

I think I should give the reason for my being in Birmingham, since you have been influenced by the argument of "outsiders coming in." I have the honor of serving as president of the Southern Christian Leadership Conference, an organization operating in every Southern state with headquarters in Atlanta, Georgia. We have some eighty-five affiliate organizations all across the South—one being the Alabama Christian Movement for Human Rights. Whenever necessary and possible we share staff, educational, and financial resources with our affiliates. Several months ago our local affiliate here in Birmingham invited us to be on call to engage in a nonviolent direct action program if such were deemed necessary. We readily consented and when the hour came we lived up to our promises. So I am here, along with several members of my staff, because we were invited here. I am here because I have basic organizational ties here. Beyond this, I am in Birmingham because injustice is here. Just as the eighth-century prophets left their little villages and carried their "thus saith the Lord" far beyond the boundaries of their home town, and just as the Apostle Paul left his little village of Tarsus and carried the gospel of Jesus Christ to practically every hamlet and city of the Graeco-Roman world, I too am compelled to carry the gospel of freedom beyond my particular home town. Like Paul, I must constantly respond to the Macedonian call for aid.

Moreover, I am cognizant of the interrelatedness of all communities and states. I cannot sit idly by in Atlanta and not be concerned about what happens in Birmingham. Injustice anywhere is a threat to justice everywhere. We are caught in an inescapable network of mutuality tied in a single garment of destiny. Whatever affects one directly affects all indirectly. Never again can we afford to live with the narrow, provincial "outside agitator" idea. Anyone who lives inside the United States can never be considered an outsider anywhere in this country.

Reasons for Demonstrations

You deplore the demonstrations that are presently taking place in Birmingham. But I am sorry that your statement did not express a similar concern for the conditions that brought the demonstrations into being. I am sure that each of you would want to go beyond the superficial social analyst who looks merely at effects, and does not grapple with underlying causes. I would not hesitate to say that it is unfortunate that so-called demonstrations are taking place in Birmingham at this time, but I would say in more emphatic terms that it is even more unfortunate that the white power structure of this city left the Negro community with no other alternative.

In any nonviolent campaign there are four basic steps: (1) collection of the facts to determine whether injustices are alive; (2) negotiation; (3) self-purification; and (4) direct action. We have gone through all of these steps in Birmingham. There can be no gainsaying of the fact that racial injustice engulfs this community. Birmingham is probably the most thoroughly segregated city in the United States. Its ugly record of police brutality is known in every section of this country. Its unjust treatment of Negroes in the courts is a notorious reality. There have been more unsolved bombings of Negro homes and churches in Birmingham than any city in this nation. These are the hard, brutal, and unbelievable facts. On the basis of these conditions Negro leaders sought to negotiate with the city fathers. But the political leaders consistently refused to engage in good faith negotiation.

Then came the opportunity last September to talk with some of the leaders of the economic community. In these negotiating sessions certain promises were made by the merchants—such as the promise to remove the humiliating racial signs from the stores. On the basis of these promises Reverend Shuttlesworth and the leaders of the Alabama Christian Movement for Human Rights agreed to call a moratorium on any type of demonstrations. As the weeks and months unfolded we realized that we were the victims of a broken promise. The signs remained. As in so many experiences of the past, we were confronted with blasted hopes, and the dark shadow of a deep disappointment settled upon us. So we had no alternative except that of preparing for direct action, whereby we would present our very bodies as a means of laying our case before the conscience of the local and national community. We were not unmindful of the difficulties involved. So we decided to go through a process of self-purification. We started having workshops on nonviolence and repeatedly asked ourselves the questions, "Are you able to accept blows without retaliating?" "Are you able to endure the ordeals of jail?"

We decided to set our direct action program around the Easter season, realizing that, with the exception of Christmas, this was the largest shopping period of the year. Knowing that a strong economic withdrawal program would be the by-product of direct action, we felt that this was the best time to bring pressure on the merchants for the needed changes. Then it occurred to us that the March election was ahead, and so we speedily decided to postpone action until after election day. When we discovered that Mr.

[Eugene "Bull"] Connor was in the run-off, we decided again to postpone action so that the demonstrations could not be used to cloud the issues. At this time we agreed to begin our nonviolent witness the day after the run-off.

This reveals that we did not move irresponsibly into direct action. We too wanted to see Mr. Connor defeated; so we went through postponement after postponement to aid in this community need. After this we felt that direct action could be delayed no longer.

The Purpose of Direct Action

You may well ask, "Why direct action? Why sit-ins, marches, etc.? Isn't negotiation a better path?" You are exactly right in your call for negotiation. Indeed, this is the purpose of direct action. Nonviolent direct action seeks to create such a crisis and establish such creative tension that a community that has constantly refused to negotiate is forced to confront the issue. It seeks so to dramatize the issue that it can no longer be ignored.

I just referred to the creation of tension as a part of the work of the nonviolent resister. This may sound rather shocking. But I must confess that I am not afraid of the word tension. I have earnestly worked and preached against violent tension, but there is a type of constructive nonviolent tension that is necessary for growth. Just as Socrates felt that it was necessary to create a tension in the mind so that individuals could rise from the bondage of myths and half-truths to the unfettered realm of creative analysis and objective appraisal, we must see the need of having nonviolent gadflies to create the kind of tension in society that will help men rise from the dark depths of prejudice and racism to the majestic heights of understanding and brotherhood. So the purpose of the direct action is to create a situation so crisis-packed that it will inevitably open the door to negotiation. We, therefore, concur with you in your call for negotiation. Too long has our beloved Southland been bogged down in the tragic attempt to live in monologue rather than dialogue.

One of the basic points in your statement is that our acts are untimely. Some have asked, "Why didn't you give the new administration time to act?" The only answer that I can give to this inquiry is that the new administration must be prodded about as much as the outgoing one before it acts. We will be sadly mistaken if we feel that the election of Mr. [Albert] Boutwell will bring the millennium to Birmingham. While Mr. Boutwell is much more articulate and gentle than Mr. Connor, they are both segregationists dedicated to the task of maintaining the status quo. The hope I see in Mr. Boutwell is that he will be reasonable enough to see the futility of massive resistance to desegregation.

But he will not see this without pressure from the devotees of civil rights.

My friends, I must say to you that we have not made a single gain in civil rights without determined legal and nonviolent pressure. History is the long and tragic story of the fact that privileged groups seldom give up their privileges voluntarily. Individuals may see the moral light and voluntarily give up their unjust posture; but as Reinhold Niebuhr has reminded us, groups are more immoral than individuals.

Why We Cannot Wait

We know through painful experience that freedom is never voluntarily given by the oppressor; it must be demanded by the oppressed. Frankly I have never yet engaged in a direct action movement that was "well timed," according to the timetable of those who have not suffered unduly from the disease of segregation. For years now I have heard the word "Wait!" It rings in the ear of every Negro with a piercing familiarity. This "wait" has almost always meant "never." It has been a tranquilizing Thalidomide, relieving the emotional stress for a moment, only to give birth to an ill-formed infant of frustration. We must come to see with the distinguished jurist of yesterday that "justice too long delayed is justice denied." We have waited for more than 340 years for our constitutional and God-given rights. The nations of Asia and Africa are moving with jet-like speed toward the goal of political independence, and we still creep at horse and buggy pace toward the gaining of a cup of coffee at a lunch counter.

I guess it is easy for those who have never felt the stinging darts of segregation to say wait. But when you have seen vicious mobs lynch your mothers and fathers at will and drown your sisters and brothers at whim; when you have seen hate-filled policemen curse, kick, brutalize, and even kill your black brothers and sisters with impunity; when you see the vast majority of your twenty million Negro brothers smothering in an air-tight cage of poverty in the midst of an affluent society; when you suddenly find your tongue twisted and your speech stammering as you seek to explain to your six-year-old daughter why she can't go to the public amusement park that has just been advertised on television, and see tears welling up in her little eyes when she is told that Funtown is closed to colored children, and see the depressing clouds of inferiority begin to form in her little mental sky, and see her begin to distort her little personality by unconsciously developing a bitterness toward white people; when you have to concoct an answer for a five-year-old son asking in agonizing pathos: "Daddy, why do white people treat colored people so mean?"; when you take a cross country drive and find it necessary to sleep night after night in the uncomfortable corners of your automobile because no motel will accept you; when you are humiliated day in and day out by nagging signs reading "white" men and "colored"; when your first name becomes "nigger" and your middle name becomes "boy" (however old you are) and your last name becomes "John," and when your wife and mother are never given the respected title "Mrs."; when you are harried by day and haunted by night by the fact that you are a Negro, living constantly at tip-toe stance never quite knowing what to expect next, and plagued with inner fears and outer resentments; when you are forever fighting a degenerating sense of "nobodiness"—then you will understand why we find it difficult to wait. There comes a time when the cup of endurance runs over, and men are no longer willing to be plunged into an abyss of injustice where they experience the bleakness of corroding despair. I hope, sirs, you can understand our legitimate and unavoidable impatience.

Just and Unjust Laws

You express a great deal of anxiety over our willingness to break laws. This is certainly a legitimate concern. Since we so diligently urge people to obey the Supreme Court's decision of 1954 outlawing segregation in the public schools, it is rather strange and paradoxical to find us consciously breaking laws. One may well ask, "How can you advocate breaking some laws and obeying others?" The answer is found in the fact that there are two types of laws: There are *just* laws and there are *unjust* laws. I would be the first to advocate obeying just laws. One has not only a legal but a moral responsibility to obey just laws. Conversely, one has a moral responsibility to disobey unjust laws. I would agree with Saint Augustine that "An unjust law is no law at all."

Now what is the difference between the two? How does one determine when a law is just or unjust? A just law is a man-made code that squares with the moral law or the law of God. An unjust law is a mode that is out of harmony with the moral law. To put it in the terms of Saint Thomas Aquinas, an unjust law is a human law that is not rooted in eternal and natural law. Any law that uplifts human personality is just. Any law that degrades human personality is unjust.

All segregation statutes are unjust because segregation distorts the soul and damages the personality. It gives the segregator a false sense of superiority and the segregated a false sense of inferiority. To use the words of Martin Buber, the great Jewish philosopher, segregation substitutes an "I-it" relationship for the "I-thou" relationship, and ends up relegating persons to the status of things. So segregation is not only politically, economically, and sociologically unsound, but it is morally wrong and sinful.

Paul Tillich has said that sin is separation. Isn't segregation an existential expression of man's tragic separation, an expression of his awful estrangement, his terrible sinfulness? So I can urge men to obey the 1954 decision of the Supreme Court because it is morally right, and I can urge them to disobey segregation ordinances because they are morally wrong.

Let us turn to a more concrete example of just and unjust laws. An unjust law is a code that a majority inflicts on a minority that is not binding on itself. This is *difference* made legal. On the other hand a just law is a code that a majority compels a minority to follow that it is willing to follow itself. This is *sameness* made legal.

Martin Luther King Jr. was arrested in Birmingham for defying a state injunction against demonstrations by leading a march on April 12 (Good Friday), 1963.

Let me give another explanation. An unjust law is a code inflicted upon a minority which that minority had no part in enacting or creating because they did not have the unhampered right to vote. Who can say the legislature of Alabama which set up the segregation laws was democratically elected? Throughout the state of Alabama all types of conniving methods are used to prevent Negroes from becoming registered voters and there are some counties without a single Negro registered to vote despite the fact that the Negro constitutes a majority of the population. Can any law set up in such a state be considered democratically structured?

These are just a few examples of unjust and just laws. There are some instances when a law is just on its face but unjust in its application. For instance, I was arrested Friday on a charge of parading without a permit. Now there is nothing wrong with an ordinance which requires a permit for a parade, but when the ordinance is used to preserve segregation and to deny citizens the First Amendment privilege of peaceful assembly and peaceful protest, then it becomes unjust.

I hope you can see the distinction I am trying to point out. In no sense do I advocate evading or defying the law as the rabid segregationist would do. This would lead to anarchy. One who breaks an unjust law must do it *openly*, *lovingly* (not hatefully as the white mothers did in New Orleans when they were seen on television screaming "nigger, nigger, nigger") and with a willingness to accept the penalty. I submit that an individual who breaks a law that conscience tells him is unjust, and willingly accepts the penalty by staying in jail to arouse the conscience of the community over its injustice, is in reality expressing the very highest respect for law. . . .

The White Moderate

First I must confess that over the last few years I have been gravely disappointed with the white moderate. I have almost reached the regrettable conclusion that the Negroes' great stumbling block in the stride toward freedom is not the White Citizens' "Counciler" or the Ku Klux Klanner, but the white moderate who is more devoted to "order" than to justice; who prefers a negative peace which is the absence of tension to a positive peace which is the presence of justice; who constantly says "I agree with you in the goal you seek, but I can't agree with your methods of direct action"; who paternalistically feels that he can set the timetable for another man's freedom; who lives by the myth of time and who constantly advises the Negro to wait until a "more convenient season." Shallow understanding from people of good will is more frustrating than absolute misunderstanding from people of ill will. Lukewarm acceptance is much more bewildering than outright rejection.

I had hoped that the white moderate would understand that law and order exist for the purpose of establishing justice, and that when they fail to do this they become the dangerously structured dams that block the flow of social progress. I had hoped that the white moderate would understand that the present tension in the South is merely a necessary phase of the transition from an obnoxious negative peace, where the Negro passively accepted his unjust plight, to a substance-filled positive peace, where all men will respect the dignity and worth of human personality.

Actually, we who engage in nonviolent direct action are not the creators of tension. We merely bring to the surface the hidden tension that is already alive. We bring it out in the open where it can be seen and dealt with. Like a boil that can never be cured as long as it is covered up but must be opened with all its pus-flowing ugliness to the natural medicines of air and light, injustice must likewise be exposed, with all of the tension its exposing creates, to the light of human conscience and the air of national opinion before it can be cured.

In your statement you asserted that our actions, even though peaceful, must be condemned because they precipitate violence. But can this assertion be logically made? Isn't this like condemning the robbed man because his possession of money precipitated the evil act of robbery? Isn't this like condemning Socrates because his unswerving commitment to truth and his philosophical delvings precipitated the misguided popular mind to make him drink the hemlock? Isn't this like condemning Jesus because His unique God consciousness and never-ceasing devotion to His will precipitated the evil act of crucifixion? We must come to see, as Federal courts have consistently affirmed, that it is immoral to urge an individual to withdraw his efforts to gain his basic constitutional rights because the quest precipitates violence. Society must protect the robbed and punish the robber. . . .

Two Opposing Forces

You spoke of our activity in Birmingham as extreme. At first I was rather disappointed that fellow clergymen would see my nonviolent efforts as those of the extremist. I started thinking about the fact that I stand in the middle of two opposing forces in the Negro community. One is a force of complacency made up of Negroes who, as a result of long years of oppression, have been so completely drained of self-respect and a sense of "somebodiness" that they have adjusted to segregation, and of a few Negroes in the middle class who, because of a degree of academic and economic security, and because at points they profit by segregation, have unconsciously become insensitive to the problems of the masses. The other force is one of bitterness and hatred and comes perilously close to advocating violence. It is expressed in the various black nationalist groups that are springing up over the nation, the largest and best known being Elijah Muhammad's Muslim movement. This movement is nourished by the contemporary frustration over the continued existence of racial discrimination. It is made up of people who have lost faith in America, who have absolutely repudiated Christianity, and who have concluded that the white man is an incurable "devil."

I have tried to stand between these two forces saying that we need not follow the "do-nothingism" of the complacent or the hatred and despair of the black nationalist. There is the more excellent way of love and nonviolent protest. I'm grateful to God that, through the Negro church, the dimension of nonviolence entered our struggle. If this philosophy had not emerged I am convinced that by now many streets of the South would be flowing with floods of blood. And I am further convinced that if our white brothers dismiss us as "rabble rousers" and "outside agitators"—those of us who are working through the channels of nonviolent direct action—and refuse to support our nonviolent efforts, millions of Negroes, out of frustration and despair, will seek solace and security in black nationalist ideologies, a development that will lead inevitably to a frightening racial nightmare.

Oppressed people cannot remain oppressed forever. The urge for freedom will eventually come. This is what has happened to the American Negro. Something within has reminded him of his birthright of freedom; something without has reminded him that he can gain it. Consciously and unconsciously, he has been swept in by what the Germans call the *Zeitgeist*, and with his black brothers of Africa, and his brown and yellow brothers of Asia, South America, and the Caribbean, he is moving with a sense of cosmic urgency toward the promised land of racial justice. Recognizing this vital urge that has engulfed the Negro community, one should readily understand public demonstrations.

The Negro has many pent-up resentments and latent frustrations. He has to get them out. So let him march sometime; let him have his prayer pilgrimages to the city hall; understand why he must have sit-ins and freedom rides. If his repressed emotions do not come out in these nonviolent ways, they will come out in ominous expressions of violence. This is not a threat; it is a fact of history. So I have not said to my people, "Get rid of your discontent." But I have tried to say that this normal and healthy discontent can be channeled through the creative outlet of nonviolent direct action. Now this approach is being dismissed as extremist. I must admit that I was initially disappointed in being so categorized.

Extremists

But as I continued to think about the matter I gradually gained a bit of satisfaction from being considered an extremist. Was not Jesus an extremist in love? "Love your enemies, bless them that curse you, pray for them that despitefully use you." Was not Amos an extremist for justice—"Let justice roll down like waters and righteousness like a mighty stream." Was not Paul an extremist for the gospel of Jesus Christ—"I bear in my body the marks of the Lord Jesus." Was not Martin Luther an extremist—"Here I stand; I can do none other so help me God." Was not John Bunyan an extremist—"I will stay in jail to the end of my days before I make a butchery of my conscience." Was not Abraham Lincoln an extremist—"This nation cannot survive half slave and half free." Was not Thomas Jefferson an extremist—"We hold these truths to be self evident that all men are created equal."

So the question is not whether we will be extremist but what kind of extremist will we be. Will we be extremists for hate or will we be extremists for love? Will we be extremists for the preservation of injustice—or will we be extremists for the cause of justice? In that dramatic scene on Calvary's hill three men were crucified. We must never forget that all three were crucified for the same crime—the crime of extremism. Two were extremists for immorality, and thus fell below their environment. The other, Jesus Christ, was an extremist for love, truth, and goodness, and thereby rose above His environment. So, after all, maybe the South, the nation, and the world are in dire need of creative extremists. . . .

The Birmingham Police

I must close now. But before closing I am impelled to mention one other point in your statement that troubled me profoundly. You warmly commended the Birmingham police force for keeping "order" and "preventing violence." I don't believe you would have so warmly commended the police force if you had seen its angry violent dogs literally biting six unarmed, nonviolent Negroes. I don't believe you would so quickly commend the policemen if you would observe their ugly and inhuman treatment of Negroes here in the city jail; if you would watch them push and curse old Negro women and young Negro girls; if you would see them slap and kick old Negro men and young Negro boys; if you will observe them, as they did on two occasions, refuse to give us food because we wanted to sing our grace together. I'm sorry that I can't join you in your praise for the police department.

It is true that they have been rather disciplined in their public handling of the demonstrators. In this sense they have been rather publicly "nonviolent." But for what purpose? To preserve the evil system of segregation. Over the last few years I have consistently preached that nonviolence demands that the means we use must be as pure as the ends we seek. So I have tried to make it clear that it is wrong to use immoral means to attain moral ends. But now I must affirm that it is just as wrong, or even more so, to use moral means to preserve immoral ends. Maybe Mr. Connor and his policemen have been rather publicly nonviolent, as Chief [Laurie] Prichett was in Albany, Georgia, but they have used the moral means of nonviolence to maintain the immoral end of flagrant racial injustice. T.S. Eliot has said that there is no greater treason than to do the right deed for the wrong reason.

I wish you had commended the Negro sit-inners and demonstrators of Birmingham for their sublime courage, their willingness to suffer, and their amazing discipline in the midst of the most inhuman provocation. One day the South will recognize its real heroes. They will be the James Merediths, courageously and with a majestic sense of purpose, facing jeering and hostile mobs and the agonizing loneliness that characterizes the life of the pioneer. They will be old, oppressed, battered Negro women, symbolized in a 72-year-old woman of Montgomery, Alabama, who rose up with a sense of dignity and with her people decided not to ride the segregated buses, and responded to one who inquired about her tiredness with ungrammatical profundity: "My feets is tired, but my soul is rested." They will be young high school and college students, young ministers of the gospel and a host of the elders, courageously and nonviolently sitting in at lunch counters and willingly going to jail for conscience sake. One day the South will know that when these disinherited children of God sat down at lunch counters they were in reality standing up for the best in the American dream and the most sacred values in our Judeo-Christian heritage, and thus carrying our whole nation back to great wells of democracy which were dug deep by the founding fathers in the formulation of the Constitution and the Declaration of Independence.

Never before have I written a letter this long (or should I say a book?). I'm afraid that it is much too long to take your precious time. I can assure you that it would have been much shorter if I had been writing from a comfortable desk, but what else is there to do when you are alone for days in the dull monotony of a narrow jail cell other than write long letters, think strange thoughts, and pray long prayers?

If I have said anything in this letter that is an overstatement of the truth and is indicative of an unreasonable impatience, I beg you to forgive me. If I have said anything in this letter that is an understatement of the truth and is indicative of my having a patience that makes me patient with anything less than brotherhood, I beg God to forgive me.

I hope this letter finds you strong in the faith. I also hope that circumstances will soon make it possible for me to meet each of you, not as an integrationist or a civil rights leader, but as a fellow clergyman and a Christian brother. Let us all hope that the dark clouds of racial prejudice will soon pass away and the deep fog of misunderstanding will be lifted from our fear-drenched communities and in some not too distant tomorrow the radiant stars of love and brotherhood will shine over our great nation with all of their scintillating beauty.

Yours for the cause of
Peace and Brotherhood,
M.L. King, Jr.

VIEWPOINT 5

"We maintain that an interracial movement for change is desirable."

White Liberals Should Play a Greater Role in the Civil Rights Movement

Anne Braden (b. 1924)

Anne Braden was one of the relatively few Southern whites active in the civil rights movement. A former newspaper reporter, she was on the staff of the Southern Conference Educational Fund, an interracial organization that worked for racial integration in the South. The following viewpoint is a condensed version of a discussion paper she and her husband, Carl Braden, prepared for a 1962 conference in Chapel Hill, North Carolina (the conference was sponsored by Students for a Democratic Society, an activist college student organization). She argues that if the goal of racial integration is to be achieved, both whites and blacks should be involved in civil rights activism. She especially calls on southern whites sympathetic to the goals of integration and racial justice to contribute more to the movement.

A few months ago we had an experience in Alabama which we think points up rather dramatically one of the basic problems in the South today.

We were helping to organize a conference to be held in Birmingham. It was conceived as—and actually turned out to be—

Anne Braden, "The White Southerner in the Integration Struggle," *Freedomways*, Winter 1963.

the first public interracial meeting of sizeable proportions in that city in two decades; and it was designed to bring together Negro and white actionists (or potential actionists) from several states to discuss ways and means to integrate the Deep South. The moving spirit behind the conference was the militant Negro leadership of Birmingham, but we also set out to draw in as many white people as possible.

One of the people we asked to appear on the program was a white man in his 30's from South Alabama. He was known as a generally liberal person and had been active in various interracial groups. The Negro leaders in Birmingham suggested him, although—significantly—they had never met him.

He responded to our invitation most cordially, but he declined to come. He said: "I'm working in the area of the uncommitted, and I think it's better to keep the two things separate." The separation he meant was between the area of action and the work of trying to reach the uncommitted, or fence-sitting, Southern white.

Then he volunteered the opinion that, while the concept of our Birmingham conference was "very good," he thought our timing was "very bad." He noted that Alabama was then in the throes of a gubernatorial campaign; all candidates were outdoing each other to prove to white voters that they knew best how to preserve segregation, but in the eyes of liberals some were worse than others. Our South Alabama friend felt that if our interracial conference created an "incident" in Birmingham, one of the "worst" candidates could seize upon this to convince the voters that they needed him as a strong man for governor.

We suggested that this sounded like the usual argument of "now is not the time"; we noted that the conference had been the idea of the Negro leaders of Birmingham, most notably the Rev. Fred L. Shuttlesworth, and that their wishes as to timetable could scarcely be ignored. Our white friend then remarked that he had never met Fred Shuttlesworth but he was sure Mr. Shuttlesworth would not want to do anything that would elect the worst man governor.

We realized that this man probably voiced the sentiments of many Alabama white liberals, so we asked Rev. Shuttlesworth for his reaction. It was immediate and uncompromising. He said:

"The conference is on. What do we care who is elected governor? One of them is as bad as the other. We have to take a position. It's time to have an interracial meeting in Birmingham. When it's time to do something, it's time to do it—regardless of the consequences. Those who aren't ready can stay home. Those who are ready go ahead."

As it turned out, of course, the conference was quite successful, there were no major incidents, and the South Alabama man's fears were all fancy. But this is not the main point. Even if the conference had created a major stir, Shuttlesworth and other Birmingham Negroes still would have felt it was the thing to do at that moment. The important thing here is the gap that exists between these Negroes and people like the South Alabamian, who probably represent the *most* decent trend in white Alabama.

The Negro Needs Allies

Bayard Rustin was the leading organizer of the August 28, 1963, March on Washington. In an article in Liberation *he argues that the march was necessary because of the need for broad-based support for civil rights.*

The March on Washington took place because the Negro needed allies. One reason he needed allies was that the Negro revolt had, quite properly, begun to become a revolution. The struggle began with the problem of buses and lunch counters and theaters—in a word, with the problem of dignity. But since the roots of discrimination are economic, and since, in the long run, the Negro, like everyone else, cannot achieve even dignity without a job, economic issues were bound to emerge, with far-reaching implications. Similarly, when the question of where Negro children go to school began to come to a head, deeper problems arose than when it was a question of a movie or a hamburger. When you touch the home and the job, you touch sensitive nerves. At the point where this happened, it became important for the Negro to have allies, for his own sake and for the sake of his white brothers as well.

Historically, the March on Washington broadened the base of the civil-rights movement. The March was not a Negro action; it was an action by Negroes and whites together. Not just the leaders of the Negro organizations, but leading Catholic, Protestant, and Jewish spokesmen called the people into the streets. And Catholics, Protestants, and Jews, white and black, responded.

In the first place, it is significant that these two men, both working for a more decent Alabama, had never met and that apparently the white man had never attended meetings of the most militant Negro civil rights groups in the state. He was honest and sincere and favored change, but he had no real comprehension of the drive that pushes the Negroes on and makes them impatient with delays and excuses. On the other hand, from the viewpoint of the Negroes this man and people like him—although obviously better than segregationists—are really of very little use in the fast-moving struggle in which they are engaged, and the world will just have to move on without them.

Alabama is an extreme case, because the terror is greater there and the lines of communication between Negro and white liberal are fewer than in less backward Southern states. But the difference is one of degree only. What is illustrated by this incident in Alabama may be the key to real Southern tragedy today. The truly depressing fact about our region is not the gap that exists between Negroes and segregationists; this is to be expected and is the root of the struggle. But the really depressing thing is the gap that exists all too often, even in the more enlightened areas, between Negro actionists and white liberals.

Ardent segregationists are in a minority now in the South. The great bulk of white Southerners would fall into the loose category of "moderate"—people who recognize change as inevitable and in some cases may even smooth its path once it gets started. Beyond this, there are the people we are referring to as liberals—a sizeable number of them: people who are honestly opposed to the whole system of segregation and want it to change. But so many of these people still set themselves in a world apart from Negroes and shrink from action. For this reason, we have the phenomenon that is the most important fact of life in the Southern cultural and social revolution today: that it is basically an all-Negro movement.

This does not mean that no white people at all are involved. Almost everywhere there are a few—on the picket lines, in the jails, just as deeply committed as the Negro actionists. But they are the exception, the relative handful. They represent no major trend, no mass movement such as the Negroes represent. The hard fact is that there is not today in the South any revolutionary interracial movement of significant size.

This situation has led many people within the movement—both the Negroes and the white people who *are* there—to wonder whether there is at this time any significant place for the white Southerner in this struggle at all. This raises certain basic questions that those involved in the movement must face and consider. We do not claim to have the final answers, but we want to suggest some tentative ones for discussion.

Three Important Questions

We think the questions boil down to three: 1. Is a truly joint interracial campaign for change in the South, if it is possible, desirable? 2. If it is desirable, what forces will have to come into play to make it a practical possibility? And 3. Assuming that there is not the possibility of a large-scale interracial movement in the foreseeable future, what should be the course of the individual white Southerner who does want to act now? Since he is so obviously the exception and can speak only for himself, does his active presence in the movement really make a contribution, or should he stay in the background and try to help there?

In regard to Question No. 1, until someone convinces us otherwise, we maintain that an interracial movement for change is desirable. Obviously we may be influenced by the fact that we are white, but we think we also speak as members of the human race. We recognize too that the important and ultimate decision on this must be made by the Negroes, who today *are* the movement. Do they want white participation? We do not presume to answer for them, but we ask that they consider the question deeply.

We suggest that before any person can formulate his own answer, he must determine what he feels is the ultimate goal of the movement. The goal in part determines the tools you use to get there. Is this a freedom movement or an integration movement—or is it both? It could not be an integration movement without also being a freedom movement because there can never be any real integration within the old paternalistic framework, but conceivably it could be a freedom movement without also being an integration movement. If it is only a freedom movement, it could well succeed as an all-Negro movement; if it is also an integration movement, it is difficult to see how it could. There can be no progress toward a new and integrated society unless some small model of the new and envisioned society is being built within the old. Otherwise, when does integration start—by some wave of a magic wand at a nebulous future time? Such changes in human relations don't come that way; they must be built by hard work and dedication, by trial and error and practice, by example; we can't let the gap we've discussed above widen and then think that some great change will suddenly seize the population in the future.

There are undoubtedly many Negroes in the current Southern movement who see only freedom as their goal, but we cannot write off the further goal of integration that inspires many of them. This is implied in the present orientation of the Southern movement to nonviolent revolution. Nonviolence means much more than the absence of the use of physical violence; it also carries with it the desire for deep and ultimate reconciliation with the opponent. In this struggle, that can only mean integration.

It has been our observation that many of the most militant Southern Negroes honestly want white participation—but with certain important provisos. They want it if it is all-out and fully committed; they don't want it if it is hedged in by ifs, ands, and buts; they don't want whites in the movement if constantly they are going to be a drag on things, pulling back, hesitating, saying to wait. And they don't want white people who are unable to accept Negro leadership; they have had enough of the old paternalistic relationships that were once prevalent even in liberal and radical organizations.

On the other hand, this raises certain problems the other way, because there are many white people who also reject the paternalistic patterns but who do not want to be just silent partners in the struggle. They want not only to act but to have some part in the planning and policy making; they too want to be accepted as human beings.

It is a touchy problem, and the most hopeful sign on the horizon is the fact that the new generation, less prisoners of old patterns, seems at times to be working it out. In some instances, through painful growth processes and in the heat of struggle, they are establishing new relationships in which Negroes and whites plan together and act together, not so much as whites and Negroes but as human beings joined by the esprit de corps of a great and historic cause.

Origins of the Present Movement

As to our second question, what forces will have to develop before there *can* be a significant interracial action movement in the South, we must recall the origin of the present nonviolent revolution among Southern Negroes. We believe history will record its moment of beginning as the Montgomery bus protest which started in December, 1955. From there it fanned out over the South and received renewed impetus with the student upsurge of 1960; after 1955, it was not possible for the South ever to be the same again. And the great change came primarily because a sizeable number of Southern Negroes made up their minds that they had had enough of second-class citizenship and that it was time to act.

Just why this mass decision was made at this particular moment is not pertinent to this discussion. What is pertinent is the paradoxical fact that it came at a time when mass movements toward social change were not prevalent in the South—or anywhere else in the United States. It was a time when the country was in something of a state of paralysis; liberalism was at a low ebb, McCarthyism was at its crest, and thousands of people had simply stopped participating in movements for social change; the labor movement—once the spearhead of a broad movement for change—had pretty much withdrawn from large social issues.

Some may say that this paralysis, while new to the rest of the country, was just a continuation of the usual situation in the South. But this is not true. There have been previous upsurges in the South. One came in the 1930's and early 1940's. It arose as a part of the New Deal upsurge; it was geared to raising economic standards in the poverty-stricken South, so it was closely tied to the labor movement; it was also concerned with equal rights for

Negroes. The important fact was that it was an interracial movement; it involved Negro and white Southerners working together for common goals.

This is not to paint an idealized image of this early movement. In terms of the 1960's, it had its shortcomings too, as much paternalism haunted it and its organizations were mostly white-led with the notable exception of the Southern Negro Youth Congress. But it is interesting to speculate on what might have developed if this movement had continued to develop along a straight line. It would probably still have been necessary for the Negro South to make an independent and dramatic breakaway, such as it did in the mid-50's, presenting a sharp challenge to the white world. But this challenge would have been presented in an entirely different frame of reference. There would have been an organized liberal movement, involving white Southerners, to hear the challenge. Some, to be sure, would have fallen away. But others would have met the challenge; and, most important, they would have had an organized framework to act in; they could not have been isolated so easily. Even more important, there would have been an organized framework of an interracial liberal movement in which a new generation, hearing the challenge, could have moved into action—could have moved more closely to the growing Negro movement. To get down to cases, the South Alabama white liberal mentioned earlier—and his counterparts all over the South—very likely would have been a part of this movement. In this context, it is unlikely that he and others ever could have been so remote from the militant Negroes that they could not even comprehend when the Negro leadership felt it was crucially important to hold a certain meeting.

As it was, the Negro challenge of the mid-50's was presented in a vacuum, insofar as liberal organizations were concerned. There have been individuals—a surprising number, considering the situation—who have responded, but what organizations existed were so under attack that they have had to use much of their energy simply to survive. In the face of this vacuum, much potential energy in the white South—which might have been mobilized directly into a nonviolent revolutionary movement—was drained off into more modest efforts to smooth the path of change. Some of these efforts have been quite constructive, but they have been so far removed from the center of the struggle that the gap we are discussing widened.

The reason for the vacuum of the mid-50's is not hard to find. It resulted from the tide of reaction that swept the entire country in the late 40's: the witch hunt, the jailing of people under the Smith Act [a 1940 sedition law], the actions of the House Un-American Activities Committee and its counterparts. All this created an atmosphere in the country in which *all* movements for social change, *all* liberal and radical people came to be identified with "subversion" or suspected of it in many quarters. Many such people and movements were destroyed, and many more were silenced.

None of this history can be undone now. But it is important to recognize it if we are to find the key to a different situation in the future. Someday there must and will be another mass interracial movement in the South. It will be on a much higher plane than before; it will not be white-led; hopefully, it will join Negroes and whites as equals in the struggle. But it may have to have some things in common with the previous great liberal upsurge. It will perhaps come as a part of a nationwide revival of liberal forces, at a time when McCarthyism is really dead. It will perhaps encompass broad social goals that touch the lives of every citizen—better housing, better education, better medical care, a higher standard of living—all this and integration too. And it most certainly must include a rejuvenated labor movement. It may be that it will be the Negroes of the South, as they organize the vote and become a political power, who will spark a new movement for such broad social growth that it can again inspire the imaginations of all men, of all colors.

We say this may be; we rather think it will be. But we dare not predict how soon. Such a movement is not on the horizon now. And so we come to our third question: What about the white Southerners who feel the present challenge deeply and want to act for integration now, who do not want to wait for mass movements or until a cause is popular? What should they do?

A Hard Choice

They face a hard choice. In most Southern communities, it is now possible to be a "moderate" on segregation—that is, attend a few interracial meetings, discuss with one's fellows the inevitability of integration—without changing one's basic pattern of life very much. But in most places, the minute a white person steps over the line and becomes an actual part of the Negro freedom movement—on the picket line, in open action—his whole life changes. And because of the nature of the changes, many have asked whether such a step does more harm than good.

In the first place, such a person may very likely lose his job—or in the case of students, his job opportunities later—and have to leave the South. In the second place, his position in the community drastically changes; in a sense he is cut off from the white community, set apart, isolated. This leads some to conclude that the white integrationist loses thereby the greatest contribution he could have made to the integration struggle—his "influence" in the white community. And then there is the question of how all this looks to the Negro actionists. Since there is no sizeable interracial movement, just how important are one or two white persons here, two or three there? Are they really worth the trouble it takes to bring them into the movement? Does one white person on a picket line make an interracial movement? Are they worth the extra attacks they cause by being there?

It is our opinion that even if only a tiny minority of white liberals can be mobilized for action, it is important that they act. In any community, if no more than one or two white persons are active, the fact that they are there changes the whole nature of the movement. One or two white people do make an interracial movement. It proves that the movement can be Negro and white together. It says something that speaks to the whole outside community, as well as to those within the movement. It is the beginning we mentioned earlier—the beginning of a new society within the framework of the old.

As to the difficulties presented: the economic risk for the white actionist is rarely greater than that for the Negro, and the decision to take the risk is basically one each individual must make for himself. If he must eventually leave the South, the loss is also social. We suggest that this might be alleviated if those in the movement will band together to help such a displaced person find other employment in the South. This is not always impossible. Where it is, we feel that each of us must make up our minds that we are not indispensable in this struggle. No person can decide that another person is expendable, but perhaps each of us must decide for ourselves that we are expendable at the point where we are and when a job needs to be done; if we are forced to leave, we must assume that we have made our contribution when it was most needed and that others will arise to take our place. If we constantly hold ourselves back—saving ourselves for that day when we can be *more* effective—we'll find that the time for action constantly recedes into the future.

In regard to the other difficulty, supposed loss of influence in the white community, we think that can be minimized too. There are many ways of influencing our fellowmen, and actions do speak louder than words. It has been well said that Negro students, sitting quietly at the lunch counters, communicated more to the white South than hundreds of so-called race-relations meetings. This may be true with the white liberal too. When he moves into action, he may no longer be able to talk like one of the boys with his old associates, but they are well aware of him. Some may come to hate him, but he remains a challenge to their conscience and their way of life; he is simply talking to them in a different way. It may not be obvious immediately, but two white people on an otherwise Negro picket line may influence a white community more profoundly than 50 white people at a discussion of "race relations" could.

This is not to say that all white liberals should move at this moment into open action. This is a many-faceted struggle, and it is undoubtedly the role of many white Southerners to play the quieter part. We suggest, however, that there is at this time relatively little shortage of persons willing to assume this latter role; the shortage is of those ready to act. The times call for action; we happen to think they call especially loud for white Southerners to act. There will be few enough right now at best; we rather feel that each of us must see himself as that one who can perhaps tip the scales as to whether it is enough.

VIEWPOINT 6

"As the Negro becomes more articulate and discerning, he insists on voicing his own aspirations, particularly in the light of what he regards as the shortcomings of liberal leadership."

White Liberals Should Play a Limited Role in the Civil Rights Movement

Loren Miller (1903–1967)

Many black civil rights activists in the early 1960s, especially those involved in mass demonstrations and civil disobedience, expressed impatience and criticism toward older legalistic strategies, and especially toward those in the white community that favored such approaches to civil rights. In the following viewpoint, taken from a 1962 article, civil rights attorney and Los Angeles municipal judge Loren Miller examines why anger is being directed at whites who were formerly considered allies of the civil rights movement. Criticizing some of the beliefs and actions of white liberals and labor leaders, Miller argues that the civil rights movement has entered an important new phase, and that whites should learn to cede control of it to emerging black leadership. Miller was a vice president of the National Association for the Advancement of Colored People (NAACP) at the time of this writing.

Loren Miller, "Farewell to Liberals: A Negro View," *Nation*, October 20, 1962. Reprinted with permission from *The Nation* magazine. Copyright © The Nation Company L.P.

Liberals who were shocked or surprised at James Baldwin's recent statement that Negroes "twenty years younger than I don't believe in liberals at all" haven't been doing their homework. Discontent with the liberal position in the area of race relations has been building up for the past several years. Of course there are liberals and liberals, ranging from Left to Right; still, there does exist a set of beliefs and attitudes, not easily defined but readily identified, constituting the liberal outlook on the race question. Simply stated, it contemplates the ultimate elimination of all racial distinctions in every phase of American life through an orderly, step-by-step process adjusted to resistance and aimed at overcoming such resistance. In the field of constitutional law, the classic liberal position, exemplified in the Supreme Court's "all deliberate speed" formula of the school-segregation cases, requires and rationalizes Negro accommodation to, and acquiescence in, disabilities imposed because of race and in violation of the fundamental law.

On his part, the Negro has to put up with such practices, but he cannot admit that they have constitutional sanction; to do so would be to give away his case and knuckle under to the revisionist theory that the Civil War Amendments conferred less than complete equality under the law. The liberal sees "both sides" of the issue: the force of the Negro's constitutional argument and the existence of customs, sometimes jelled into law, that justify the gradualist approach. He is impatient with "extremists on both sides."

Freedom Now

The Negro is outraged at being called an extremist. Since he takes the position that the Constitution confers complete equality on all citizens, he must rest his case on the proposition that there is only one side: his side, the constitutional side. That his attitude in that respect is firming up is evidenced by the fact that Negro spokesmen who once won applause by claiming that their activities made for progress in race relations are being elbowed aside by others whose catchword is Freedom Now. "We want our Freedom Here; we want it Now, not tomorrow; we want it All, not just a part of it," Martin Luther King tells receptive audiences. Whoever opposes, or even doubts, that doctrine is cast in the role of a foe, whether he calls himself conservative or liberal. The middle ground on which the traditional liberal has taken his stand is being cut from beneath him.

Every civil-rights victory adds to the Negro's intransigence; he becomes ever more impatient and demanding. To the extent that this attitude tends to precipitate racial conflict, a substantial number of liberals shy away. As they see it, their role is to ease, not heighten, racial tensions while they create a climate in which progress is possible. But the new militants don't want *progress*; they *demand* Freedom: "The courts take time and we want Freedom Now—Today," the Rev. Ralph Abernathy told cheering Georgians last month. Abernathy's cry, echoing King and the student leaders, underscores the strong trend away from dependence on legalistic methods and, equally important, implies rejection of the dogma that racial reforms must await a change in the hearts and minds of men—the so-called educational approach that once numbered many adherents.

Different Goals

In his 1964 book Crisis in Black and White *author Charles E. Silberman argues that white liberals and Negroes have fundamentally different goals.*

There is another source of strain between Negroes and white liberals that is likely to take on more importance as the years go by: the fact that when the struggle for Negro rights moves into the streets, the majority of liberals are reluctant to move along with it. They are all for the Negroes' *objectives*, they say, but they cannot go along with the *means*. Rightly or wrongly, Negroes receive this sort of statement with a good deal of cynicism; as Bismarck once remarked, "When you say that you agree to a thing in principle, you mean that you have not the slightest intention of carrying it out in practice."

The problem is a real one. There is a fundamental difference in the situation of Negroes and of whites that leads almost inevitably to conflict over tactics and strategy: Negroes are outside the mainstream of middle-class American life, whereas their liberal allies are on the inside. Hence the latter have a deep interest in preserving the status quo, in the sense of maintaining peace and harmony.

The swing away from major reliance on legal methodology and the educational approach poses new problems for liberals. It was easy and comfortable to wait for the filing of civil-rights cases or proposals for anti-discriminatory legislation and then lend support to those causes, or an even greater mark of liberalism to initiate them. However, the persistence of discriminatory practices in the wake of the NAACP's sweeping court victories which have destroyed the legal base of the Southern segregation system, and in the face of an upsurge of civil-rights legislation in the North, has shaken the faith of the Negro in the efficacy of the law. It is significant that King abjures his followers to disobey "unjust laws" and ironic that some segregationists, harried by the direct actionists, now argue that racial issues should be left to the courts. The plea for civil disobedience flies in the face of liberal doctrine of respect for the law; direct action in the form of sit-ins or stand-ins is seen by many as raising grave questions as to infringements of personal and property rights.

The liberal dilemma does not spring solely from doubts as to the advisability of direct action or the disobedience doctrine. The hard core of the difficulty lies in the circumstance that in the eighty years since the failure of Reconstruction, racial discrimination has become deeply rooted and thoroughly institutionalized in governmental agencies (local, state and federal), in the civil service and in churches, labor unions, political parties, professional organizations, schools, trade associations, service groups and in that vast array of voluntary organizations which play such a vital role in our society. Racial discrimination can't be uprooted unless governmental agencies are administered with that purpose in mind and unless voluntary organizations exert constant and consistent pressure to that end on local, state and federal governments, and at the same time accord Negroes all of the privileges and benefits that accrue from membership in such organizations. Those requirements aren't being met. Negroes are dismayed as they observe that liberals, even when they are in apparent control, not only do not rally their organizations for an effective role in the fight against discrimination, but even tolerate a measure of racial discrimination in their own jurisdictions.

Liberal Vacillation

Again, the liberal is restrained by his historical choice of seeing "both sides" of the issue. He understands the justice of the Negro's claim, but he argues that as a responsible administrator, he must reckon with deep-seated resistance to quick change and with the breakdown that might follow precipitate disruption of institutionalized practices. He may vacillate, as the President has done in the case of the Executive housing order, in an attempt to coax a consensus favorable to a change in policy. In any event, he is not, he says, as free as the Negro thinks; he must gauge the situation and settle for progress in the face of Negro clamor for immediate action.

Take the case of a liberal administrator of a government agency. He may owe his eminence to a political victory insured by a four- or five-to-one vote cast by urban Negroes. He now finds himself head of an agency mired in civil service and hobbled by a heritage of discriminatory practices. His underlings are apt to be wedded to that past; they helped frame the rules. He is a new broom that can hardly sweep at all, let alone sweep clean. Ordinarily, he appoints a few Negroes and institutes such reforms as will not call down upon his head the wrath of Congress, the state legislature or the Chamber of Commerce. Not personal cowardice makes him fear that wrath, but concern lest the opposition—through a crippling withdrawal of funds from his agency, perhaps—might make *all* reform impossible.

He may have done the best he could, but he hasn't endeared himself to Negroes, who contrast performance to pre-election speeches and campaign promises.

Civil service is a trap for unwary Negroes who enter it and find themselves frozen in its lower reaches. The United States Civil Rights Commission has found that, just as in private industry, there are "Negro" jobs and"white" jobs with Negroes at the bottom of the civil-service heap. The liberal who comes to head a civil service–staffed department of government is caught in a web of rules and regulations deliberately designed, in some instances, to institutionalize racial discrimination, or having that effect. Again there may be token appointments and token promotions, but the establishment yields slowly. The Negro looks for results and what he sees often makes him take the cynical position that the liberal differs no whit from his conservative predecessor.

Or take the situation in the AFL-CIO, where discrimination is rife in craft unions. The federation professes an inability to compel constituent unions to abandon time-honored racial practices. That is bad enough. What is worse is the stance of liberal-led industrial unions. The Steelworkers maintain Jim Crow locals in the South, where union halls double in brass as meeting places for White Citizens Councils. It is an open secret that Negroes have next to nothing to say in the policy-making bodies of unions, craft or industrial, on local, state or national levels. When the Pullman Porters' A. Philip Randolph, the only Negro member of the AFL-CIO Executive Board, urged reforms in federation, George Meany, described in labor circles as a liberal, shouted at him, "Who the hell gave you the right to speak for Negroes?" and accused him of attacking the labor movement. The Executive Board at Meany's urging, then censured Randolph for anti-union activities—without a dissent from such liberals as Walter Reuther or David Dubinsky. Randolph's answer was the formation of a *Negro* labor council; he was denounced again by labor leaders of all shades of opinion on the ground that he was fathering "Jim Crow in reverse." Yet for many years, the AFL-CIO has thrown its official weight behind state and federal fair housing, fair employment and other civil-rights legislation and has assisted in tests of segregatory laws.

An examination of the practices of other voluntary organizations, including churches, would produce a similar yield of institutionalized discriminatory practices. In almost every case in which the leadership of such organizations is classified as liberal, there has been announced public support of civil-rights objectives. Everybody seems to want everybody else to practice what he preaches and nobody seems to be able, or willing, to practice what everybody else preaches.

An End to Paternalism

It is very easy to charge hypocrisy in the situation, but what is really at play here is a cleavage between the burgeoning Freedom Now thinking of the Negro and the old progress concept to which liberals still cling. That conflict flares into the open when liberals exercise the prerogative, long held by them, of speaking *for* the Negro, and of espousing views which the Negro is abandoning. The liberal custom of speaking for the Negro is rooted in history; there was a time when the Negro needed spokesmen. Inevitably, a measure of paternalism and a father-knows-best attitude developed. But as the Negro becomes more articulate and discerning, he insists on voicing his own aspirations, particularly in the light of what he regards as the shortcomings of liberal leadership.

When the Negro insists on speaking for himself, the rebuffed liberal may shout as Meany did at Randolph that the dissenters are agitators or troublemakers (another replication, in a liberal context, of a familiar Southern cliché). Others take the tack popularized by John Fischer in *Harper's* and, transforming themselves into spokesmen for all whites, issue stern warnings that discrimination will prevail until all Negroes conform to middle-class standards of morality—a cozy variant of the theme that all Negroes are chargeable with the sins of every Negro. Negroes aren't dismayed at the opposition to their taking matters into their own hands. Detroit Negroes, led by unionists, revolted against the UAW's mayoralty endorsement in that city and turned the tide against the union's choice; the NAACP and the AFL-CIO are increasingly at odds over the treatment of Negroes in the labor movement; Roy Wilkins defended bloc voting by Negroes in his Atlanta keynote speech. Muslims are drawing substantial urban support by proposing to have done with all "white devils."

There is a growing cynicism about the current stress being laid on absolute fairness in public and private employment and in political appointments—beginning as of today. The Negro wants a little more than that. One hundred years of racial discrimination have produced a wide gap between him and white Americans. The Negro wants that gap closed in political appointments, in civil service, in schools and in private industry. He sees no way to close it unless he gets preferential treatment. Logic favors his position, but such a proposal runs into opposition from those who argue, correctly, that preferential treatment cannot be extended to a Negro without impinging on the personal rights of the white person over whom he will be preferred.

In truth, the impasse between liberals and Negroes is the end-product of a long historical process in which Americans of African, or partially African, descent have been treated as Negroes rather than as individuals, in legal lore as well as in popular concept. But constitutional protections run to persons—individuals—rather than to groups; American idealism exalts the individual and insists that group identification is an irrelevance. The liberal's historic concern is with individual rights and he seeks to apply that formula in the area of race relations. The Negro, whose ultimate ideal is the attainment of the right to be treated as an individual without reference to his racial identification, sees his immediate problem as that of raising the status of the group to which he has been consigned by popular attitude and action and by laws which permit racial classification. The liberal sees progress in the admission of a few select Negro children to a hitherto white school; the Negro wants all Negro children admitted and spurns the concession as mere tokenism.

The Negro's quarrel with liberal leadership does not portend his subscription to conservative or radical philosophies of race relations. Indeed, the Negro revolt, as [*The Negro Revolt* author] Louis Lomax has pointed out, is a rebellion against white leadership, whether that leadership is asserted directly or filtered down through Negroes who accept it. There is a certain irony in the fact that liberals are the targets of Negro displeasure precisely because of their long association in the quest for equality. It is the ally, not the enemy, who gets the blame when the alliance fails to gain its objectives. Rejection of liberal leadership does not mean that Negroes do not want, and expect, continued liberal aid. But they want it on their own terms and they are too sophisticated to believe that liberals can resign a battle involving fundamental equalitarian issues out of pique at the rejection of their leadership.

A Grand Strategy

It is against this background, and to some extent because of it, that the young Negro militants "don't believe in liberals at all." Profoundly influenced by the overthrow of white colonialism in Asia and Africa, they not only want Freedom Now, but insist on substituting a grand strategy for the liberal tactics of fighting one civil-rights battle at a time. They are determined to plot the strategy and dictate the tactics of the campaign. The details of the grand strategy haven't been blueprinted as yet, but in bold outline it calls for direct action by way of sit-ins, stand-ins, kneel-ins, boycotts, freedom rides, civil disobedience and as-yet-unheard-of techniques as the occasion demands, with resort to legal action when expedient—all under Negro leadership, all calculated to produce immediate results. Heavy stress is being laid on voter registration in the Deep South and it is significant that student leaders make no bones about the fact that *Negro* voting is seen as a device to elect *Negroes* to public office. The very choice of weapons, incidentally, requires action by Negroes. Only Negroes can desegregate a cafe or a hotel or an airport by a sit-in, or a beach by a wade-in, or a church by a kneel-in or withdraw Negro patronage through a boycott.

It would not be accurate to say that the direct actionists speak for all Negroes under all circumstances. It is fair to say that their philosophy is ascendant, that their influence is becoming pervasive and that their voices are heard with increasing respect and diminishing dissent in Negro communities. Those voices are harsh and strident, and jarring to the liberal ear. Their message is plain: To liberals a fond farewell, with thanks for services rendered, until you are ready to re-enlist as foot soldiers and subordinates in a Negro-led, Negro-officered army under the banner of Freedom Now.

Viewpoint 7

"The philosophy of non-violent resistance . . . says that the means must be as pure as the end."

Nonviolent Resistance Must Remain a Civil Rights Principle

Martin Luther King Jr. (1929–1968)
and Horace Julian Bond (b. 1940)

Nonviolent protest was a central component of the civil rights movement beginning in December 1955 with the Montgomery bus boycott and continuing during the student-led sit-ins and protests of the early 1960s. The following two-part viewpoint expresses the views of two leaders who played leading roles in both the bus boycott and the sit-ins.

Part I of the viewpoint is taken from a speech by Martin Luther King Jr. A Baptist preacher, King was thrust into national prominence when he helped lead the successful campaign of black citizens in Montgomery, Alabama, to boycott the city buses to protest racial discrimination. King later founded and led the Southern Christian Leadership Conference (SCLC), helped organize other nonviolent protests, and traveled and spoke widely on civil rights. In a 1961 speech before the Presbyterian Fellowship of the Concerned, an interracial group supportive of civil rights (but some members of which had also criticized nonviolent protest as being too extreme), King defends nonviolence. He tells of the inspiration he received from the example of Indian independence leader Mohandas K. Gandhi, and he expresses his belief that nonviolent resistance can help gain civil rights for blacks.

Martin Luther King Jr., speech delivered to the Presbyterian Fellowship of the Concerned, November 16, 1961. Reprinted by arrangement with The Heirs to the Estate of Martin Luther King Jr., c/o Joan Daves Agency as agent for the proprietor. Copyright 1961 by Martin Luther King Jr.; copyright renewed 1989 by Coretta Scott King. Horace Julian Bond, "Nonviolence: An Interpretation," *Freedomways*, Spring 1963.

Part II of the viewpoint is taken from an article by Horace Julian Bond, who from 1961 to 1966 was the communications director of the Student Nonviolent Coordinating Committee (SNCC), one of the leading organizations of the civil rights movement. He describes the experiences of members of the student-run organization working for civil rights in southern communities and their commitment to nonviolence. Bond was later elected to the Georgia state legislature.

I

Now there are three ways that oppressed people have generally dealt with their oppression. One way is the method of acquiescence, the method of surrender; that is, the individuals will somehow adjust themselves to oppression, they adjust themselves to discrimination or to segregation or colonialism or what have you. The other method that has been used in history is that of rising up against the oppressor with corroding hatred and physical violence. Now of course we know about this method in western civilization, because in a sense it has been the hallmark of its grandeur, and the inseparable twin of western materialism. But there is a weakness in this method because it ends up creating many more social problems than it solves. And I am convinced that if the Negro succumbs to the temptation of using violence in his struggle for freedom and justice, unborn generations will be the recipients of a long and desolate night of bitterness. And our chief legacy to the future will be an endless reign of meaningless chaos.

But there is another way, namely the way of non-violent resistance. This method was popularized in our generation by a little man from India, whose name was Mohandas K. Gandhi. He used this method in a magnificent way to free his people from the economic exploitation and the political domination inflicted upon them by a foreign power.

This has been the method used by the student movement in the South and all over the United States. And naturally whenever I talk about the student movement I cannot be totally objective. I have to be somewhat subjective because of my great admiration for what the students have done. For in a real sense they have taken our deep groans and passionate yearnings for freedom, and filtered them in their own tender souls, and fashioned them into a creative protest which is an epic known all over our nation. As a result of their disciplined, non-violent, yet courageous struggle, they have been able to do wonders in the South, and in our nation. But this movement does have an underlying philosophy, it has certain ideas that are attached to it, it has certain philosophical precepts. These are the things that I would like to discuss for the few moments left.

SNCC Statement of Purpose

The Student Nonviolent Coordinating Committee (SNCC) was formed in April 1960 when close to 175 students met at a leadership conference at Shaw University at Raleigh, North Carolina. Among the actions of the students in founding SNCC was the adoption of a statement of purpose, drafted by divinity student James Lawson, that expressed their nonviolent philosophy.

We affirm the philosophical or religious ideal of nonviolence as the foundation of our purpose, the presupposition of our faith, and the manner of our action. Nonviolence as it grows from Judaic-Christian tradition seeks a social order of justice permeated by love. Integration of human endeavor represents the crucial first step toward such a society.

Through nonviolence, courage displaces fear; love transforms hate. Acceptance dissipates prejudice; hope ends despair. Peace dominates war; faith reconciles doubt. Mutual regard cancels enmity. Justice for all overthrows injustice. The redemptive community supersedes systems of gross social immorality.

Love is the central motif of nonviolence. Love is the force by which God binds man to Himself and man to man. Such love goes to the extreme; it remains loving and forgiving even in the midst of hostility. It matches the capacity of evil to inflict suffering with an even more enduring capacity to absorb evil, all the while persisting in love.

By appealing to conscience and standing on the moral nature of human existence, nonviolence nurtures the atmosphere in which reconciliation and justice become actual possibilities.

I would say that the first point or the first principle in the movement is the idea that means must be as pure as the end. This movement is based on the philosophy that ends and means must cohere. Now this has been one of the long struggles in history, the whole idea of means and ends. Great philosophers have grappled with it, and sometimes they have emerged with the idea, from Machiavelli on down, that the end justifies the means. There is a great system of thought in our world today, known as Communism. And I think that with all of the weakness and tragedies of Communism, we find its greatest tragedy right here, that it goes under the philosophy that the end justifies the means that are used in the process. So we can read or we can hear the Lenins say that lying, deceit, or violence, that many of these things justify the ends of the classless society.

This is where the student movement and the non-violent movement that is taking place in our nation would break with Communism and any other system that would argue that the end justifies the means. For in the long run, we must see that the end represents the means in process and the ideal in the making. In other words, we cannot believe, or we cannot go with the idea that the end justifies the means because the end is pre-existent in the means. So the idea of non-violent resistance, the philosophy of non-violent resistance, is the philosophy which says that the means must be as pure as the end, that in the long run of history, immoral destructive means cannot bring about moral and constructive ends.

There is another thing about this philosophy, this method of non-violence which is followed by the student movement. It says that those who adhere to or follow this philosophy must follow a consistent principle of non-injury. They must consistently refuse to inflict injury upon another. Sometimes you will read the literature of the student movement and see that, as they are getting ready for the sit-in or stand-in, they will read something like this, "if you are hit do not hit back, if you are cursed do not curse back." This is the whole idea, that the individual who is engaged in a non-violent struggle must never inflict injury upon another. Now this has an external aspect and it has an internal one. From the external point of view it means that the individuals involved must avoid external physical violence. So they don't have guns, they don't retaliate with physical violence. If they are hit in the process, they avoid external physical violence at every point. But it also means that they avoid internal violence of spirit. This is why the love ethic stands so high in the student movement. We have a great deal of talk about love and non-violence in this whole thrust. . . .

There is something else: that one seeks to defeat the unjust system, rather than individuals who are caught in that system. And that one goes on believing that somehow this is the important thing, to get rid of the evil system and not the individual who happens to be misguided, who happens to be misled, who was taught wrong. The thing to do is to get rid of the system and thereby create a moral balance within society.

Another thing that stands at the center of this movement is another idea: that suffering can be a most creative and powerful social force. Suffering has certain moral attributes involved, but it can be a powerful and creative social force. Now, it is very interesting at this point to notice that both violence and non-violence agree that suffering can be a very powerful social force. But there is this difference: violence says that suffering can be a powerful social force by inflicting the suffering on somebody else; so this is what we do in war, this is what we do in the whole violent thrust of the violent movement. It believes that you achieve some end by inflicting suffering on another. The non-violent say that suffering becomes a powerful social force when you willingly accept that violence on yourself, so that self-suffering stands at the center of the non-violent movement and the individuals involved are able to suffer in a creative manner, feeling that unearned suffering is redemptive, and that suffering may serve to transform the social situation.

Another thing in this movement is the idea that there is within human nature an amazing potential for goodness. There is within human nature something that can respond to goodness. I know somebody's liable to say that this is an unrealistic movement if it goes on believing that all people are good. Well, I didn't say that. I think the students are realistic enough to believe that there is a strange dichotomy of disturbing dualism within human nature. Many of the great philosophers and thinkers through the ages have seen this. It caused Ovid the Latin poet to say, "I see and approve the better things of life, but the evil things I do." It caused even St. Augustine to say, "Lord, make me pure, but not yet." So that that is in human nature. Plato, centuries ago said that the human personality is like a charioteer with two headstrong horses, each wanting to go in different directions, so that within our own individual lives we see this conflict and certainly when we come to the collective life of man, we see a strange badness. But in spite of this there is something in human nature that can respond to goodness. So that man is neither innately good nor is he innately bad; he has potentialities for both. So in this sense, [Thomas] Carlyle was right when he said that "there are depths in man which go down to the lowest hell, and heights which reach the highest heaven, for are not both heaven and hell made out of him, everlasting miracle and mystery that he is?" Man has the capacity to be good, man has the capacity to be evil.

And so the non-violent resister never lets this idea go, that there is something within human nature that can respond to goodness. So that a Jesus of Nazareth or a Mohandas Gandhi can appeal to human beings and appeal to that element of goodness within them, and a Hitler can appeal to the element of evil within them. But we must never forget that there is something within human nature that can respond to goodness, that man is not totally depraved, to put it in theological terms, the image of God is never totally gone. And so the individuals who believe in this movement and who believe in non-violence and our struggle in the

South somehow believe that even the worst segregationist can become an integrationist. Now sometimes it is hard to believe that this is what this movement says, and it believes it firmly, that there is something within human nature that can be changed, and this stands at the top of the whole philosophy of the student movement and the philosophy of non-violence.

II

. . . we are holding nonviolent workshops in the smaller Delta towns. Several people in Shaw have, on their own, asked us to tell them how to go about registering. . . . We have mentioned voting only in passing. We have been working on the theory that if you can make a man feel like a whole person and realize his own worth and dignity and if you make him understand his plight better he will want to vote on his own accord.—from a SNCC secretary in the Mississippi Delta.

The adherents of nonviolence as a means to achieve social change fall into two categories. One group, containing most of the activists working in the South today, believes in and has seen the proof of nonviolent direct action as an effective means of protest and as a method of achieving change; the other group, smaller in number, believes in nonviolence not only as a tactic but as a way of life and a philosophy of living. (Let us realize here that no social action method in or by itself is sufficient to successfully integrate the nation's Negro masses. The power of the boycott, legalistic procedures, and mediation are all employed by America's protesting Negroes.)

Opponents of the nonviolent method have yet to offer a suitable alternative. Many point with pride to Robert Williams, ex-President of the Monroe, North Carolina NAACP branch, who was hounded from the United States by racists after he encouraged Negroes in Monroe to defend their homes against night riders. But what they fail to recall is that Williams believed in nonviolence, participated in nonviolent demonstrations in Monroe, and was charged with kidnapping a white couple he had taken into his home—in the spirit of nonviolence—to protect them from a Negro mob.

A statistical listing of the successes of nonviolence as typified by the student sit-in movement which began in February, 1960, is impressive. The number of facilities integrated, jobs secured and oppressive laws lifted is great.

But the believers in nonviolence say that it goes further than "just a hamburger." The critic of the students' methods who thinks that these young militants are interested only in dime store lunch counters and movie theaters is seriously mistaken.

"I was in New York the other day," one student said, "and read

151

the inscription on the Statue of Liberty. 'Give me your tired, your poor, your hungry masses yearning to be free,' it read. I thought, 'Well, baby, here we are!'"

The young nonviolent protestors who are working in the rural counties of Mississippi's Delta, Alabama's Black Belt and Georgia's cotton country are not aiming at a world where all men can eat together at the same lunch counter. Their aim is to change a society which lets some men keep others from eating where they choose, to develop the "beloved community" they speak of.

Two Purposes

To these students, nonviolent protest methods serve two purposes. The method and technique of nonviolence integrate a given lunch counter or movie theater, and the philosophy of nonviolence affords men—those involved in the rights struggle and those opposed to it—a chance at confrontation and exchange of ideas that will certainly make the former stronger and perhaps will convert the latter.

"I know that a person who has a real commitment to nonviolence will never leave the movement," William Porter said. Porter, who headed the youth group of the Albany (Georgia) Movement, said that Albany's success "cannot be measured with Montgomery's where nonviolent protests, and the Supreme Court, brought bus segregation to an end. Our victory here has been over the minds and hearts of Albany's Negro masses, who now not only know how to get their rights, but are determined to do so!"

Porter is one of forty-two college age young people, Negroes and whites, who make up the staff of the Student Nonviolent Coordinating Committee (SNCC). They are all former participants in student sit-in demonstrations in their own homes and college towns, but they have all left their schools, families and in some cases, jobs, to work for SNCC at a $15 a week "subsistence" wage.

They work in Arkansas, Mississippi, Alabama, Georgia, and South Carolina on direct action and voter registration projects designed, as *Saturday Evening Post* writer Ben Bagdikian put it, "to upset the social structure of the deep South and to change party politics in the United States."

The historic alignment of Southern Dixiecrats and Northern Republicans, the hypocrisy of both parties in dealing with civil rights, and the lack of any real advancement for Negroes beyond the 1954 Supreme Court's decision motivate these students.

Through their nonviolent workshops in the cotton towns of the rural South, they are spreading a message which transcends lunch counter integration.

SNCC staffer Mrs. Diane Nash Bevel, expecting her first child last summer, surrendered herself to a Mississippi judge who had charged her with "contributing to the delinquency of minors" because she had encouraged young Negroes in Jackson, Mississippi to join the Freedom Rides.

The Perils of Using Violence

In an article in the October 1959 issue of Liberation, *Martin Luther King Jr. argues that violence is of little use in the civil rights struggle.*

There are three different views on the subject of violence. One is the approach of pure nonviolence, which cannot readily or easily attract large masses, for it requires extraordinary discipline and courage. The second is violence exercised in self-defense, which all societies, from the most primitive to the most cultured and civilized, accept as moral and legal. . . . The third is the advocacy of violence as a tool of advancement, organized as in warfare, deliberately and consciously. To this tendency many Negroes are being tempted today. There are incalculable perils in this approach. It is not the danger or sacrifice of physical being which is primary, though it cannot be contemplated without a sense of deep concern for human life. The greatest danger is that it will fail to attract Negroes to a real collective struggle, and will confuse the large uncommitted middle group, which as yet has not supported either side. Further, it will mislead Negroes into the belief that this is the only path and place them as a minority in a position where they confront a far larger adversary than it is possible to defeat in this form of combat. When the Negro uses force in self-defense he does not forfeit support—he may even win it, by the courage and self-respect it reflects. When he seeks to initiate violence he provokes questions about the necessity for it, and inevitably is blamed for its consequences. It is unfortunately true that however the Negro acts, his struggle will not be free of violence initiated by his enemies, and he will need ample courage and willingness to sacrifice to defeat this manifestation of violence. But if he seeks it and organizes it, he cannot win.

Mrs. Bevel said, "I refuse to cooperate any longer with what I consider to be an immoral court system." The judge, perhaps aware of the hue that would arise were he to sentence an expectant mother to a three-year jail term, refused to sentence her.

Her refusal "to cooperate" with Mississippi's segregated and prejudiced courts stems from her readings and training in nonviolence. Just as the students consider it wrong to inflict harm on another, they consider it evil to participate in any way with a system built on wrong.

For this reason, the workers in SNCC Atlanta office refuse to shop in any of the city's Woolworth's stores. Although the Woolworth's branches here integrated a year ago, students in Pine Bluff, Arkansas are currently staging sit-ins at a Woolworth's there.

For this reason, several have registered as conscientious objectors with their draft boards; at least one student, working in the North, has refused to register at all.

"This movement is bigger than a civil rights fight," one of SNCC's Southwest Georgia staffers said. "We're fighting for basic civil liberties. That's what the whole Albany Movement is about, whether the First Amendment applies in Albany or not."

Building Courage

Ruby Doris Smith, a former Freedom Rider who worked on SNCC's first voter registration campaign in Amite County, Mississippi in 1961, says that nonviolence helped build up the courage of the rural Negroes she worked with.

"They had never heard of Martin Luther King or the Montgomery boycott," she says. "But one young girl told me that she wasn't afraid of the police in McComb when she and 112 of her classmates staged a protest march through the town. The older people too, are deeply religious, and find courage in nonviolence. We reminded them that Christ had been nonviolent on the cross, and I think that now, the kids and their parents, realize that not only can they do something to change the system, but that they have an obligation to change it."

One of the tragedies of nonviolence is that the biggest critics are those who understand it least.

Some northern liberals look upon the students as a bunch of modern "Uncle Toms," praying for deliverance while white mobs ravish and beat them. The reverse is true. The students who are working today in Dawson and Leesburg, Georgia, in Shaw, Leland, and Greenwood, Mississippi, and in Gee's Bend, Alabama are daily placing their lives on the line.

When trouble threatens, as it does with unsettling certainty almost every day, they draw upon the inner courage which wells from practicing what they preach: that every man has his own worth, and that all men must strive together to develop the "beloved community."

To a northerner reading of arrests and beatings such a statement may sound trite or even naive, but to the young militants who know it to be true, it is a simple statement of fact.

"I no longer hold that a simple repetition of . . . nonviolent demonstrative action . . . will bring victory."

Nonviolent Resistance May Not Be Enough

Howard Zinn (b. 1922)

The effectiveness of nonviolence was frequently debated and criticized within the black community and the civil rights movement, especially in the face of violent and sometimes murderous actions from the Ku Klux Klan and other sources of resistance. The following viewpoint is by Howard Zinn, who at the time of its writing was a former chairman of the history department at Spellman College and a close observer of the civil rights movement. He later became a professor of political science at Boston University and the author of several noted books, including *SNCC: The New Abolitionists* and *A People's History of the United States.*

In this 1964 article Zinn questions the efficacy of nonviolent protest as a civil rights tactic in some parts of the South. He argues that the pressures exerted on communities through lawsuits, sit-ins, demonstrations, and other measures are inadequate in many southern locations where racial segregation and white violence are particularly severe. The experiences at Albany, Georgia, in 1962, in which a campaign of nonviolent resistance accomplished little in ending racial segregation practices, further undermined his confidence in nonviolence. He warns that if the federal government does not intervene in these areas to keep local policemen and politicians from depriving blacks of their civil rights, an armed black revolt could result.

Howard Zinn, "The Limits of Nonviolence," *Freedomways*, Winter 1964. Reprinted by permission of the author.

When I went to Albany, Georgia, during the first wave of demonstrations and mass arrests in December of 1961, I had been in Atlanta for five years and thought I had learned some important things about the South, as observer and minor participant in the civil rights struggle. I had written an optimistic article for *Harper's Magazine* about the possibility of changing the *behavior* (not immediately his *thinking*) of the white southerner without violence, by playing upon his self-interest, whether through economic pressure or other means which would forcefully confront him with hard choices. And in Atlanta, I saw such changes come about, through the pressure of lawsuits, sit-ins, boycotts, and sometimes by just the threat of such actions. Nonviolence was not only hugely appealing as a concept. It worked.

And then I took a good look at Albany, and came back troubled. Eight months later, when the second crisis broke out in Albany, in the summer of 1962, I drove down again from Atlanta. The picture was the same. Again, mass demonstrations and mass arrests. Again, the federal government stood by impotent while the chief of police took control of the constitutional rights of citizens.

My optimism was shaken but still alive. To those people around me who said that Albany was a huge defeat, I replied that you could not measure victories and defeats only by tangible results in the desegregation of specific facilities, that a tremendous change had taken place in the thinking of Albany's Negroes, that expectations had been raised which could not be stilled until the city was transformed.

Today, over a year later, after studying events in Birmingham and Gadsden and Danville and Americus, after interviewing staff workers of the Student Nonviolent Coordinating Committee just out of jail in Greenwood, Mississippi, watching state troopers in action in Selma, Alabama, and talking at length to voter registration workers in Greenville, Mississippi, I am rethinking some of my old views. Albany, it seems to me, was the first dramatic evidence of a phenomenon which now has been seen often enough to be believed: that there is a part of the South impermeable by the ordinary activities of nonviolent direct action, a monolithic South completely controlled by politicians, police, dogs, and prod sticks. And for this South, special tactics are required.

One portion of the South has already been removed from the old Confederacy. This part of the South, represented by places like Richmond, Memphis, Nashville, Louisville, and Atlanta, is still fundamentally segregationist—as is the rest of the nation, North and South—but the first cracks have appeared in a formerly solid social structure. In these places, there is fluidity and promise, room for maneuver and pressure and accommodation; there is an economic elite sophisticated enough to know how badly it can be hurt by outright resistance, and political leaders shrewd enough to take cognizance of a growing Negro electorate. There will be much conflict yet in Atlanta and in Memphis. But the tactics of nonviolent direct action can force ever greater gains there.

Where Slavery Still Lingers

Then there is the South of Albany and Americus, Georgia; of Gadsden and Selma, Alabama; of Danville, Virginia; of Plaquemine, Louisiana; of Greenwood and Hattiesburg and Yazoo City, Mississippi—and a hundred other towns of the Black Belt. Here, where the smell of slavery still lingers, politicians are implacable, plantation owners relentless, policemen unchecked by the slightest fear of judgment. In these towns of the Black Belt, a solid stone wall separates black from white, and reason from fanaticism; nonviolent demonstrations smash themselves to bits against this wall, leaving pain, frustration, bewilderment, even though the basic resolve to win remains alive, and some kind of ingenuous optimism is left untouched by defeat after defeat.

I still believe that the Albany Movement, set back again and again by police power, has done a magnificent service to the Negroes of Albany—and ultimately, to the whites who live in that morally cramped town. I still believe that the three hundred Negroes who waited on line near the county courthouse in Selma, Alabama from morning to evening in the shadow of clubs and guns to register to vote, without even entering the doors of that courthouse, accomplished something. But I no longer hold that a simple repetition of such nonviolent demonstrative action—which effectively broke through barriers in the other part of the South—will bring victory. I am now convinced that the stone wall which blocks expectant Negroes in every town and village of the hard-core South, a wall stained with the blood of children, as well as others, and with an infinite capacity to absorb the blood of more victims—will have to be crumbled by hammer blows.

Federal Government Must Act

This can be done, it seems to me, in one of two ways. The first is a Negro revolt, armed and unswerving, in Mississippi, Alabama and southwest Georgia, which would result in a terrible waste of human life. That may be hard to avoid unless the second alternative comes to pass: the forceful intervention of the national government, to smash, with speed and efficiency, every attempt by local policemen or politicians to deprive Negroes (or others) of the rights supposedly guaranteed by the Constitution.

Unaware of the distinction between the two Souths, not called upon for such action in places like Atlanta and Nashville, and uncommitted emotionally and ideologically to racial equality as a first-level value, the national government has played the role of a hesitant, timorous observer. It will have to move into bold action, or face trouble such as we have not seen yet in the civil rights crisis. This is my thesis here, and the story of Albany, Georgia may help illustrate it.

Federal law was violated again and again in Albany, yet the federal government did not act. In effect, over a thousand Negroes spent time in prison, and thousands more suffered and sacrificed, in ways that cannot be expressed adequately on paper, as a mass substitute for federal action.

Judicial decisions in this century have made it clear that the Fourteenth Amendment, besides barring officials from dispensing unequal treatment on the basis of race, also prohibits them from interfering with the First Amendment rights of free speech, petition, and assembly. Yet in Albany over one thousand Negroes were locked up in some of the most miserable jails in the country for peacefully attempting to petition the local government for a redress of grievances. *And the Justice Department did nothing.*

Section 242 of the U.S. Criminal Code, which comes from the Civil Rights Act of 1866 and the Enforcement Act of 1870, creates a legal basis for prosecution of: "Whoever, under color of any law . . . wilfully subjects . . . any inhabitant of any State . . . to the deprivation of any rights, privileges, or immunities secured or protected by the Constitution and laws of the United States. . . ." Three times in succession, in November and December 1961, the police of the city of Albany, by arresting Negroes and whites in connection with their use of the terminal facilities in that city, violated a right which has been made clear beyond a shadow of a doubt. Yet the federal government took no action.

Today, the wheels of the nonviolent movement are churning slowly, in frustration, through the mud of national indifference which surrounds the stone wall of police power in the city of Albany. As if to give a final blow to the Albany Movement, the Department of Justice is now prosecuting nine of its leaders and members, who face jail sentences up to ten years, in connection with the picketing of a white grocer who had served on a federal jury. One of the defendants is Dr. W. G. Anderson, former head of the Albany Movement. Another is Slater King, now heading the Movement. *It is the bitterest of ironies that Slater King, who pleaded in vain for federal action while he himself was jailed, while his wife was beaten by a deputy sheriff, while his brother was beaten, is now being vigorously prosecuted by the U.S. Department of Justice on a charge which can send him to jail for five years.*

The simple and harsh fact, made clear in Albany, and reinforced by events in Americus, Georgia, in Selma and Gadsden, Alabama, in Danville, Virginia, in every town in Mississippi, is that the Federal Government abdicated its responsibility in the Black Belt. The Negro citizens of that area were left to the local police. The United States Constitution was left in the hands of Neanderthal creatures who cannot read it, and whose only response to it has been to grunt and swing their clubs.

Federal Presence Must Be Felt

The responsibility is that of the president of the United States, and no one else. It is his job to enforce the law. And the law is clear. Previously the civil rights movement joined in thrusting the responsibility on Congress when the president himself, without any new legislation, had the constitutional power to enforce the 14th Amendment in the Black Belt.

The immediate necessity is for a *permanent* federal presence in the Deep South. I am not talking of occupation by troops, except as an ultimate weapon. I am suggesting the creation of a special force of federal agents, stationed throughout the Deep South, and authorized to make immediate on-the-spot arrests of any local official who violates federal law. The action would be preventive, before a crisis has developed, and would snuff out incipient fires before they got going, by swift, efficient action. Such a force would have taken Colonel Al Lingo into custody as he was preparing to use his electric prod sticks on the Freedom Walkers crossing the border into Alabama. Such a force would have taken Governor [George] Wallace to the nearest federal prison the very first time he blocked the entrance of a Negro student into the University of Alabama, and would have arrested Sheriff Jim Clark as he moved to drag those two SNCC youngsters off the steps of the federal building in Selma.

Many liberals are affronted by such a suggestion; they worry about civil war. My contention is that the white southerner submits—as do most people—to a clear show of authority; note how

Why Violence Is Necessary

Zinn's warning of a possible black revolt is supported by sentiments expressed by Robert F. Williams in the following passage. Williams, a former U.S. Marine and head of the National Association for the Advancement of Colored People (NAACP) chapter in Monroe, North Carolina, was suspended in 1959 by the NAACP because of his remarks condoning violence. In this excerpt from the September 1959 issue of Liberation, *Williams defends his views.*

On May 5, 1959, while president of the Union County [North Carolina] branch of the NAACP, I made a statement to the United Press International after a trial wherein a white man was supposed to have been tried for kicking a Negro maid down a flight of stairs in a local white hotel. In spite of the fact that there was an eyewitness, the defendant failed to show up for his trial, and was completely exonerated.

Another case in the same court involved a white man who had come to a pregnant Negro mother's home and attempted to rape her. In recorder's court the only defense offered for the defendant was that "he's not guilty. He was just drunk and having a little fun." A white woman neighbor testified that the woman had come to her house excited, her clothes torn, her feet bare and begging her for assistance; the court was unmoved.

This great miscarriage of justice left me sick inside, and I said then what I say now. I believe Negroes must be willing to defend themselves, their women, their children and their homes. They must be willing to die and to kill in repelling their assailants. Negroes *must* protect themselves, it is obvious that the federal government will not put an end to lynching; therefore it becomes necessary for us to stop lynching with violence.

Some Negro leaders have cautioned me that if Negroes fight back, the racist will have cause to exterminate the race.

This government is in no position to allow mass violence to erupt, let alone allow twenty million Negroes to be exterminated.

It is instilled at an early age that men who violently and swiftly rise to oppose tyranny are virtuous examples to emulate. I have been taught by my government to fight. Nowhere in the annals of history does the record show a people delivered from bondage by patience alone.

Governors Wallace and [Ross] Barnett gave in at the last moment rather than go to jail. Once southern police officials realize that the club is in the other hand, that *they* will be behind bars, that *they* will have to go through all the legal folderal of getting bond and filing appeal, etc. which thousands of Negroes have had to endure these past few years—things will be different. The national government needs to drive a wedge, as it began to do in the First Reconstruction, between the officialdom and the ordinary white citizen of the South, who is not a rabid brute but a vacillating conformist.

Burke Marshall, head of the Civil Rights Division of the Department of Justice, has been much disturbed by this suggestion of "a national police force or some other such extreme alternative." If a national police force is extreme, then the United States is already "extremist," because the Federal Bureau of Investigation is just that. It is stationed throughout the country and has the power to arrest anyone who violates federal law. Thus, it arrests those who violate the federal statutes dealing with bank robberies, interstate auto thefts and interstate kidnapping. But it does *not* arrest those who violate the civil rights laws. I am suggesting an organization of special agents, who will arrest violators of civil rights laws the way the F.B.I. arrests bank robbers.

The continued dependence on nonviolence by the civil rights movement is now at stake. Nonviolent direct action can work in social situations where there are enough apertures through which economic and political and moral pressure can be applied. But it is ineffective in a totally closed society, in those Black Belt towns of the Deep South where Negroes are jailed and beaten and the power structure of the community stands intact.

The late President Kennedy's political style was one of working from crisis to crisis rather than undertaking fundamental solutions—like a man who settles one debt by contracting another. This can go on and on, until the day of reckoning. And that day may come, in the civil rights crisis, this summer just before the election.

There is a strong probability that this July and August will constitute another "summer of discontent." The expectations among Negroes in the Black Belt have risen to the point where they cannot be quieted. CORE (Congress of Racial Equality), SCLC (Southern Christian Leadership Conference) and the intrepid youngsters of the Student Nonviolent Coordinating Committee, are determined to move forward.

With the probability high of intensified activity in the Black Belt this summer, the President will have to decide what to do. He can stand by and watch Negro protests smashed by the local police, with mass jailings, beatings, and cruelties of various kinds. Or he can take the kind of firm action suggested above, which would simply establish clearly what the Civil War was fought for a hundred years ago, the supremacy of the U.S. Constitution over the entire nation. If he does not act, the Negro community may be pressed by desperation to move beyond the nonviolence which it has maintained so far with amazing self-discipline.

Thus, in a crucial sense, the future of nonviolence as a means for social change rests in the hands of the President of the United States. And the civil rights movement faces the problem of how to convince him of this, both by words and by action. For, if nonviolent direct action seems to batter itself to death against the police power of the Deep South, perhaps its most effective use is against the national government. The idea is to persuade the executive branch to use its far greater resources of nonviolent pressure to break down the walls of totalitarian rule in the Black Belt.

The latest victim of this terrible age of violence—which crushed the life from four Negro girls in a church basement in Birmingham, and in this century has taken the lives of over fifty million persons in war—is President John F. Kennedy, killed by an assassin's bullet. To President Johnson will fall the unfinished job of ending the violence and fear of violence which has been part of the everyday life of the Negro in the Deep South.

VIEWPOINT 9

"The Negro woman can no longer postpone or subordinate the fight against discrimination because of sex to the civil rights struggle but must carry on both fights simultaneously."

Black Women Should Seek Gender Equality

Pauli Murray (1910–1985)

Pauli Murray was a longtime activist in both civil rights and women's rights, having faced discrimination in both areas. In 1938 she was denied admission to the law school of the University of North Carolina because of her race, and in 1944 she was denied admission into the Harvard Law School because of her sex. Despite these setbacks she obtained law degrees from Howard University, the University of California, and Yale University, served as deputy attorney general of the state of California, and worked as a lawyer and law professor. She later became an Episcopal priest.

The following viewpoint is excerpted from a 1964 article in which Murray examines the dual burden of racism and sexism that black women face. She argues that gender discrimination is a serious problem not only in American society, but within the civil rights movement itself, and concludes that black women should not subordinate the fight against discrimination based on sex to the struggle against racial discrimination.

From Pauli Murray, "The Negro Woman in the Quest for Equality," *Acorn*, June 1964; ©1964 by Pauli Murray. Reprinted with permission.

Negro women, historically, have carried the dual burden of Jim Crow and Jane Crow. They have not always carried it graciously, but they have carried it effectively. They have shared with their men a partnership in a pioneer life on spiritual and psychological frontiers not inhabited by any other group in the United States. For Negroes have had to hack their way through the wilderness of racism produced by the accumulated growth of nearly four centuries of a barbarous international slave trade, two centuries of chattel slavery and a century of illusive citizenship in a desperate effort to make a place of dignity for themselves and their children.

In this bitter struggle, into which has been poured most of the resources and much of the genius of successive generations of American Negroes, these women have often carried disproportionate burdens in the Negro family as they strove to keep its integrity intact against the constant onslaught of indignities to which it was subjected. Not only have they stood shoulder to shoulder with Negro men in every phase of the battle, but they have also continued to stand when their men were destroyed by it. Who among us is not familiar with that heroic, if formidable, figure exhorting her children to overcome every disappointment, humiliation and obstacle. This woman's lullaby was very often "Be something!" "Be somebody!". . .

Negro women have had to fight against the stereotypes of "female dominance" on the one hand and loose morals on the other hand, both growing out of the roles forced upon them during the slavery experience and its aftermath. But out of their struggle for human dignity, they also developed a tradition of independence and self-reliance. This characteristic, said the late Dr. E. Franklin Frazier, sociologist, "has provided generally a pattern of equalitarian relationship between men and women in America." Like the Western pioneer settlements, the embattled Negro society needed the strength of all of its members in order to survive. The economic necessity for the Negro woman to earn a living to help support her family— if indeed she was not the sole support—fostered her independence and equalitarian position. . . .

Not only have women whose names are well known given this great human effort [the civil rights movement] its peculiar vitality but women in many communities whose names will never be known have revealed the courage and strength of the Negro woman. These are the mothers who have stood in school yards with their children, many times alone. These are the images which have touched America's heart. Painful as these experiences have been, one cannot help asking: would the Negro struggle have come this far without the indomitable determination of its women?

In the larger society, Negro and white women share a common burden because of traditional discriminations based upon sex. Dr. Gunnar Myrdal pointed out the similarities between the Negro problem and the women's problem in *An American Dilemma*. What he saw is common knowledge among Negro women, but it is interesting to see the United States through the eyes of a foreign observer. He said:

> As in the Negro problem, most men have accepted as self-evident, until recently, the doctrine that women had inferior endowments in most of those respects which carry prestige, power and advantages in society. . . . The arguments were used, have been about the same: smaller brains, scarcity of geniuses and so on. . . . As in the case of the Negro, women themselves have often been brought to believe in their inferiority of endowment. As the Negro was awarded his 'place' in society, so there was a 'woman's place.' . . . The myth of the 'contented women' who did not want to have suffrage or other civil rights and equal opportunities had the same social function as the myth of the 'contented Negro.'

Despite the common interests of Negro and white women, however, the dichotomy of the segregated society has prevented them from cementing a natural alliance. Communication and cooperation between them have been hesitant, limited and formal. Negro women have tended to identify all discrimination against them as racial in origin and to accord high priority to the civil rights struggle. They have had little time or energy for consideration of women's rights. But as the civil rights struggle gathers momentum, they begin to recognize the similarities between paternalism and racial arrogance. They also begin to sense that the struggle into which they have poured their energies may not afford them rights they assumed would be theirs when the civil rights cause has triumphed.

Women in the Civil Rights Movement

Recent disquieting events have made imperative an assessment of the role of the Negro woman in the quest for equality. The civil rights revolt, like many social upheavals, has released powerful pent-up emotions, cross currents, rivalries, and hostilities. . . . There is much jockeying for position as ambitious men push and elbow their way to leadership roles. Part of this upsurge reflects the Negro male's normal desire to achieve a sense of personal worth and recognition of his manhood by a society which has so long denied it. One aspect is the wresting of the initiative of the civil rights movement from white liberals. Another is the backlash of a new male aggressiveness against Negro women.

What emerges most clearly from events of the past several

months is the tendency to assign women to a secondary, ornamental or "honored" role instead of the partnership role in the civil rights movement which they have earned by their courage, intelligence and dedication. It was bitterly humiliating for Negro women on August 28 [1963] to see themselves accorded little more than token recognition in the historic March on Washington. Not a single woman was invited to make one of the major speeches or to be part of the delegation of leaders who went to the White House. This omission was deliberate. Representations for recognition of women were made to the policy-making body sufficiently in advance of the August 28 arrangements to have permitted the necessary adjustments of the program. What the Negro women leaders were told is revealing: that no representation was given to them because they would not be able to agree on a delegate. How familiar was this excuse! It is a typical response from an entrenched power group. . . .

It is also pointedly significant that in the great mass of magazine and newsprint expended upon the civil rights crisis, national editors have selected Negro men almost exclusively to articulate the aspirations of the Negro community. There has been little or no public discussion of the problems, aspirations and role of Negro women. Moreover, the undertone of news stories of recent efforts to create career opportunities for Negroes in government and industry seems to be that what is being talked about is jobs for Negro men only. The fact that Negro women might be available and, as we shall see, are qualified and in need of employment, is ignored. While this is in keeping with the tenor of a male-dominated society, it has grave consequences for Negro women. . . .

At the very moment in history when there is an international movement to raise the status of women and a recognition that women generally are underemployed, are Negro women to be passed over in the social arrangements which are to create new job opportunities for Negroes? Moreover, when American women are seeking partnership in our society, are Negro women to take a backward step and sacrifice their equalitarian tradition? . . .

Family Life

A fact of enormous importance to the whole discussion of Negro family life and one which has received little analysis up to now is the startling 1960 census figure showing an excess of 648,000 Negro females over Negro males. More than a half million of these were 14 years and over. In the past century, the ratio of Negro males to females has decreased steadily. In 1960 there were only 93.3 Negro males to every 100 females.

The statistical profile of a Negro woman which emerges from the latest census reports is that she has a harder time finding a mate, remains single more often, bears more children, is in the labor market longer, has less education, earns less, is widowed earlier and carries a heavier economic burden as a family head than her white sister.

A Caste System

The role of women within the civil rights movement was the subject of an internal memo written by Casey (Sandra) Hayden and Mary King, longtime SNCC activists.

There seem to be many parallels that can be drawn between treatment of Negroes and treatment of women in our society as a whole. But in particular, women we've talked to who work in the [civil rights] movement seem to be caught up in a common-law caste system that operates, sometimes subtly, forcing them to work around or outside hierarchical structures of power which may exclude them. Women seem to be placed in the same position of assumed subordination in personal situations too. It is a caste system which, at its worst, uses and exploits women. . . .

The caste-system perspective dictates the roles assigned to women in the movement, and certainly even more to women outside the movement. Within the movement, questions arise in situations ranging from relationships of women organizers to men in the community, to who cleans the freedom house, to who holds leadership positions, to who does secretarial work and to who acts as spokesman for groups. Other problems arise between women with varying degrees of awareness of themselves as being capable as men but are held back from full participation, or between women who see themselves as needing more control of their work than other women demand. And there are problems with relationships between white women and black women.

Moreover, while it is now generally known that women are constitutionally stronger than men, that male babies are more fragile than female babies, that boys are harder to rear than girls, that the male death rate is slightly higher and life expectancy for males is shorter than that of females, the numerical imbalance between the sexes in the Negro group is more dramatic than in any group in the United States. Within the white population the excess of women shows up in the middle and later years. In the Negro population, the excess is present in every age group over 14 and is greatest in the 15–44 age group which covers the college years and the age when most marriages occur. Consider, for example, the fact that in the 15–24 age group, there are only 96.7 nonwhite males for every 100 females. This ratio drops to 88.4 in the 25-44 age group. Compare this with the white population in which the ratios for these two age groups are 102.2 and 98, respectively.

The explosive social implications of an excess of more than half a million Negro girls and women over 14 years of age are obvious. . . . The problem of an excess female population is a familiar one in European countries which have experienced heavy male casualties during wars, but an excess female ethnic minority as an enclave within a larger population raises important social issues. What is there in the American environment which is hostile to both the birth and survival of Negro males? How much of the tensions and conflicts traditionally associated with the matriarchal frame-work of Negro society are in reality due to this imbalance and the pressure it generates? Does this excess explain the active competition between Negro professional men and women seeking employment in markets which have limited or excluded Negroes? And does this competition intensify the stereotype of the matriarchal society and female dominance? . . .

Fate of Women Transcends Civil Rights

I have stressed the foregoing figures, however, because it seems to me that the Negro woman's fate in the United States, while inextricably bound with that of the Negro male in one sense, transcends the issue of civil rights. Equality for the Negro woman must mean equal opportunity to compete for jobs and to find a mate in the total society. For as long as she is confined to an area in which she must compete fiercely for a mate, she will remain the object of sexual exploitation and the victim of all of the social evils which such exploitation involves.

In short, many of the 645,000 excess Negro women will never marry at all unless they marry outside of the Negro community. And many others will marry men whose educational and cultural standards may not be the same as their own. Add to the large reservoir of unmarried white women (22.3%), a higher proportion of widowed, separated and divorced nonwhite women than of white women, and you have factors which have combined to make the Negro woman the responsible family head in more than one fifth of all nonwhite families.

The point I am trying to make here is that the Negro woman cannot assume with any degree of confidence that she will be able to look to marriage for either economic or emotional support. She must prepare to be self-supporting and to support others, perhaps, for a considerable period or for life. . . . Bearing in mind that everything possible must be done to encourage Negro males to develop their highest educational potential and to accept their family responsibilities and feel secure in their marital relationships, Negro women have no alternative but to insist upon equal opportunities without regard to sex in training, education and employment at every level. This may be a matter of sheer survival. And these special needs must be articulated by the civil rights movement so that they are not overlooked. . . .

One thing is crystal clear. The Negro woman can no longer postpone or subordinate the fight against discrimination because of sex to the civil rights struggle but must carry on both fights simultaneously. She must insist upon a partnership role in the integration movement.

VIEWPOINT 10

"Black women feel resentful that white women are raising issues of oppression . . . because black women do not see white women in any kind of classic oppressed position."

Black Women Should Seek Racial Equality

Charlayne Hunter (b. 1942)

The 1960s saw the rise of a revitalized feminist movement whose inspiration and organizational and tactical methods were modeled largely on the black civil rights movement. However, most feminist organizations had few black members, and many people questioned whether the predominantly white feminist movement adequately addressed the needs of black women. The following viewpoint is taken from a 1970 *New York Times* article in which several key black women leaders express their views on the relationship between the organized feminist movement and black women. Some of them argue that racism is a more serious problem than sexism.

The author of the viewpoint, *New York Times* reporter Charlayne Hunter (now Charlayne Hunter-Gault), became in 1963 the first black person to earn a degree from the University of Georgia. She later became the national correspondent for "The MacNeil/Lehrer Newshour" on public television.

Charlayne Hunter, "Many Blacks Wary of 'Women's Liberation' Movement," *New York Times*, November 17, 1970. Reprinted by permission of the *New York Times*. Copyright ©1970 by The New York Times Company, Inc.

Despite the fact that a black woman, Aileen Hernandez, heads one of the largest "women's liberation" groups in the country (the National Organization for Women), black women have been conspicuously absent from such groups. And while liberation is being discussed by black women—in workshops, liberation groups and privately—it is usually in a context different from that of white women.

The kind of liberation that black women are talking about raises some of the same questions being posed by the white groups. They include such issues as a guaranteed adequate income; day-care centers controlled and administered by the community they serve and the role of the woman in the relation to her man.

The differences are rooted in historical traditions that have placed black women—in terms of work, family life, education and men—in a relationship quite apart from that of white women. To militant black women—such as Frances Beal, a member of the newly formed Third World Women's Alliance—the white women's liberation charge of "sexism" is irrelevant; blackness is more important than maleness.

The Hostile Male

"Often, as a way of escape," she said in an interview, "black men have turned their hostility toward their women. But this is what we have to understand about him. It is a long, slow and sometimes painful process for the black man who has been so oppressed. But as black women, we have to have a conciliatory attitude. Firm, but creating together."

Such different perspectives make it all but impossible for some black women to relate to the white "women's lib" movement.

Mrs. Hernandez, as head of the National Organization for Women, which has a membership of roughly 10,000, said she was dismayed that "people are making a lot of generalizations about the movement and not getting an accurate portrayal."

"It is a predominantly white and middle-class movement—which all movements are," she asserted in a telephone interview from her San Francisco office. "But we feel an identity with all women."

Mrs. Hernandez, former Commissioner of the Federal Equal Employment Opportunity Commission, said she felt that "many more young women and many more black and Chicano women" are becoming active in NOW, "particularly in the Southern chapters."

"I find it strange that people are having to make a decision about which to be involved in," she said.

Miss Dorothy I. Height, president of the National Council of

Negro Women—a coalition of more than 25 black women's groups, representing about four million black women—said that she hoped eventually to have a "dialogue" with women's liberation groups. But even though she participated as a speaker in the Women's Liberation Day Program last August, she felt the presence of a wide gulf between them.

The Black Experience

Dorothy I. Height, leader of the National Council of Negro Women, argues in a speech at the 1970 convention of the Young Women's Christian Association (YWCA) that black and white women have had fundamentally different experiences.

While the whole culture downgrades women, the Black experience is different from the white. The Black woman's problem in her relationship to the Black man has not been subservience, but a forced position of responsibility that has made her seem a domineering matriarch. Ever since slavery, she has had to hold the family together, while her mate has been kept in a demoralizing, psychologically emasculating position of economic powerlessness. The feminists' call for deliberate competition with men and shaking up of the traditional family patterns cannot be highest in the present order of priorities of a woman who has been struggling to stabilize her family without flaunting the great strength required for that task.

"Fifty years ago all women got suffrage," Miss Height said she reminded the group, "but it took lynching, bombing, the civil-rights movement, and then the Voting Rights Act of 1965 to get it for black women and black people."

Miss Height said she felt it absolutely essential that "special attention be paid" to black women.

"With all the advances that black women have made—and we are in every field occupied by women—it is still true that we are in predominantly household and related services, with a median income of $1,523," she said.

Eleanor Holmes Norton, chairman of New York City's Commission on Human Rights, supplied another economic statistic concerning the black female labor force. Almost 70 per cent of black women with children between the ages of 6 and 18 work, she said.

Resentment

"Black women feel resentful that white women are raising issues of oppression even, because black women do not see white women in any kind of classic oppressed position," Mrs. Norton said.

Miss Beal recalled, for example, that the Third World Women's

Alliance had been against marching in the women's "Liberation Day" parade last August. But "at the last minute," she said, they decided that marching might be a way of letting other minority-group women who might be standing on the sidelines know of their organization.

"We had signs reading 'Hands Off Angela Davis' [a controversial black radical professor then under indictment for conspiracy to murder]—that was before her capture—and one of the leaders of NOW ran up to us and said angrily, 'Angela Davis has nothing to do with women's liberation.' And that's really the difference right there.

"It has nothing to do with the kind of liberation you're talking about," Miss Beal said she told the woman, "but it has everything to do with the kind of liberation we're talking about."

The Third World group, which has a New York City membership of about 200, and is establishing chapters in other states, includes young women who were formerly in the Black Women's Alliance of the Student National Coordinating Committee as well as a wide range of non-affiliated women. They see themselves as "part of the national liberation struggle" and, as such, believe that "the struggle against racism and imperialism must be waged simultaneously with the struggle for women's liberation."

Miss Beal, who is the mother of two daughters, said: "When white women demand from men an equal part of the pie, we say, 'Equal to what? What makes us think that white women, given the positions of white men in the system, would not turn around and use their white skin for the same white privileges? This is an economy that favors whites. And white women would have the privilege of their class.'"

A Rough Equality

While class and sex distinction undoubtedly exist in the black community, there are those like Mrs. Norton who declare that the distinctions are minimized by the experience of slavery and of discrimination.

"The black women already have a rough equality which came into existence out of necessity and is now ingrained in the black life style," said Mrs. Norton, a Yale law school graduate, and mother of a 3-month-old child. "Black women had to work with or beside their men, because work was necessary to survival. As a result, that give the black family very much of a headstart on egalitarian family life."

What about black women's attitudes toward black men?

According to Mrs. Norton: "Black men are the one group accustomed to women who are able and assertive, because their mothers and sisters were that way. And I don't think they reject their

173

mothers and sisters and wives. I don't think they want wives to be like the white suburban chocolate eaters who live in Larchmont."

Mrs. Shirley Lacy, director of training for the Scholarship Education and Defense Fund for Racial Equality—an integrated civil rights leadership training organization—has been called in by some black women's groups to hold workshops that include discussions on the black woman's role in the feminist movement.

Mrs. Lacy said that it was terribly important for black women to look at where they are in this time and say: "Given what I've got, how can I best use that in the context of the black struggle?"

"And if it means that today I walk behind the black man," she said, "that's what I do today, but that may not be true tomorrow. It may be that tomorrow he's going to fall, and I'm going to have to jump in there and be the leader. And the black man is going to have to understand that kind of juxtaposition too."

Chapter 4

Debates on National Civil Rights Acts

Chapter Preface

Among the highlights of the civil rights movement were two major pieces of national legislation passed by Congress: the Civil Rights Act of 1964 and the Voting Rights Act of 1965. The Civil Rights Act of 1964, signed by President Lyndon B. Johnson on July 2, guaranteed equal access to hotels, restaurants, and other facilities that served the general public. The act also authorized greater federal government involvement in combating school segregation and voting discrimination and prohibited discrimination based on race, religion, and gender in the workplace. The Voting Rights Act, signed by Johnson on August 6, 1965, further expanded the powers of the federal government to eliminate discrimination in voting. It empowered the U.S. attorney general to authorize federal voting officials to register black voters where discrimination existed, and it outlawed literacy test requirements for voter registration in some southern states. Federal officials registered hundreds of thousands of black and Hispanic voters in the following three years.

The debates held in the nation's capital over these pieces of legislation were highly influenced by the activities of the civil rights movement. In 1963 a series of civil rights demonstrations in Birmingham, Alabama, drew national attention when demonstrators were subject to mass arrests and physical attacks by local authorities. Many opponents of civil rights legislation sought to portray the civil rights demonstrators as dangerous and law-breaking radicals. However, most of the outrage expressed by many Americans who viewed the Birmingham events on television was aimed at segregationists rather than civil rights activists—a development that helped build support for the 1964 Civil Rights Act. A similar wave of demonstrations and white reprisals in Selma, Alabama, in early 1965 played a similar role in the debate over the Voting Rights Act. The viewpoints in this chapter present differing opinions both on the merits of federal civil rights legislation and on the activities of the civil rights movement.

"We have a right to expect that the Negro community will be responsible, will uphold the law, but they have a right to expect that the law will be fair."

America Should Support Federal Civil Rights Legislation

John F. Kennedy (1917–1963)

John F. Kennedy's election to the presidency in 1960 raised hopes among many blacks that the federal government would take a more active role in protecting their civil rights. But during his first years in office he placed a higher priority on other items of his domestic and foreign agenda. He did not propose any significant civil rights legislation, nor did he address the nation on the issue of racial inequality. However, events of the civil rights struggle—especially the confrontations between demonstrators and police in Birmingham, Alabama, in 1963—placed the issue of civil rights squarely before the American public. Responding both to the Birmingham demonstrations and Alabama governor George Wallace's continuing defiance of university desegregation, Kennedy delivered a nationally televised address on civil rights on June 11, 1963.

His speech, from which this viewpoint is taken, was one of the most significant presidential speeches on civil rights in American history. In it, Kennedy strongly endorses the goals of racial equality in the United States and praises civil rights demonstrators.

John F. Kennedy, "Radio and Television Report to the American People on Civil Rights," in *Public Papers of the President of the United States, John F. Kennedy*, vol. 3, 1963. Washington, DC: GPO, 1964.

The following day Kennedy proposed significant civil rights legislation that would prohibit racial discrimination in voting, education, employment, and access to public facilities. His proposals were signed into law as the Civil Rights Act of 1964 less than a year after Kennedy was assassinated in November 1963.

Good evening, my fellow citizens.

This afternoon, following a series of threats and defiant statements, the presence of Alabama National Guardsmen was required on the University of Alabama to carry out the final and unequivocal order of the United States District Court of the Northern District of Alabama. That order called for the admission of two clearly qualified young Alabama residents who happened to have been born Negro.

That they were admitted peacefully on the campus is due in good measure to the conduct of the students of the University of Alabama, who met their responsibilities in a constructive way.

I hope that every American, regardless of where he lives, will stop and examine his conscience about this and other related incidents. This Nation was founded by men of many nations and backgrounds. It was founded on the principle that all men are created equal, and that the rights of every man are diminished when the rights of one man are threatened.

Today we are committed to a worldwide struggle to promote and protect the rights of all who wish to be free. And when Americans are sent to Viet-Nam or West Berlin, we do not ask for whites only. It ought to be possible, therefore, for American students of any color to attend any public institution they select without having to be backed up by troops.

It ought to be possible for American consumers of any color to receive equal service in places of public accommodation, such as hotels and restaurants and theaters and retail stores, without being forced to resort to demonstrations in the street, and it ought to be possible for American citizens of any color to register and to vote in a free election without interference or fear of reprisal.

It ought to be possible, in short, for every American to enjoy the privileges of being American without regard to his race or his color. In short, every American ought to have the right to be treated as he would wish to be treated, as one would wish his children to be treated. But this is not the case.

The Negro baby born in America today, regardless of the section of the Nation in which he is born, has about one-half as

178

much chance of completing a high school as a white baby born in the same place on the same day, one-third as much chance of completing college, one-third as much chance of becoming a professional man, twice as much chance of becoming unemployed, about one-seventh as much chance of earning $10,000 a year, a life expectancy which is 7 years shorter, and the prospects of earning only half as much.

"It's A Hell Of A Note — No Accomodations Available!"

© 1965 Herblock in the *Washington Post*

This is not a sectional issue. Difficulties over segregation and discrimination exist in every city, in every State of the Union, producing in many cities a rising tide of discontent that threatens the public safety. Nor is this a partisan issue. In a time of domestic crisis men of good will and generosity should be able to unite regardless of party or politics. This is not even a legal or legislative issue alone. It is better to settle these matters in the courts than on the streets, and new laws are needed at every level, but law alone cannot make men see right.

We are confronted primarily with a moral issue. It is as old as the scriptures and is as clear as the American Constitution.

The heart of the question is whether all Americans are to be afforded equal rights and equal opportunities, whether we are going to treat our fellow Americans as we want to be treated. If an American, because his skin is dark, cannot eat lunch in a restaurant open to the public, if he cannot send his children to the best public school available, if he cannot vote for the public officials who represent him, if, in short, he cannot enjoy the full and free life which all of us want, then who among us would be content to have the color of his skin changed and stand in his place? Who among us would then be content with the counsels of patience and delay?

One hundred years of delay have passed since President Lincoln freed the slaves, yet their heirs, their grandsons, are not fully free. They are not yet freed from the bonds of injustice. They are not yet freed from social and economic oppression. And this Nation, for all its hopes and all its boasts, will not be fully free until all its citizens are free.

We preach freedom around the world, and we mean it, and we cherish our freedom here at home, but are we to say to the world, and much more importantly, to each other that this is a land of the free except for the Negroes; that we have no second-class citizens except Negroes; that we have no class or caste system, no ghettoes, no master race except with respect to Negroes?

The Nation's Promise

Now the time has come for this Nation to fulfill its promise. The events in Birmingham and elsewhere have so increased the cries for equality that no city or State or legislative body can prudently choose to ignore them.

The fires of frustration and discord are burning in every city, North and South, where legal remedies are not at hand. Redress is sought in the streets, in demonstrations, parades, and protests which create tensions and threaten violence and threaten lives.

We face, therefore, a moral crisis as a country and as a people. It cannot be met by repressive police action. It cannot be left to increased demonstrations in the streets. It cannot be quieted by token moves or talk. It is a time to act in the Congress, in your State and local legislative body and, above all, in all of our daily lives.

It is not enough to pin the blame on others, to say this is a problem of one section of the country or another, or deplore the fact that we face. A great change is at hand, and our task, our obligation, is to make that revolution, that change, peaceful and constructive for all.

Those who do nothing are inviting shame as well as violence. Those who act boldly are recognizing right as well as reality.

Next week I shall ask the Congress of the United States to act, to make a commitment it has not fully made in this century to the proposition that race has no place in American life or law. The Federal judiciary has upheld that proposition in a series of forth-right cases. The executive branch has adopted that proposition in the conduct of its affairs, including the employment of Federal personnel, the use of Federal facilities, and the sale of federally financed housing.

But there are other necessary measures which only the Congress can provide, and they must be provided at this session. The old code of equity law under which we live commands for every wrong a remedy, but in too many communities, in too many parts of the country, wrongs are inflicted on Negro citizens and there are no remedies at law. Unless the Congress acts, their only remedy is in the street.

A Call for Legislation

I am, therefore, asking the Congress to enact legislation giving all Americans the right to be served in facilities which are open to the public—hotels, restaurants, theaters, retail stores, and similar establishments.

This seems to me to be an elementary right. Its denial is an arbitrary indignity that no American in 1963 should have to endure, but many do.

I have recently met with scores of business leaders urging them to take voluntary action to end this discrimination and I have been encouraged by their response, and in the last two weeks over 75 cities have seen progress made in desegregating these kinds of facilities. But many are unwilling to act alone, and for this reason, nationwide legislation is needed if we are to move this problem from the streets to the courts.

I am also asking Congress to authorize the Federal Government to participate more fully in lawsuits designed to end segregation in public education. We have succeeded in persuading many districts to desegregate voluntarily. Dozens have admitted Negroes without violence. Today a Negro is attending a State-supported institution in every one of our 50 States, but the pace is very slow.

Too many Negro children entering segregated grade schools at the time of the Supreme Court's decision 9 years ago will enter segregated high schools this fall, having suffered a loss which can never be restored. The lack of an adequate education denies the Negro a chance to get a decent job.

The orderly implementation of the Supreme Court decision, therefore, cannot be left solely to those who may not have the economic resources to carry the legal action or who may be subject to harassment.

Other features will be also requested, including greater protection for the right to vote. But legislation, I repeat, cannot solve this problem alone. It must be solved in the homes of every American in every community across our country.

Praising Civil Rights Workers

In this respect, I want to pay tribute to those citizens North and South who have been working in their communities to make life better for all. They are acting not out of a sense of legal duty but out of a sense of human decency.

Like our soldiers and sailors in all parts of the world they are meeting freedom's challenge on the firing line, and I salute them for their honor and their courage.

My fellow Americans, this is a problem which faces us all—in every city of the North as well as the South. Today there are Negroes unemployed, two or three times as many compared to whites, inadequate in education, moving into the large cities, unable to find work, young people particularly out of work without hope, denied equal rights, denied the opportunity to eat at a restaurant or lunch counter or go to a movie theater, denied the right to a decent education, denied almost today the right to attend a State university even though qualified. It seems to me that these are matters which concern us all, not merely Presidents or Congressmen or Governors, but every citizen of the United States.

This is one country. It has become one country because all of us and all the people who came here had an equal chance to develop their talents.

We cannot say to 10 percent of the population that you can't have that right; that your children can't have the chance to develop whatever talents they have; that the only way that they are going to get their rights is to go into the streets and demonstrate. I think we owe them and we owe ourselves a better country than that.

Therefore, I am asking for your help in making it easier for us to move ahead and to provide the kind of equality of treatment which we would want ourselves; to give a chance for every child to be educated to the limit of his talents.

As I have said before, not every child has an equal talent or an equal ability or an equal motivation, but they should have the equal right to develop their talent and their ability and their motivation, to make something of themselves.

We have a right to expect that the Negro community will be responsible, will uphold the law, but they have a right to expect that the law will be fair, that the Constitution will be color blind, as Justice [John] Harlan said at the turn of the century.

This is what we are talking about and this is a matter which concerns this country and what it stands for, and in meeting it I ask the support of all our citizens.

Thank you very much.

"The President's [civil rights] proposals are clearly destructive of the American system and the constitutional rights of American citizens."

America Should Not Support Federal Civil Rights Legislation

Richard B. Russell (1897–1971)

Richard B. Russell, a Georgia Democrat, served in the U.S. Senate from 1932 until his death in 1971. He was one of several southern senators who, by virtue of their seniority and legislative skills, rose to powerful positions within the U.S. Senate, and who used that power to delay or prevent the passage of national civil rights legislation.

The following viewpoint is taken from a public statement made by Russell on June 12, 1963, in response to President John F. Kennedy's nationally televised call for civil rights legislation. Russell argues that legislation mandating racial integration is unconstitutional. He asserts that blacks already possess full legal equal rights, and criticizes the president for not condemning the mass demonstrations of civil rights activists that were then being carried out in Birmingham, Alabama, and other parts of the South.

The President's speech appealed eloquently to the emotions but completely disregarded reason, human experience and true equality under the Constitution.

Richard B. Russell, public statement of June 12, 1963; reprinted in the June 24, 1963, *U.S. News & World Report* under the headline "The South States Its Case."

The fact that every citizen has the same right to own and operate a swimming pool or dining hall constitutes equality. The use of federal power to force the owner of a dining hall or swimming pool to unwillingly accept those of a different race as guests creates a new and special right for Negroes in derogation of the property rights of all of our people to own and control the fruits of their labor and ingenuity.

The outstanding distinction between a government of free men and a socialistic or communistic state is the fact that free men can own and control property, whereas statism denies property rights.

"From each according to his ability and to each according to his need" may have greater emotional appeal than "work hard to acquire property and the law will protect you in its enjoyment." However, Marxism has not worked and can never work because it does not take human nature into account. To rebut the emotional appeal, we have the hard, undeniable fact that in our free-enterprise system we have plenty, whereas the Marxists—though they have never been able to apply literally their avowed creed—all suffer from scarcity and privation.

Our American system has always rejected the idea that one group of citizens may deprive another of legal rights in property by process of agitation, demonstration, intimidation, law defiance and civil disobedience.

I do not believe that the American people will be easily frightened into discarding our system for adventures into socialism that have been discredited wherever tried.

The highest office of the land should symbolize respect for law, whether it be legally enacted ordinances of the meanest hamlet in the land or the written word of our national charter—the Constitution.

I was, therefore, shocked to hear the President justify, if not encourage, the present wave of mass demonstrations, accompanied by the practices of sitting or lying in public streets and blocking traffic: forming human walls before the doors of legal businesses and assaulting with deadly weapons officers of the law whose only offense was undertaking to maintain order and protect private property.

The South has its shortcomings as well as other areas. But a calculated campaign waged by the metropolitan press, television and radio has magnified the unfortunate occurrences in the South while crimes of violence in other areas have been minimized. This has generated bitterness and hatred against the white people of the Southern States almost amounting to a national disease. It is also encouraging a condition bordering on anarchy in many communities. These terrible conditions are sure to further deteriorate with increasing disorder unless the President of the United

States desists from using threats of mass violence to rush his social equality legislation through the Congress.

No American citizen has the right to select the laws he will obey and those he will disobey.

The President of the United States has a higher call to leadership than to use threats of mass violence and disregard of reasonable local laws as a means of securing action in the courts and Congress, however desirable he may regard it to be.

Turmoil in Birmingham

In an editorial published in the Wall Street Journal *on May 9, 1963, associate editor Joseph E. Evans questions the tactics of civil rights leaders in Birmingham, Alabama.*

From the small, sporadic, scattered and relatively quiet sit-ins of a few years ago have grown large organized marches on cities. The invasion of Birmingham came under the label of non-violent demonstrating, but it was all too likely to degenerate into violence by the very nature of the undertaking.

Without question, the Birmingham authorities have long been intransigent. Without question, the jailing of little children is a sorry spectacle. But it must also be asked who first threw the little children against the police lines.

Or can it seriously be argued that a community should do nothing whatsoever when a couple of thousand organized people—be they women ban-the-bomb marchers or Negroes with a cause—come in, parade up and down the streets and finally erupt in a spree of stoning the police? That can only be an argument for anarchy.

The Congress of the United States, by an enactment of March 1, 1875, declared that all persons were entitled "to the full and equal enjoyment of the accommodations, advantages, facilities and privileges of inns, public conveyances on land or water, theaters and other places of public amusement." The Supreme Court of the United States on Oct. 15, 1883, declared this federal restriction upon the use and control of private property to be unconstitutional. In accordance with the contentions of those who would use federal power to mix the races socially, this has been the "law of the land" from that date and still applies today.

The President and the Attorney General now say that they will predicate this new thrust for race mixing on the already tortured commerce clause of the Constitution. If the commerce clause will sustain an act to compel the white owner of a dining hall to accept a Negro against his wishes, it can be used to sustain the validity of legislation that will compel his admittance into the living room or bedroom of any citizen.

I believe in equality before the law for every American. In equal measure, I reject the idea that federal power may be invoked to compel the mingling of the races in social activities to achieve the nebulous aim of social equality.

Every Negro citizen possesses every legal right that is possessed by any white citizen, but there is nothing in either the Constitution or Judaeo-Christian principles or common sense and reason which would compel one citizen to share his rights with one of another race at the same place and at the same time. Such compulsion would amount to a complete denial of the inalienable rights of the individual to choose or select his associates.

I hope that the American people will not be swept further down the road to socialism by the present unprecedented wave of propaganda. To me, the President's legislative proposals are clearly destructive of the American system and the constitutional rights of American citizens. I shall oppose them with every means and resource at my command. I do not believe a majority of the Congress will be frightened by thinly veiled threats of violence.

"We cannot, we must not refuse to protect the right of every American to vote in every election that he may desire to participate in."

The Voting Rights Act Should Be Passed

Lyndon B. Johnson (1908–1973)

Lyndon B. Johnson became president of the United States following the assassination of John F. Kennedy on November 22, 1963. Johnson, a Texas native who had been the Senate majority leader prior to his election as vice president in 1960, was able to marshal enough support in Congress to pass most of Kennedy's proposed civil rights legislation, and signed the Civil Rights Act of 1964 into law on July 2. Elected president by a wide margin in the 1964 election, Johnson continued to support civil rights as part of his general legislative effort to create what he called the "Great Society."

The following viewpoint is excerpted from an address before a joint session of Congress on March 15, 1965, in which Johnson calls for the passing of new federal legislation to secure the voting rights of blacks. Despite voting rights provisions in the Civil Rights Acts of 1957, 1960, and 1964, many southern blacks attempting to vote still faced significant harassment and opposition from local authorities. Eight days before Johnson's speech, in Selma, Alabama, state police armed with clubs and tear gas attacked hundreds of civil rights activists who were attempting to march from Selma to Montgomery as part of a longstanding campaign to register blacks and publicize continuing discrimination. Two days later, on March 9, a white civil rights activist was fatally assaulted by local whites. The events in Selma, much like similar incidents in Birmingham, Alabama, in 1963, received national

From Lyndon B. Johnson, *Congressional Record*, 89th Cong., 1st sess., vol. 3, no. 47 (March 15, 1965).

media coverage and focused the nation's attention on the problem of civil rights. Referring to incidents in Selma and adopting the civil rights slogan "we shall overcome," Johnson makes an impassioned plea for voting rights and an end to racism. Johnson's televised address was seen by approximately seventy million Americans.

I speak tonight for the dignity of man and the destiny of democracy. I urge every member of both parties, Americans of all religions and of all colors, from every section of this country, to join me in that cause.

At times history and fate meet at a single time in a single place to shape a turning point in man's unending search for freedom. So it was at Lexington and Concord. So it was a century ago at Appomattox. So it was last week in Selma, Alabama.

There, long-suffering men and women peacefully protested the denial of their rights as Americans. Many were brutally assaulted. One good man, a man of God, was killed.

There is no cause for pride in what has happened in Selma. There is no cause for self-satisfaction in the long denial of equal rights of millions of Americans.

But there is cause for hope and for faith in our democracy in what is happening here tonight.

For the cries of pain and the hymns and protests of oppressed people have summoned into convocation all the majesty of this great government of the greatest nation on earth.

Our mission is at once the oldest and the most basic of this country: to right wrong, to do justice, to serve man.

In our time we have come to live with the moments of great crisis. Our lives have been marked with debate about great issues, issues of war and peace, issues of prosperity and depression. But rarely in any time does an issue lay bare the secret heart of America itself. Rarely are we met with a challenge, not to our growth or abundance, or our welfare or our security, but rather to the values and the purposes and the meaning of our beloved nation.

The issue of equal rights for American Negroes is such an issue. And should we defeat every enemy, and should we double our wealth and conquer the stars and still be unequal to this issue, then we will have failed as a people and as a nation.

For with a country as with a person, "What is a man profited, if he shall gain the whole world, and lose his own soul?"

There is no Negro problem. There is no Southern problem. There is no Northern problem. There is only an American problem. And we are met here tonight as Americans, not as Democrats or Republicans, we are met here as Americans to solve that problem.

America's Promise

This was the first nation in the history of the world to be founded with a purpose. The great phrases of that purpose still sound in every American heart, North and South: "All men are created equal"—"government by consent of the governed"—"give me liberty or give me death." Those are not just clever words. Those are not just empty theories. In their name Americans have fought and died for two centuries, and tonight around the world they stand there as guardians of our liberty, risking their lives.

Those words are a promise to every citizen that he shall share in the dignity of man. This dignity cannot be found in a man's possessions. It cannot be found in his power or in his position. It really rests on his right to be treated as a man equal in opportunity to all others. It says that he shall share in freedom, he shall choose his leaders, educate his children, provide for his family according to his ability and his merits as a human being.

To apply any other test—to deny a man his hopes because of his color or race, or his religion, or the place of his birth—is not only to do injustice, it is to deny America and to dishonor the dead who gave their lives for American freedom.

Our fathers believed that if this noble view of the rights of man was to flourish, it must be rooted in democracy. The most basic right of all was the right to choose your own leaders. The history of this country in large measure is the history of expansion of that right to all of our people.

The Right to Vote

Many of the issues of civil rights are very complex and most difficult. But about this there can and should be no argument. Every American citizen must have an equal right to vote. There is no reason which can excuse the denial of that right. There is no duty which weighs more heavily on us than the duty we have to ensure that right.

Yet the harsh fact is that in many places in this country men and women are kept from voting simply because they are Negroes.

Every device of which human ingenuity is capable has been used to deny this right. The Negro citizen may go to register only to be told that the day is wrong, or the hour is late, or the official in charge is absent. And if he persists and if he manages to present himself to the registrar, he may be disqualified because he did not spell out his middle name or because he abbreviated a word on the application. And if he manages to fill out an application he is

Is This America?

One of the heroes of the civil rights movement was Fannie Lou Hamer, a Mississippi sharecropper who was active in the movement for black voting registration. Her testimony at the 1964 Democratic National Convention describing her experiences was nationally televised. Ironically, her plea that the Mississippi Freedom Democrat Party be seated at the convention instead of the state's regular Democratic Party slate (which had excluded blacks from participation) was opposed by President Lyndon B. Johnson, causing many civil rights activists to be embittered against the president.

In June the 9th, 1963, I had attended a voter-registration workshop, was returning back to Mississippi. Ten of us was traveling by the Continental Trailway bus. When we got to Winona, Mississippi, which is Montgomery County, four of the people got off to use the washroom, and two of the people—to use the restaurant—two of the people wanted to use the washroom. The four people that had gone in to use the restaurant was ordered out. During this time I was on the bus. But when I looked through the window and saw they had rushed out, I got off of the bus to see what had happened, and one of the ladies said, "It was a state highway patrolman and a chief of police ordered us out."

I got back on the bus and one of the persons had used the washroom got back on the bus, too. As soon as I was seated on the bus, I saw when they began to get the four people in a highway patrolman's car. I stepped off the bus to see what was happening and somebody screamed from the car that the four workers was in and said, "Get that one there," and when I went to get in the car, when the man told me I was under arrest, he kicked me.

I was carried to the county jail, and put in the booking room. They left some of the people in the booking room and began to place us in cells. I was placed in a cell with a young woman called Miss Euvester Simpson. After I was placed in the cell I began to hear sounds of licks and screams. I could hear the sounds of licks and horrible screams, and I could hear somebody say, "Can you say, yes sir, nigger? Can you say yes, sir?". . .

And it wasn't too long before three white men came to my cell. One of these men was a State Highway Patrolman and he asked me where I was from, and I told him Ruleville. He said, "We are going to check this." And they left my cell and it wasn't too long before they came back. He said, "You are from Ruleville all right," and he used a curse word, and he said, "We are going to make you wish you was dead.". . .

All of this is on account we want to register, to become first-class citizens, and if the Freedom Democratic Party is not seated now, I question America, is this America, the land of the free and the home of the brave where we have to sleep with our telephones off the hooks because our lives be threatened daily because we want to live as decent human beings, in America?

given a test. The registrar is the sole judge of whether he passes this test. He may be asked to recite the entire constitution, or explain the most complex provisions of state laws. And even a college degree cannot be used to prove that he can read and write.

For the fact is that the only way to pass these barriers is to show a white skin.

Experience has clearly shown that the existing process of law cannot overcome systematic and ingenious discrimination. No law that we now have on the books—and I have helped to put three of them there—can ensure the right to vote when local officials are determined to deny it.

In such a case our duty must be clear to all of us. The Constitution says that no person shall be kept from voting because of his race or his color. We have all sworn an oath before God to support and to defend that Constitution. We must now act in obedience to that oath.

A New Law

Wednesday I will send to Congress a law designed to eliminate illegal barriers to the right to vote.

The broad principle of that bill will be in the hands of the Democratic and Republican leaders tomorrow. After they have reviewed it, it will come here formally as a bill. I am grateful for this opportunity to come here tonight at the invitation of the leadership to reason with my friends, to give them my views and to visit with my former colleagues.

I have had prepared a more comprehensive analysis of the legislation which I have intended to transmit to the clerks tomorrow, but which I will submit to the clerks tonight; but I want to really discuss with you now briefly the main proposals of this legislation.

This bill will strike down restrictions to voting in all elections—Federal, State, and local—which have been used to deny Negroes the right to vote.

This bill will establish a simple, uniform standard which cannot be used however ingenious the effort to flout our Constitution.

It will provide for citizens to be registered by officials of the United States government, if the state officials refuse to register them.

It will eliminate tedious, unnecessary lawsuits which delay the right to vote.

Finally, this legislation will ensure that properly registered individuals are not prohibited from voting.

I will welcome the suggestions from all of the members of Congress. I have no doubt that I will get some on ways and means to strengthen this law and to make it effective. But experience has plainly shown that this is the only path to carry out the command of the Constitution.

To those who seek to avoid action by their national government in their own communities, who want to and who seek to maintain purely local control over elections, the answer is simple.

Open your polling places to all your people.

Allow men and women to register and vote whatever the color of their skin.

Extend the rights of citizenship to every citizen of this land.

There is no constitutional issue here. The command of the Constitution is plain.

There is no moral issue. It is wrong to deny any of your fellow Americans the right to vote in this country.

There is no issue of states rights or national rights. There is only the struggle for human rights.

I have not the slightest doubt what will be your answer.

But the last time a President sent a civil rights bill to the Congress it contained a provision to protect voting rights in Federal elections. That civil rights bill was passed after eight long months of debate. And when that bill came to my desk from the Congress for my signature, the heart of the voting provision had been eliminated.

This time, on this issue, there must be no delay, or no hesitation or no compromise with our purpose.

We cannot, we must not refuse to protect the right of every American to vote in every election that he may desire to participate in. And we ought not, we must not wait another eight months before we get a bill. We have already waited a hundred years and more and the time for waiting is gone.

So I ask you to join me in working long hours, nights, and weekends if necessary, to pass this bill. And I don't make that request lightly. Far from the window where I sit with the problems of our country, I recognize that from outside this chamber is the outraged conscience of a nation, the grave concern of many nations and the harsh judgment of history on our acts.

But even if we pass this bill, the battle will not be over. What happened in Selma is part of a far larger movement which reaches into every section and state of America. It is the effort of American Negroes to secure for themselves the full blessings of American life.

Our Cause

Their cause must be our cause too. Because it is not just Negroes, but really it is all of us, who must overcome the crippling legacy of bigotry and injustice. And we shall overcome.

As a man whose roots go deeply into Southern soil I know how agonizing racial feelings are. I know how difficult it is to reshape the attitudes and the structure of our society.

But a century has passed, more than a hundred years, since the Negro was freed. And he is not fully free tonight.

It was more than a hundred years ago that Abraham Lincoln, the great President of the Northern party, signed the Emancipation Proclamation, but emancipation is a proclamation and not a fact.

A century has passed, more than a hundred years since equality was promised. And yet the Negro is not equal.

A century has passed since the day of promise. And the promise is unkept.

The time of justice has now come. I tell you that I believe sincerely that no force can hold it back. It is right in the eyes of man and God that it should come. And when it does, I think that day will brighten the lives of every American. . . .

The real hero of this struggle is the American Negro. His actions and protests, his courage to risk safety and even to risk his life, have awakened the conscience of this nation. His demonstrations have been designed to call attention to injustice, designed to provoke change, designed to stir reform. He has called upon us to make good the promise of America. And who among us can say that we would have made the same progress were it not for his persistent bravery, and his faith in American democracy.

VIEWPOINT 4

"The government of the United States appears to have bowed to a new set of extremists."

The Voting Rights Act Should Not Be Passed

David Lawrence (1888–1973)

In a nationally televised address on March 15, 1965, President Lyndon B. Johnson called on Congress to pass new voting rights legislation that would strengthen the federal government's powers to prevent blacks from being denied the right to vote. The legislation was specifically aimed at parts of the South where blacks faced numerous obstacles in registering to vote, including discriminatory practices by local voting officials.

While Congress debated the measure, more than three thousand civil rights activists led by Martin Luther King Jr. successfully completed a five-day march from Selma to Montgomery, Alabama. The oft-delayed march, escorted by army troops and federalized units of the Alabama National Guard, was completed on March 25 without incidence of violence. However, following a rally in Montgomery in which King addressed fifty thousand people, Viola Liuzzo, a white housewife and civil rights activist, was shot by Klansmen while driving marchers from Montgomery back to Selma.

The dramatic events in Alabama helped build public and congressional support for the federal voting rights legislation. However, the proposed bill was not without its critics. The following viewpoint is taken from an editorial by David Lawrence, founder and editor of the newsmagazine *U.S. News & World Report*. Lawrence argues that the proposed legislation is unconstitutional because of its federal usurpation of state authority in regulating voting procedures. He also asserts that reasoned debate was impossible because of pressure from "extremist" groups whose tactics include "organized incitement to violence." Despite the objections of Lawrence and others, the Voting Rights Act was overwhelmingly passed by Congress on August 3, 1965.

The government of the United States appears to have bowed to a new set of extremists.

The President, in an emotional address to a joint session of both houses of Congress, described in general terms an unprecedented piece of legislation on voting rights and demanded that it be promptly passed. The text of the bill, however, wasn't even made public until later in the week. Members of the Supreme Court, attired in their judicial robes, sat in the front row in the House chamber during the proceedings and joined in the applause for the President's speech.

The sweeping proposals which the President virtually ordered Congress to pass were pressured by street demonstrations, violent and nonviolent, sit-ins and lie-ins in many parts of the country and even inside the White House, as well as the Capitol and other federal buildings. All this was designed to stampede the Chief Executive and Congress to brush aside the Constitution and to accept the extremist doctrine that "the end justifies the means." The tactics of the demonstrators triumphed.

Violating the Constitution

The Constitution explicitly gives to each State the power to determine the qualifications of voters in national, State and local elections. The Constitution also declares that the right of citizens to vote shall not be denied or abridged on account of race or color.

The new proposal arbitrarily singles out those States in the Union which, on Nov. 1, 1964, happened to have registered less than 50 per cent of the persons of voting age residing in the State or in any political subdivision, or in which less than 50 per cent of such residents voted in the presidential election last November.

This is a statistical yardstick which would automatically adjudge as guilty of discrimination a State which had used any literacy test if in such a State less than half of the population of voting age had been registered to vote or if "any person acting under color of law" had in the previous 10 years engaged in any act denying the right to vote because of race or color.

An appeal to a three-judge court—only in Washington—would

Why Blacks Were Denied the Vote

James J. Kilpatrick was a Virginia newspaper editor who wrote many articles and editorials questioning the Brown v. Board of Education *decision and defending school segregation. He later became a syndicated columnist. In this excerpt from a* National Review *article published on April 20, 1965, he expresses his views on voting rights legislation proposed by President Lyndon B. Johnson, and he explains why blacks have in the past been denied the vote in the South.*

The President's bill, with a few perfecting amendments, will be passed. Yet it is important to say for the record that the bill is a bad bill, rightly motivated but wrongly drawn. It undertakes to remedy a perversion of the Constitution by perverting the Constitution; it piles wrong upon wrong; it strikes with the brute and clumsy force of a wrecking ball at the very foundations of American federalism. Our body politic suffers, it is true, from a few tumors in the lower South, but the condition is operable and may be cured by careful surgery. This bill is a bill for disemboweling.

No reasonable man would deny that in times past, the South has sinned against the Negro; here and there, in times present, the abuse continues. For the better part of a century, much of the South has engaged in systematic, deliberate, ingenious and effective devices to deny the colored citizen his constitutional right to register and to vote. The whole course of conduct stands in wilful defiance of the plain language of the Fifteenth Amendment to the Constitution.

To this indictment, the South can enter but one honest plea—guilty, with extenuating circumstances. Over most of this century, the great bulk of Southern Negroes have been genuinely unqualified for the franchise. They emerged illiterate from slavery; they remained for generations, metaphorically, under the age of twenty-one. To this day, such is the apathetic state of rural politics in the South, the problem is not merely that registrars deny, but that Negroes seldom ask. The evidence would show this.

There is another line of defense, but it is a defense in equity, not in law. Throughout most of this period, whatever social and economic and political values have been created in the "Black Belt" counties through the machinery of local government, the white property owner has created them. In those rural counties where white families have been outnumbered three and four to one by Negroes, it has been the white leadership that has kept the machinery going—paid the taxes, provided the capital, met the bills. To have yielded political control of these functions to a mass of relatively uneducated Negro voters, easily led, unequipped for public administration, would have meant total disintegration of the whole establishment.

be allowed. Instead of the usual presumption of innocence for a defendant, the bill would establish a presumption of guilt for the suspected State or county. The governmental body not only would have to prove that it was not guilty of an act of discrimination on a specific date but also of any other such act on any other date in the preceding 10 years.

The bill, moreover, would strike down in those States any "test or device" that may have been used in past years, even though State laws may have sought to establish whether or not an applicant had the ability to read and write, or may have prescribed some other standard test of literacy such as the Supreme Court of the United States itself upheld as recently as 1959.

To select certain States or areas and apply one kind of law to them while permitting other States and subdivisions to be immune from such interference is a conspicuous violation of the Constitution.

The whole controversy has revealed a disregard of basic constitutionalism. It is motivated by the reasoning of those who have argued that two wrongs make a right. It grows out of the rationalization, which so many people are making today, that, because injustices have been committed and discrimination has once been practiced on a wide scale in certain areas of the country, it is permissible now to diminish the rights of the States themselves.

Reliving a Tragic Era

Have we come to the point where the Congress of the United States may decide on whether a State will be permitted to remain in the Union? Have we reached a position where the national legislative body will do again what it did 100 years ago after the War Between the States had ended? The same State legislatures which had ratified the Thirteenth Amendment, abolishing slavery, were suddenly declared illegal by Congress when they rejected the Fourteenth Amendment. New legislatures were ordered to assemble and in some instances federal troops were sent into the legislative chambers to compel "ratification" of the Fourteenth and later the Fifteenth Amendment.

This was what happened in the Reconstruction period in American history. Are we to go through another such tragic era because of the submissiveness of both a Congress and a President to the dictates of pressure groups whose emotional demonstrations cause friction and disorder?

It is a sad story. Organized incitement to violence has swept many areas of the country. To yield to such demonstrations is to weaken the whole fabric of democracy and to encourage mobocracy.

It is a time for the processes of reason to supersede the hysteria of impassioned groups of citizens. For, granting that they have been unjustly treated, are there no ways to accomplish effective reforms except by violent demonstrations and a distortion of the basic provisions of the Constitution? Or must we continue to bow to the new extremists?

CHAPTER 5

From Civil Rights to Black Power

Chapter Preface

On August 6, 1965, President Lyndon B. Johnson signed the Voting Rights Act, marking what many observers viewed as a triumph for the civil rights movement and an indication that blacks were moving closer to equality than ever before. Five days later riots broke out in the predominantly black Watts section of Los Angeles, resulting in thirty-four deaths and $40 million in property damage. The immediate cause of the riots was a confrontation between young blacks and white police officers; the underlying causes included frustration and despair created by unemployment, poverty, poor living conditions, and other social problems that were largely untouched by the civil rights movement. Riots would continue to plague American cities over the next several years, peaking in 1967, when 128 cities were affected.

Seeking in part to address the problems facing northern urban blacks and to recreate his successes in combating segregation in the South, Martin Luther King Jr. led a series of protest marches and demonstrations in the city of Chicago, Illinois, in 1966 to protest segregated housing and ghetto conditions. But his nonviolent confrontation techniques proved unsuccessful in dealing with the economic problems faced by poor northern blacks. Some black leaders, such as Stokely Carmichael and H. Rap Brown, openly questioned King's philosophy of nonviolence.

Many of the civil rights activists that formed the backbone of the movement in the early 1960s were also disillusioned by events at the Democratic National Convention in 1964. Workers who had spent that summer registering blacks in Mississippi had organized the Mississippi Freedom Democratic Party (MFDP) and had enrolled in it 60,000 blacks who had been barred from participating in the state's Democratic Party. The MFDP sent 68 delegates to the convention in Atlantic City, New Jersey, with the aim to challenge the seating of the regular all-white Mississippi delegation. But President Johnson, anxious to preserve party unity and ensure a smooth convention, instead proposed a compromise granting the MFDP two at-large seats and admitting the other delegates as "guests." Despite the entreaties of many civil rights leaders and white liberals, the MFDP delegates rejected the compromise. The experience created bitterness and mistrust among many civil rights activists toward the white political establishment.

The political disappointments of Atlantic City, the urban riots, and the persistence of problems facing blacks in America despite the passage of national civil rights legislation all contributed to greater divisions within the civil rights movement. In 1966 these divisions came to a head in the controversy over "black power"—a phrase popularized by Carmichael during a civil rights march in Mississippi as a slogan of defiance and outrage against the continuing mistreatment of blacks in the South. Black power later became a political doctrine that meant different things to different people. Many whites equated black power with the disorder and violence of the urban riots. Some blacks, such as Martin Luther King Jr., rejected black power as a detour from their goal of an integrated, color-blind society, while other blacks, impatient with the slow progress in improving their own lives amidst expectations raised by the civil rights movement, seized on the idea of gaining greater control over their own communities. The controversy polarized the nation and the civil rights movement itself. Some civil rights organizations, notably SNCC and CORE, took steps to exclude whites from leadership positions and ultimately from membership. The debate over black power is one issue discussed in the following chapter on the evolution of the civil rights movement during the mid-1960s.

VIEWPOINT 1

"The future of the Negro struggle depends on whether the contradictions of this society can be resolved by a coalition of progressive forces."

Blacks Should Engage in Coalition Politics

Bayard Rustin (1910–1987)

Bayard Rustin was an advocate of pacifism and nonviolent direct action as early as the 1940s; he spent over two years in prison as a conscientious objector during World War II. One of the founders of the Southern Christian Leadership Conference (SCLC), he was also an early advisor to Martin Luther King Jr. and the principal organizer of the 1963 March on Washington. In the following viewpoint, excerpted from a widely discussed 1965 article in *Commentary*, Rustin charts what he believes should be the future course of the civil rights movement following the passage of the 1964 Civil Rights Act and the 1965 Voting Rights Act. Rustin argues that blacks in America still face significant social and economic hurdles before achieving true equality with whites, and that these problems will be best addressed through the formation of a political coalition with organized labor, white liberals, and other elements of American society supportive of reform. He especially sees the 1964 presidential election (in which Democrat Lyndon B. Johnson, with overwhelming black support, won a massive victory over Republican Barry Goldwater) as a promising turning point in American politics, and he urges blacks to work within the Democratic Party.

From Bayard Rustin, "From Protest to Politics: The Future of the Civil Rights Movement," *Commentary*, February 1965. Reprinted by permission of Walter Naegle, on behalf of the estate of Bayard Rustin.

The decade spanned by the 1954 Supreme Court decision on school desegregation and the Civil Rights Act of 1964 will undoubtedly be recorded as the period in which the legal foundations of racism in America were destroyed. To be sure, pockets of resistance remain; but it would be hard to quarrel with the assertion that the elaborate legal structure of segregation and discrimination, particularly in relation to public accommodations, has virtually collapsed. On the other hand, without making light of the human sacrifices involved in the direct-action tactics (sit-ins, freedom rides, and the rest) that were so instrumental to this achievement, we must recognize that in desegregating public accommodations, we affected institutions which are relatively peripheral both to the American socio-economic order and to the fundamental conditions of life of the Negro people. In a highly industrialized, 20th-century civilization, we hit Jim Crow precisely where it was most anachronistic, dispensable, and vulnerable—in hotels, lunch counters, terminals, libraries, swimming pools, and the like. For in these forms, Jim Crow does impede the flow of commerce in the broadest sense: it is a nuisance in a society on the move (and on the make). Not surprisingly, therefore, it was the most mobility-conscious and relatively liberated groups in the Negro community—lower-middle-class college students—who launched the attack that brought down this imposing but hollow structure.

The term "classical" appears especially apt for this phase of the civil rights movement. But in the few years that have passed since the first flush of sit-ins, several developments have taken place that have complicated matters enormously. One is the shifting focus of the movement in the South, symbolized by Birmingham; another is the spread of the revolution to the North; and the third, common to the other two, is the expansion of the movement's base in the Negro community. To attempt to disentangle these three strands is to do violence to reality. David Danzig's perceptive [1964] article, "The Meaning of Negro Strategy," correctly saw in the Birmingham events the victory of the concept of collective struggle over individual achievement as the road to Negro freedom. And Birmingham remains the unmatched symbol of grass-roots protest involving all strata of the black community. It was also in this most industrialized of Southern cities that the single-issue demands of the movement's classical stage gave way to the "package deal." No longer were Negroes satisfied with integrating lunch counters. They now sought advances in employment, housing, school integration, police protection, and so forth.

Thus, the movement in the South began to attack areas of discrimination which were not so remote from the Northern experience as were Jim Crow lunch counters. At the same time, the interrelationship of these apparently distinct areas became increasingly evident. What is the value of winning access to public accommodations for those who lack money to use them? The minute the movement faced this question, it was compelled to expand its vision beyond race relations to economic relations, including the role of education in modern society. And what also became clear is that all these interrelated problems, by their very nature, are not soluble by private, voluntary efforts but require government action—or politics. Already Southern demonstrators had recognized that the most effective way to strike at the police brutality they suffered from was by getting rid of the local sheriff—and that meant political action, which in turn meant, and still means, political action within the Democratic party where the only meaningful primary contests in the South are fought.

And so, in Mississippi, thanks largely to the leadership of Bob Moses, a turn toward political action has been taken. More than voter registration is involved there. A conscious bid for *political power* is being made, and in the course of that effort a tactical shift is being effected: direct-action techniques are being subordinated to a strategy calling for the building of community institutions or power bases. Clearly, the implications of this shift reach far beyond Mississippi. What began as a protest movement is being challenged to translate itself into a political movement. Is this the right course? And if it is, can the transformation be accomplished? . . .

The civil rights movement is evolving from a protest movement into a full-fledged *social movement*—an evolution calling its very name into question. It is now concerned not merely with removing the barriers to full *opportunity* but with achieving the fact of *equality*. From sit-ins and freedom rides we have gone into rent strikes, boycotts, community organization, and political action. As a consequence of this natural evolution, the Negro today finds himself stymied by obstacles of far greater magnitude than the legal barriers he was attacking before: automation, urban decay, *de facto* school segregation. These are problems which, while conditioned by Jim Crow, do not vanish upon its demise. They are more deeply rooted in our socio-economic order; they are the result of the total society's failure to meet not only the Negro's needs, but human needs generally.

Moderates and Militants

These propositions have won increasing recognition and acceptance, but with a curious twist. They have formed the common premise of two apparently contradictory lines of thought which

203

simultaneously nourish and antagonize each other. On the one hand, there is the reasoning of the New York *Times* moderate who says that the problems are so enormous and complicated that Negro militancy is a futile irritation, and that the need is for "intelligent moderation." Thus, during the first New York school boycott, the *Times* editorialized that Negro demands, while abstractly just, would necessitate massive reforms, the funds for which could not realistically be anticipated, therefore the just demands were also foolish demands and would only antagonize white people. Moderates of this stripe are often correct in perceiving the difficulty or impossibility of racial progress in the context of present social and economic policies. But they accept the context as fixed. They ignore (or perhaps see all too well) the potentialities inherent in linking Negro demands to broader pressures for radical revision of existing policies. They apparently see nothing strange in the fact that in the last twenty-five years we have spent nearly a trillion dollars fighting or preparing for wars, yet throw up their hands before the need for overhauling our schools, clearing the slums, and really abolishing poverty. My quarrel with these moderates is that they do not even envision radical changes; their admonitions of moderation are, for all practical purposes, admonitions to the Negro to adjust to the status quo, and are therefore immoral.

The more effectively the moderates argue their case, the more they convince Negroes that American society will not or cannot be reorganized for full racial equality. Michael Harrington has said that a successful war on poverty might well require the expenditure of a $100 billion. Where, the Negro wonders, are the forces now in motion to compel such a commitment? If the voices of the moderates were raised in an insistence upon a reallocation of national resources at levels that could not be confused with tokenism (that is, if the moderates stopped being moderates), Negroes would have greater grounds for hope. Meanwhile, the Negro movement cannot escape a sense of isolation.

It is precisely this sense of isolation that gives rise to the second line of thought I want to examine—the tendency within the civil rights movement which, despite its militancy, pursues what I call a "no-win" policy. Sharing with many moderates a recognition of the magnitude of the obstacles to freedom, spokesmen for this tendency survey the American scene and find no forces prepared to move toward radical solutions. From this they conclude that the only viable strategy is shock; above all, the hypocrisy of white liberals must be exposed. These spokesmen are often described as the radicals of the movement, but they are really its moralists. They seek to change white hearts—by traumatizing them. Frequently abetted by white self-flagellants, they may gleefully applaud (though not really agreeing with) Malcolm X because, while they admit he has no program, they think he can frighten white people into doing the right thing. To believe this, of course, you must be convinced, even if unconsciously, that at the core of the white man's heart lies a buried affection for Negroes—a proposition one may be permitted to doubt. But in any case, hearts are not relevant to the issue; neither racial affinities nor racial hostilities are rooted there. It is institutions—social, political, and economic institutions—which are the ultimate molders of collective sentiments. Let these institutions be reconstructed *today*, and let the ineluctable gradualism of history govern the formation of a new psychology.

My quarrel with the "no-win" tendency in the civil rights movement (and the reason I have so designated it) parallels my quarrel with the moderates outside the movement. As the latter lack the vision or will for fundamental change, the former lack a realistic strategy for achieving it. For such a strategy they substitute militancy. But militancy is a matter of posture and volume and not of effect.

A Revolutionary Struggle

I believe that the Negro's struggle for equality in America is essentially revolutionary. While most Negroes—in their hearts—unquestionably seek only to enjoy the fruits of American society as it now exists, their quest cannot *objectively* be satisfied within the framework of existing political and economic relations. The young Negro who would demonstrate his way into the labor market may be motivated by a thoroughly bourgeois ambition and thoroughly "capitalist" considerations, but he will end up having to favor a great expansion of the public sector of the economy. At any rate, that is the position the movement will be forced to take as it looks at the number of jobs being generated by the private economy, and if it is to remain true to the masses of Negroes.

The revolutionary character of the Negro's struggle is manifest in the fact that this struggle may have done more to democratize life for whites than for Negroes. Clearly, it was the sit-in movement of young Southern Negroes which, as it galvanized white students, banished the ugliest features of McCarthyism from the American campus and resurrected political debate. It was not until Negroes assaulted *de facto* school segregation in the urban centers that the issue of quality education for *all* children stirred into motion. Finally, it seems reasonably clear that the civil rights movement, directly and through the resurgence of social conscience it kindled, did more to initiate the war on poverty than any other single force.

It will be—it has been—argued that these by-products of the

Negro struggle are not revolutionary. But the term revolutionary, as I am using it, does not connote violence; it refers to the qualitative transformation of fundamental institutions, more or less rapidly, to the point where the social and economic structure which they comprised can no longer be said to be the same. The Negro struggle has hardly run its course; and it will not stop moving until it has been utterly defeated or won substantial equality. But I fail to see how the movement can be victorious in the absence of radical programs for full employment, abolition of slums, the reconstruction of our educational system, new definitions of work and leisure. Adding up the cost of such programs, we can only conclude that we are talking about a refashioning of our political economy. It has been estimated, for example, that the price of replacing New York City's slums with public housing would be $17 billion. Again, a multi-billion dollar federal public-works program, dwarfing the currently proposed $2 billion program, is required to reabsorb unskilled and semi-skilled workers into the labor market—and this must be done if Negro workers in these categories are to be employed. "Preferential treatment" cannot help them.

Political Power

I am not trying here to delineate a total program, only to suggest the scope of economic reforms which are most immediately related to the plight of the Negro community. One could speculate on their political implications—whether for example, they do not indicate the obsolescence of state government and the superiority of regional structures as viable units of planning. Such speculations aside, it is clear that Negro needs cannot be satisfied unless we go beyond what has so far been placed on the agenda. How are these radical objectives to be achieved? The answer is simple, deceptively so: *through political power.*

There is a strong moralistic strain in the civil rights movement which would remind us that power corrupts, forgetting that the absence of power also corrupts. But this is not the view I want to debate here, for it is waning. Our problem is posed by those who accept the need for political power but do not understand the nature of the object and therefore lack sound strategies for achieving it; they tend to confuse political institutions with lunch counters.

A handful of Negroes, acting alone, could integrate a lunch counter by strategically locating their bodies so as *directly* to interrupt the operation of the proprietor's will; their numbers were relatively unimportant. In politics, however, such a confrontation is difficult because the interests involved are merely *represented.* In the execution of a political decision a direct confrontation may ensue (as when federal marshals escorted James Meredith into the

University of Mississippi—to turn from an example of non-violent coercion to one of force backed up with the threat of violence). But in arriving at a political decision, numbers and organizations are crucial, especially for the economically disenfranchised. (Needless to say, I am assuming that the forms of political democracy exist in America, however imperfectly, that they are valued, and that elitist or putschist conceptions of exercising power are beyond the pale of discussion for the civil rights movement.)

Neither that movement nor the country's twenty million black people can win political power alone. We need allies. The future of the Negro struggle depends on whether the contradictions of this society can be resolved by a coalition of progressive forces which becomes the *effective* political majority in the United States. I speak of the coalition which staged the March on Washington, passed the Civil Rights Act, and laid the basis for the Johnson land-slide—Negroes, trade unionists, liberals, and religious groups.

A Coalition Strategy

There are those who argue that a coalition strategy would force the Negro to surrender his political independence to white liberals, that he would be neutralized, deprived of his cutting edge, absorbed into the Establishment. Some who take this position urged last year that votes be withheld from the Johnson-Humphrey ticket as a demonstration of the Negro's political power. Curiously enough, these people who sought to demonstrate power through the non-exercise of it, also point to the Negro "swing vote" in crucial urban areas as the source of the Negro's independent political power. But here they are closer to being right: the urban Negro vote will grow in importance in the coming years. If there is anything positive in the spread of the ghetto, it is the potential political power base thus created, and to realize this potential is one of the most challenging and urgent tasks before the civil rights movement. If the movement can wrest leadership of the ghetto vote from the machines, it will have acquired an organized constituency such as other major groups in our society now have.

But we must also remember that the effectiveness of a swing vote depends solely on "other" votes. It derives its power from them. In that sense, it can never be "independent," but must opt for one candidate or the other, even if by default. Thus coalitions are inescapable, however tentative they may be. And this is the case in all but those few situations in which Negroes running on an independent ticket might conceivably win. "Independence," in other words, is not a value in itself. The issue is which coalition to join and how to make it responsive to your program. Necessarily there will be compromise. But the difference between expediency and morality in politics is the difference between selling out a principle and making smaller concessions to win larger ones. The leader who shrinks from this task reveals not his purity but his lack of political sense.

No Group Can Make It Alone

Martin Luther King Jr. expressed views similar to Bayard Rustin on coalition politics in his 1967 book Where Do We Go from Here: Chaos or Community?

However much we pool our resources and "buy black," this cannot create the multiplicity of new jobs and provide the number of low-cost houses that will lift the Negro out of the economic depression caused by centuries of deprivation. Neither can our resources supply quality integrated education. All of this requires billions of dollars which only an alliance of liberal-labor-civil-rights forces can stimulate. In short, the Negroes' problem cannot be solved unless the whole of American society takes a new turn toward greater economic justice.

In a multiracial society no group can make it alone. It is a myth to believe that the Irish, the Italians and the Jews—the ethnic groups that Black Power advocates cite as justification for their views—rose to power through separatism. It is true that they stuck together. But their group unity was always enlarged by joining in alliances with other groups such as political machines and trade unions. To succeed in a pluralistic society, and an often hostile one at that, the Negro obviously needs organized strength, but that strength will only be effective when it is consolidated through constructive alliances with the majority group.

The task of molding a political movement out of the March on Washington coalition is not simple, but no alternatives have been advanced. We need to choose our allies on the basis of common political objectives. It has become fashionable in some no-win Negro circles to decry the white liberal as the main enemy (his hypocrisy is what sustains racism); by virtue of this reverse recitation of the reactionary's litany (liberalism leads to socialism, which leads to Communism) the Negro is left in majestic isolation, except for a tiny band of fervent white initiates. But the objective fact is that [Senators James] *Eastland* and [Barry] *Goldwater* are the main enemies—they and the opponents of civil rights, of the war on poverty, of medicare, of social security, of federal aid to education, of unions, and so forth. The labor movement, despite its obvious faults, has been the largest single organized force in this country pushing for progressive social legislation. And where the Negro-labor-liberal axis is weak, as in the farm belt, it was the religious groups that were most influential in rallying support for the Civil Rights Bill.

The durability of the coalition was interestingly tested during the election. I do not believe that the Johnson landslide proved the "white backlash" to be a myth. It proved, rather that economic interests are more fundamental than prejudice: the backlashers decided that loss of social security was, after all, too high a price to pay for a slap at the Negro. This lesson was a valuable first step in re-educating such people, and it must be kept alive, for the civil rights movement will be advanced only to the degree that social and economic welfare gets to be inextricably entangled with civil rights.

The 1964 Elections

The 1964 elections marked a turning point in American politics. The Democratic landslide was not merely the result of a negative reaction to Goldwaterism; it was also the expression of a majority liberal consensus. The near unanimity with which Negro voters joined in that expression was, I am convinced, a vindication of the July 25th statement by Negro leaders calling for a strategic turn toward political action and a temporary curtailment of mass demonstrations. Despite the controversy surrounding the statement, the instinctive response if met with in the community is suggested by the fact that demonstrations were down 75 per cent as compared with the same period in 1963. But should so high a percentage of Negro voters have gone to Johnson, or should they have held back to narrow his margin of victory and thus give greater visibility to our swing vote? How has our loyalty changed things? Certainly the Negro vote had higher visibility in 1960, when a switch of only 7 per cent from the Republican column of 1956 elected President Kennedy. But the slimness of Kennedy's victory—of his "mandate"—dictated a go-slow approach on civil rights, at least until the Birmingham upheaval.

Although Johnson's popular majority was so large that he could have won without such overwhelming Negro support, that support was important from several angles. Beyond adding to Johnson's total national margin, it was specifically responsible for his victories in Virginia, Florida, Tennessee, and Arkansas. Goldwater took only those states where fewer than 45 per cent of eligible Negroes were registered. That Johnson would have won those states had Negro voting rights been enforced is a lesson not likely to be lost on a man who would have been happy with a unanimous electoral college. In any case, the 1.6 million Southern Negroes who voted have had a shattering impact on the Southern political party structure, as illustrated in the changed composition of the Southern congressional delegation. The "backlash" gave the Republicans five House seats in Alabama, one in Georgia, and one in Mississippi. But on the Democratic side, seven segregationists were defeated while all nine Southerners who voted for the Civil Rights Act were re-elected. It may be premature to predict a Southern Democratic party of Negroes and white moderates and a Republican party of refugee racists and economic conservatives, but there certainly is a strong tendency toward such a realignment; and an additional 3.6 million Negroes of voting age in the eleven Southern states are still to be heard from. Even the *tendency* toward disintegration of the Democratic party's racist wing defines a new context for Presidential and liberal strategy in the congressional battles ahead. Thus the Negro vote (North as well as South), while not *decisive* in the Presidential race, was enormously effective. It was a dramatic element of a historic mandate which contains vast possibilities and dangers that will fundamentally affect the future course of the civil rights movement.

The liberal congressional sweep raises hope for an assault on the seniority system, Rule Twenty-two, and other citadels of Dixiecrat-Republican power. The overwhelming of this conservative coalition should also mean progress on much bottlenecked legislation of profound interest to the movement. . . . Moreover, the irrelevance of the South to Johnson's victory gives the President more freedom to act than his predecessors had and more leverage to the movement to pressure for executive action in Mississippi and other racist strongholds.

Reshaping the Democratic Party

None of this *guarantees* vigorous executive or legislative action, for the other side of the Johnson landslide is that it has a Gaullist quality. Goldwater's capture of the Republican party forced into the Democratic camp many disparate elements which do not belong there. Big Business being the major example. Johnson, who wants to be President "of all people," may try to keep his new coalition together by sticking close to the political center. But if he decides to do this, it is unlikely that even his political genius will be able to hold together a coalition so inherently unstable and rife with contradictions. It must come apart. Should it do so while Johnson is pursuing a centrist course, then the mandate will have been wastefully dissipated. However, if the mandate is seized upon to set fundamental changes in motion, then the basis can be laid for a new mandate, a new coalition including hitherto inert and dispossessed strata of the population.

Here is where the cutting edge of the civil rights movement can be applied. We must see to it that the reorganization of the "consensus party" proceeds along lines which will make it an effective vehicle for social reconstruction, a role it cannot play so long as it furnishes Southern racism with its national political power. (One of Barry Goldwater's few attractive ideas was that the Dixiecrats belong with him in the same party.) And nowhere has the civil rights movement's political cutting edge been more magnificently demonstrated than at Atlantic City, where the Mississippi Freedom Democratic party not only secured recognition as a bona fide component of the national party, but in the process routed the representatives of the most rabid racists—the white Mississippi and Alabama delegations. While I still believe that the FDP made a tactical error in spurning the compromise, there is no question that they launched a political revolution whose logic is the displacement of Dixiecrat power. They launched that revolution within a major political institution and as part of a coalitional effort.

The role of the civil rights movement in the reorganization of American political life is programmatic as well as strategic. We are challenged now to broaden our social vision, to develop functional programs with concrete objectives. We need to propose alternatives to technological unemployment, urban decay, and the rest. We need to be calling for public works and training, for national economic planning, for federal aid to education, for attractive public housing—all this on a sufficiently massive scale to make a difference. We need to protest the notion that our integration into American life, so long delayed, must now proceed in an atmosphere of competitive scarcity instead of in the security of abundance which technology makes possible. We cannot claim to have answers to all the complex problems of modern society. That is too much to ask of a movement still battling barbarism in Mississippi. But we can agitate the right questions by probing at the contradictions which still stand in the way of the "Great Society." The questions having been asked, motion must begin in the larger society, for there is a limit to what Negroes can do alone.

"What is needed . . . is independent political action through indigenous political organizations."

Blacks Should Seek Independent Political Power

James Farmer and the Black Panther Party

While some black leaders of the 1960s, including Bayard Rustin, advocated the formation of political coalitions in the struggle for civil rights, others favored the exercise of black political power independent of the government, the major political parties, and indeed of all white allies. Major civil rights organizations such as SNCC and CORE dropped their prior prohibitions against partisan political activity in order to mobilize the black vote in southern states and northern ghetto areas, and new organizations such as the Mississippi Freedom Democratic Party were organized as a political alternative for blacks. Among the most widely known of these organizations was the Black Panther Party, founded in Oakland, California, in 1966. It gained national notoriety for its revolutionary rhetoric and its black armed patrols that followed police into black communities to combat police brutality.

The following viewpoint is in two parts. Part I is an address to CORE's 1965 annual convention by its director, James Farmer. He argues that the civil rights movement in its new phase must emphasize local political mobilization of black communities. Part II is the manifesto of the Black Panther Party, drafted by founders Huey P. Newton and Bobby Seale, which spells out what they see as the primary problems blacks still face in America.

James Farmer, annual report to CORE National Convention, July 1, 1965. Reprinted with permission. From "What We Want. What We Believe," in the October 1966 Black Panther Party Platform and Program.

I

As CORE meets at its 23rd Annual Convention, we have behind us many successes achieved and victories won. But this report will not be a recounting of past successes, to rest on one's laurels is to atrophy and die. Past victories—in public accommodations, in voting rights, in the support of law and public policy—have been in battles preceding the major encounter.

The major war now confronting us is aimed at harnessing the awesome political potential of the black community in order to effect basic social and economic changes for all Americans, to alter meaningfully the lives of the Black Americans (our plight has not been and will not be changed by past victories), and to bring about a real equality of free men.

The Government Cannot Help

This job cannot be done for us by the Government. In the first place, the establishments—Federal, State, and Local—have too much built-in resistance to fundamental change. Any establishment by definition seeks its own perpetuation and rejects that which threatens it. For example, politicians take over and seek to make the anti-poverty programs an adjunct of their political aspirations. They attack community action programs of the anti-poverty war as being anti-city hall. School Boards, which have already lost the drop-outs and other under-privileged youth, reach out greedily to control community education programs and see that they do not shake up the school systems. Powerful lobbies, such as the financial and the real estate interests, exert tremendous pressure to see that programs to relieve poverty do not threaten their interests.

Further, it is impossible for the Government to mount a decisive war against poverty and bigotry in the United States while it is pouring billions down the drain in a war against people in Viet Nam. The billion dollars available to fight poverty is puny compared with the need and insignificant compared with the resources expended in wars.

Thus, we must be constructive critics of the anti-poverty program, using its resources for our fight where we can, insisting that local anti-poverty boards be truly representatives of the deprived communities and the minorities which they are supposed to help, and attacking waste and pork-barreling wherever it occurs.

Yet it would be fatal to think that the anti-poverty program alone can make the necessary changes in the social and economic life of Black Americans. It can be no more a solution to our problems than the Civil Rights Acts of 1957, 1960, 1964 were, or the

Voter Rights Act of 1965 will be. Like those laws, the anti-poverty program has to be seen as no more than a tool, useful at times but inadequate at best to do the job.

We can rely upon none but ourselves as a catalyst in the development of the potential power of the black community in its own behalf and in behalf of the nation. . . .

It is clear that the objectives we seek—in the wiping out of poverty and unemployment, elimination of bad housing, city planning for integration in housing and schools, quality education—are political objectives depending upon responses we can exact from political machinery. We can no longer rely on pressuring and cajoling political units toward desired actions. We must be in a position of power, a position to change those political units when they are not responsive.

The only way to achieve political objectives is through power, political power. Only diminishing returns can be achieved through the pressure of demonstrations not backed up by political muscle. . . .

As we organize the community through directed centers, so we must seek to organize the community politically—or, more accurately, to *reorganize* it politically. For the bosses and the machines have already organized it after a fashion with their ward heelers and their petty precinct captains. The greatest tragedy of all would be for the existing black vote to remain in, and the new black vote to be dumped into the general political soup now brewed by the machine bosses—black or white.

Independent Political Action

What is needed, I believe, is independent political action through indigenous political organizations. This is the Freedom Democratic Party in Mississippi and CORE is supporting it fully, including its challenge. After the Summer CORE Project in Louisiana, if activated communities articulate the desire we will help them organize a Louisiana Freedom Democratic Party.

In the North, independent political voices are needed too. When the black ghetto communities with which CORE chapters have dialogued articulate the desire, we must take the lead in helping them develop Freedom Democratic Movements to serve as a political voice for their awakening self-expression.

Only through such independent action can the growing black vote achieve maximum effectiveness in moving toward the goals we seek. Freedom Democratic Movements must not be racist and should not exclude whites. But their base must be in the black ghetto, else they will be merely another exercise in liberal futility!

We must be prepared to put up candidates for nomination, when necessary, through such political vehicles, and to endorse or oppose candidates for election. A few of our chapters, Brooklyn, for example, are already doing this. Brooklyn CORE took the initiative in helping people in the Bedford-Stuyvesant ghetto in setting up the Brooklyn Freedom Democratic Movement. The CORE Chairman, Major Owens, is a candidate for nomination to the City Council under the BFDM banner (with the backing of the national organization)—challenging an incumbent machine politician. And Owens has a fighting chance to win the nomination [in the Democratic Primary].

Audacious Power

Adam Clayton Powell Jr. represented the Harlem area of New York City in Congress from 1944 to 1970, and became one of the most powerful black political figures in America. Speaking at Ebenezer Missionary Baptist Church in Chicago, Illinois, on May 28, 1965, Powell argues that blacks should emphasize political power and economic self-sufficiency.

Black leadership in the North and the South must differentiate between and work within the two-pronged thrust of the Black Revolution: economic self-sufficiency and political power. The Civil Rights Act of 1964 has absolutely no meaning for black people in New York, Chicago, or any of the Northern cities. *De jure* school segregation, denial of the right to vote, or barriers to public accommodations are no longer sources of concern to Northern Negroes. Civil rights in the North means more jobs, better education, manpower retraining, and development of new skills. As Chairman of the House Committee on Education and Labor, I control all labor legislation such as minimum wage, all education legislation, including aid to elementary schools and higher education, the manpower training and redevelopment program, vocational rehabilitation and of greater importance today, the "War on Poverty." This is legislative power. This is political power. I use myself as an example because this is the *audacious power* I urge every black woman and man in this audience to seek—the kind of political clout needed to achieve greater economic power and bring the black Revolution into fruition.

This is, of course, a new departure in CORE policy. But the old policy is no longer applicable to the needs of the movement. We may as well admit that the old policy is dead, and move boldly on with the new.

Such ghetto-oriented political movements must avoid, at all costs, becoming an adjunct to, or a tool of, any political party, bloc, or machine. They must be controlled by the interests of the black ghetto alone. They must be in a position to make alliances when called for, and break them when necessary. There should be no

215

binding Grand Alliances where the black ghetto becomes a tail to some other kite, or a dancer to some other political fiddler's tune!

Now, it will be a disservice to the ghetto community if we seek to be its manipulators, to substitute CORE as the boss of a political machine which will, in the very nature of the case, become corrupt and oppressive, as boss-ridden machines always are. CORE bossism may be *benevolent* despotism, but it would be despotism nonetheless, and essentially no different from any other.

What is called for, instead, is *dialogue* and *interaction* between CORE and the community to determine goals. We must listen to them, and have the machinery for doing so, and hope that they will listen to us. But the community must be the boss, not we! . . . And through the ghetto's emerging voice we must speak to the nation—and to the world.

Similar Problems North and South

Such new directions are developing in the South and being groped for in the North. In North and South, now, we must get moving with no further delay if the civil rights revolution is to succeed in this enormously difficult and highly complex new phase into which our past successes have thrust us.

In the North our chapters must make quick transitions from the old phase to the new if we are to remain relevant to the needs of the struggle. In the South, except for Klanism and massive police violence, our problems are not vastly different from the North. The South is becoming, and will become, increasingly like the North with *de facto* segregation substituted for *de jure* with the black man confined to a status of built in low-man on the economic, social and political totem pole—able to eat a hamburger, but not to have a rewarding life.

II

What We Want
What We Believe

1. We want freedom. We want power to determine the destiny of our Black Community.

We believe that black people will not be free until we are able to determine our destiny.

2. We want full employment for our people.

We believe that the federal government is responsible and obligated to give every man employment or a guaranteed income. We believe that if the white American businessmen will not give full employment, then the means of production should be taken from the businessmen and placed in the community so that the people of the community can organize and employ all of its people and give a high standard of living.

3. We want an end to the robbery by the white man of our Black Community.

We believe that this racist government has robbed us and now we are demanding the overdue debt of forty acres and two mules. Forty acres and two mules was promised 100 years ago as restitution for slave labor and mass murder of black people. We will accept the payment in currency which will be distributed to our many communities. The Germans are now aiding the Jews in Israel for the genocide of the Jewish people. The Germans murdered six million Jews. The American racist has taken part in the slaughter of over fifty million black people; therefore, we feel that this is a modest demand that we make.

4. We want decent housing, fit for shelter of human beings.

We believe that if the white landlords will not give decent housing to our black community, then the housing and the land should be made into cooperatives so that our community, with government aid, can build and make decent housing for its people.

5. We want education for our people that exposes the true nature of this decadent American society. We want education that teaches us our true history and our role in the present-day society.

We believe in an educational system that will give to our people a knowledge of self. If a man does not have knowledge of himself and his position in society and the world, then he has little chance to relate to anything else.

6. We want all black men to be exempt from military service.

We believe that black people should not be forced to fight in the military service to defend a racist government that does not protect us. We will not fight and kill other people of color in the world who, like black people, are being victimized by the white racist government of America. We will protect ourselves from the force and violence of the racist police and the racist military, by whatever means necessary.

7. We want an immediate end to POLICE BRUTALITY and MURDER of black people.

We believe we can end police brutality in our black community by organizing black self-defense groups that are dedicated to defending our black community from racist police oppression and brutality. The Second Amendment to the Constitution of the United States gives a right to bear arms. We therefore believe that all black people should arm themselves for self-defense.

8. We want freedom for all black men held in federal, state, county and city prisons and jails.

We believe that all black people should be released from the many jails and prisons because they have not received a fair and impartial trial.

9. We want all black people when brought to trial to be tried in court by a jury of their peer group or people from their black communities, as defined by the Constitution of the United States.

We believe that the courts should follow the United States Constitution so that black people will receive fair trials. The 14th Amendment of the U.S. Constitution gives a man a right to be tried by his peer group. A peer is a person from a similar economic, social, religious, geographical, environmental, historical and racial background. To do this the court will be forced to select a jury from the black community from which the black defendant came. We have been, and are being tried by all-white juries that have no understanding of the "average reasoning man" of the black community.

10. We want land, bread, housing, education, clothing, justice and peace. And as our major political objective, a United Nations–supervised plebiscite to be held throughout the black colony in which only black colonial subjects will be allowed to participate, for the purpose of determining the will of black people as to their national destiny.

When, in the course of human events, it becomes necessary for one people to dissolve the political bands which have connected them with another, and to assume, among the powers of the earth, the separate and equal station to which the laws of nature and nature's God entitle them, a decent respect to the opinions of mankind requires that they should declare the causes which impel them to the separation.

We hold these truths to be self-evident, that all men are created equal; that they are endowed by their Creator with certain unalienable rights; that among these are life, liberty, and the pursuit of happiness. *That, to secure these rights, governments are instituted among men, deriving their just powers from the consent of the governed; that, whenever any form of government becomes destructive of these ends, it is the right of the people to alter or to abolish it, and to institute a new government, laying its foundation on such principles, and organizing its powers in such form, as to them shall seem most likely to effect their safety and happiness.* Prudence, indeed, will dictate that governments long established should not be changed for light and transient causes; and, accordingly, all experience hath shown, that mankind are more disposed to suffer, while evils are sufferable, than to right themselves by abolishing the forms to which they are accustomed. *But, when a long train of abuses and usurpations, pursuing invariably the same object, evinces a design to reduce them under absolute despotism, it is their right, it is their duty, to throw off such government, and to provide new guards for their future security.*

VIEWPOINT 3

"The racial and cultural personality of the black community must be preserved and the community must win its freedom while preserving its cultural integrity. This is the essential difference between integration as it is currently practiced and the concept of Black Power."

Blacks Should Aim for Black Power

Stokely Carmichael (Kwame Ture) (b. 1941)

In 1966 some of the divisions within the civil rights movement came out in the open in the controversy over the slogan "black power." Disagreement existed both as to the precise meaning of the term and its utility in the movement. Some civil rights leaders and supporters embraced the term as a necessary next step for blacks in their quest for racial equality, arguing that blacks needed more political power in their communities and pride in their cultural heritage. Others, both within and outside the civil rights movement, decried the slogan as having ominous overtones of antiwhite racism and violence.

The following viewpoint is by Stokely Carmichael, one of the foremost exponents of black power. Carmichael replaced John Lewis as chairman of the Student Nonviolent Coordinating Committee (SNCC) in 1966, after being active in the organization and in other civil rights activities for several years. Under his leadership SNCC excluded whites from its membership and de-emphasized racial integration as a goal for blacks. He popularized the slogan of black power during a civil rights march through Mississippi in 1966, and spent the following several months writing and speaking about the concept. He wrote *Black*

Stokely Carmichael, "Toward Black Liberation," *The Massachusetts Review*, September 1966; ©1966 The Student Nonviolent Coordinating Committee.

Power: The Politics of Liberation in America with Charles V. Hamilton in 1967. In an article that appeared in the *Massachusetts Review* in 1966 (and which he frequently used as his text when speaking before predominantly white audiences), Carmichael explains and defends what he means by black power. He argues that the tactics and philosophy that have guided the civil rights movement have accomplished all they can, and that blacks must use their political and economic power to take control of their own communities.

Carmichael left SNCC in 1967 and briefly joined the Black Panther Party. He later moved to Guinea, Africa, and adopted the African name Kwame Ture.

One of the most pointed illustrations of the need for Black Power, as a positive and redemptive force in a society degenerating into a form of totalitarianism, is to be made by examining the history of distortion that the concept has been given by the national media of publicity. In this "debate," as in everything else that affects our lives, Negroes are dependent on, and at the discretion of, forces and institutions within the white society that have little interest in representing us honestly. Our experience with the national press has been that when they have managed to escape a meretricious special interest in "Git Whitey" sensationalism and race-war mongering, individual reporters and commentators have been conditioned by the enveloping racism of the society to the point where they are incapable of objective observation and reporting of racial *incidents*, much less the analysis of *ideas*. But this limitation of vision and perceptions is an inevitable consequence of the dictatorship of definition, interpretation, and consciousness, along with the censorship of history that the society has inflicted upon the Negro—and itself.

Our concern for Black Power addresses itself directly to this problem: the necessity to reclaim our history and our identity from the cultural terrorism and depredation of self-justifying white guilt.

To do this we shall have to struggle for the right to create our own terms to define ourselves and our relationship to the society, and to have these terms recognized. This is the first necessity of a free people, and the first right that any oppressor must suspend. The white fathers of American racism knew this—instinctively it seems—as is indicated by the continuous record of the distortion and omission in their dealings with the red and black men. In the same way that Southern apologists for the "Jim Crow" society have so obscured, muddied and misrepresented the record of the Reconstruction period, until it is almost impossible to tell what really happened, their contemporary counterparts are busy with the recent history of the civil rights movement.

A native of Trinidad who grew up in New York City, Stokely Carmichael was one of the most charismatic and controversial leaders of the civil rights movement.

In 1964, for example, the National Democratic Party, led by L. B. Johnson and Hubert H. Humphrey, cynically undermined the efforts of Mississippi's black population to achieve some degree of political representation. Yet, whenever the events of that convention are recalled by the press, one sees only the version fabricated by the press agents of the Democratic Party. A year later the House representatives in an even more vulgar display of political racism made a mockery of the political rights of Mississippi's Negroes when it failed to unseat the Mississippi delegation to the House—which had been elected through a process that methodically and systematically excluded over 450,000 voting-age Negroes, almost one-half of the total electorate of the state. Whenever this event is mentioned in print, it is in terms that leave one with the rather curious impression that somehow the oppressed Negro people of Mississippi are at fault for confronting the Congress with a situation in which they had no alternative but to endorse Mississippi's racist political practices. I am speaking now of the Mississippi Freedom Democratic Party.

I mention these two examples because, having been directly involved in them, I can see very clearly the discrepancies between what happened and the versions that are finding their way into general acceptance as a kind of popular mythology. The victimization of the Negro takes place in two phases: first it occurs in fact and deed; then, and this is equally sinister, in the official recording of those facts.

The Black Power program and concept being articulated by SNCC, CORE, and a host of community organizations in the ghettos of the North and South, has not escaped that process. The white press has been busy articulating their own analyses, their own interpretations and criticisms. For example, while the press has given wide and sensational dissemination to attacks made by figures in the civil rights movement—foremost among them are Roy Wilkins of the NAACP and Whitney Young of the Urban League—and to the hysterical ranting about black racism made by that political chameleon, Vice-President Humphrey, it has generally failed to give accounts of the reasonable and productive dialogue that is taking place in the Negro community, and in certain important areas in the white religious and intellectual community. A national committee of influential Negro churchmen affiliated with the National Council of Churches, despite their obvious respectability and responsibility, had to resort to a paid advertisement to articulate their position, while anyone shouting the hysterical yappings of "black racism" got ample space. Thus the American people have got at best a superficial and misleading account of the very terms and tenor of this debate. I wish to quote briefly from the statement by the national committee of churchmen, which I suspect the majority of Americans will not have seen. This statement appeared in the *New York Times*, July 31, 1966:

> We, an informal group of Negro Churchmen in America, are deeply disturbed about the crisis brought upon our country by historic distortions of important human realities in the controversy about "black power." What we see shining through the variety of rhetoric is not anything new but the same old problem of power and race which has faced our beloved country since 1619.
>
> . . . The conscience of black men is corrupted because, having no power to implement the demands of conscience, the concern for justice in the absence of justice becomes a chaotic self-surrender. Powerlessness breeds a race of beggars. We are faced now with a situation where powerless conscience meets conscience-less power, threatening the very foundations of our Nation.
>
> . . . We deplore the overt violence of riots, but we feel it is more important to focus on the real sources of these eruptions. These sources may be abetted inside the Ghetto, but their basic cause lies in the silent and covert violence which white middle-class America inflicts upon the victims of the inner city.
>
> . . . In short, the failure of American leaders to use American power to create equal opportunity in life as well as law, this is

the real problem and not the anguished cry for black power.

. . . Without the capacity to participate with power, i.e., to have some organized political and economic strength to really influence people with whom one interacts—integration is not meaningful.

. . . America has asked its Negro citizens to fight for opportunity as individuals, whereas at certain points in our history what we have needed most has been opportunity for the whole group, not just for selected and approved Negroes.

. . . We must not apologize for the existence of this form of group power, for we have been oppressed as a group and not as individuals. We will not find our way out of that oppression until both we and America accept the need for Negro Americans, as well as for Jews, Italians, Poles, and white Anglo-Saxon Protestants, among others, to have and to wield group power.

Traditionally, for each new ethnic group, the route to social and political integration in America's pluralistic society has been through the organization of their own institutions with which to represent their communal needs within the larger society. This is simply stating what the advocates of Black Power are saying. The strident outcry, *particularly* from the liberal community, that has been evoked by this proposal can be understood only by examining the historic relationship between Negro and white power in this country.

Negroes are defined by two forces: their blackness and their powerlessness. There have been, traditionally, two communities in America: the white community, which controlled and defined the forms that all institutions within the society would take, and the Negro community, which has been excluded from participation in the power decisions that shaped the society, and has traditionally been dependent upon and subservient to the white community.

This has not been accidental. The history of every institution of this society indicates that a major concern in the ordering and structuring of the society has been the maintaining of the Negro community in its condition of dependence and oppression. This has not been on the level of individual acts of discrimination—individual whites against individual Negroes—but total acts by the white community against the Negro community. This fact cannot be too strongly emphasized—that racist assumptions of white superiority have been so deeply ingrained in the structure of the society that it infuses its entire functioning, and is so much a part of the national subconscious that it is taken for granted and is frequently not even recognized. It is more than a figure of speech to say that the Negro community in America is the victim of white imperialism and colonial exploitation.

It is white power that makes the laws, and it is violent white power in the form of armed white cops that enforces those laws with guns and nightsticks. The vast majority of Negroes in this country live in captive communities and must endure these conditions of oppression because, and only because, *they are black and powerless*. Without bothering to go into the historic factors that contribute to this pattern—economic exploitation, political impotence, discrimination in employment and education—one can see that to correct this pattern will require far-reaching changes in the basic power-relationships and the ingrained social patterns within the society. The question, of course, is: What kinds of changes are necessary, and how is it possible to bring them about?

Integration and the Civil Rights Movement

In recent years the answer to these questions that has been given by most articulate groups of Negroes and their white allies, the "liberals" of all stripes, has been in terms of something called "integration." According to the advocates of integration, social justice will be accomplished by "integrating the Negro into the mainstream institutions of the society from which he has been traditionally excluded." It is very significant that each time I have heard this formulation it has been in terms of "the Negro," the individual Negro, rather than in terms of the community.

This concept of integration had to be based on the assumption that there was nothing of value in the Negro community, so the thing to do was to siphon off the "acceptable" Negroes into the surrounding middle-class white community. It is true that the student demonstrations in the South during the early sixties, out of which SNCC came, had a similar orientation. But while it is hardly a concern of a black sharecropper, dishwasher, or welfare recipient whether a certain fifteen-dollar-a-day motel offers accommodations to Negroes, the overt symbols of white superiority and the imposed limitations on the Negro community had to be destroyed. Now black people must look beyond these goals, to the issue of collective power.

Such a limited class orientation was reflected not only in the program and goals of the civil rights movement, but in its tactics and organization. It is very significant that the two oldest and most "respectable" civil rights organizations have constitutions which *specifically* prohibit partisan political activity. CORE once did, but changed that clause when it changed its orientation toward Black Power. But this is perfectly understandable in terms of the strategy and goals of the older organizations. The civil rights movement saw its role as a kind of liaison between the powerful white community and the dependent Negro one. The dependent status of the black community apparently was unimportant since—if the movement was successful—it was going to blend into the white community anyway. We made no pretense of organizing and developing institutions of community power in the Negro community, but appealed to the conscience of white institutions of power. The posture of the civil rights movement was that of the dependent, the suppliant. The theory was that without attempting to create any organized base of political strength itself, the civil rights movement could influence national legislation and national social patterns by forming coalitions with various "liberal" pressure organizations in the white community—liberal reform clubs, labor unions, church groups, progressive civic groups, and at times one or other of the major political parties.

Black Power

Speaking before a black audience in Detroit on July 30, 1966, Stokely Carmichael expresses disillusionment with the civil rights movement and racial integration.

Let it be known that we don't need threats. This is 1966. It's time out for beautiful words. It's time out for euphemistic statements. And it's time out for singing "We Shall Overcome." It's time to get some Black Power. It's time to get some Black Power.

Now they take our kids out of our community, and they pick the best. You got to be the best to get next to them. You got to be the best to get next to them; they pick the best. The five or six out of every school and send them to their school, and they call that integration. And they tell us that that's the way we going to solve our problem. They leave the rest of our children to stay in the filthy ghettos that they took the money from, and the rest of us get up and say, "Yeah, they working on solving the problem!" Baby, they ain't doing nothing but absorbing the best that we have. It's time that we bring them back into our community.

You need to tell Lyndon Baines Johnson, and all them white folk, that we don't have to move into white schools to get a better education. We don't have to move into white suburbs to get a better house. All they need to do is stop exploiting and oppressing our communities, and we going to take care of our communities. That's what you've got to tell them. You've got to tell them that when a lot of black people get together it doesn't mean that the slum area's going to develop. It's only because we don't own and control our communities that they are the way they are. You've got to tell them that.

I think we all have seen the limitations of this approach. We have repeatedly seen that political alliances based on appeals to conscience and decency are chancy things, simply because institutions and political organizations have no consciences outside their own special interests. The political and social rights of Negroes have been and always will be negotiable and expendable the moment they conflict with the interests of our "allies." If we do not learn from history, we are doomed to repeat it, and that is precisely the lesson of the Reconstruction. Black people were allowed to register, vote, and participate in politics because it was to the advantage of powerful white allies to promote this. But this was the result of white decision, and it was ended by other white men's decision before any political base powerful enough to challenge that decision could be established in the Southern Negro community. (Thus at this point in the struggle Negroes have no assurance—save a kind of idiot optimism and faith in a society whose history is one of racism—that if it were to become necessary, even the painfully limited gains thrown to the civil rights movement by the Congress will not be revoked as soon as a shift in political sentiments should occur.)

The major limitation of this approach was that it tended to maintain the traditional dependence of Negroes, and of the movement. We depended upon the good will and support of various groups within the white community whose interests were not always compatible with ours. To the extent that we depended on the financial support of other groups, we were vulnerable to their influence and domination.

Also, the program that evolved out of this coalition was really limited and inadequate in the long term, and one which affected only a small select group of Negroes. Its goal was to make the white community accessible to "qualified" Negroes and presumably each year a few more Negroes armed with their passport—a couple of university degrees—would escape into middle-class America and adopt the attitudes and life styles of that group; and one day the Harlems and the Watts would stand empty, a tribute to the success of integration. This is simply neither realistic nor particularly desirable. You can integrate communities, but you assimilate individuals. Even if such a program were possible its result would be, not to develop the black community as a functional and honorable segment of the total society, with its own cultural identity, life patterns, and institutions, but to abolish it—the final solution to the Negro problem. Marx said that the working class is the first class in history that ever wanted to abolish itself. If one listens to some of our "moderate" Negro leaders it appears that the American Negro is the first *race* that ever wished to abolish itself. The fact is that what must be abolished is not the black community, but the dependent colonial status that has been inflicted upon it. The racial and cultural personality of the black community must be preserved and the community must win its freedom while preserving its cultural integrity. This is the essential difference between integration as it is currently practiced and the concept of Black Power.

What has the movement for integration accomplished to date? The Negro graduating from M.I.T. with a doctorate will have better job opportunities available to him than to Lynda Bird Johnson. But the rate of unemployment in the Negro community is steadily increasing, while that in the white community decreases. More educated Negroes hold executive jobs in major corporations and federal agencies than ever before, but the gap between white income and Negro income has almost doubled in the last twenty years. More suburban housing is available to Negroes, but housing conditions in the ghetto are steadily declining. While the infant mortality rate of New York City is at its lowest rate ever in the city's history the infant mortality rate of Harlem is steadily climbing. There has been an organized national resistance to the Supreme Court's order to integrate the schools, and the federal government has not acted to enforce that order. Less than 15 per cent of black children in the South attend integrated schools; and Negro schools, which the vast majority of black children still attend, are increasingly decrepit, overcrowded, understaffed, inadequately equipped and funded.

The rate of school dropouts is increasing among Negro teenagers, who then express their bitterness, hopelessness, and alienation by the only means they have—rebellion. As long as people in the ghettos of our large cities feel that they are victims of the misuse of white power without any way to have their needs represented—and these are frequently simple needs (to get the welfare inspectors to stop kicking down your doors in the middle of the night, the cops to stop beating your children, to get the landlord to exterminate the vermin in your home, the city to collect your garbage)—we will continue to have riots. These are not the products of Black Power, but of the absence of any organization capable of giving the community the power, the Black Power, to deal with its problems.

SNCC proposes that it is now time for the black freedom movement to stop pandering to the fears and anxieties of the white middle class in the attempt to earn its "good will," and to return to the ghetto to organize these communities to control themselves. This organization must be attempted in Northern and Southern urban areas as well as in the rural black-belt counties of the South. The chief antagonist to this organization is, in the South, the overtly racist Democratic Party, and in the North the equally corrupt big city machines.

The standard argument presented against independent political organization is, "But you are only 10 per cent." I cannot see the relevance of this observation, since no one is talking about taking over the country, but taking control over our own communities.

The fact is that the Negro population, 10 per cent or not, is very strategically placed because of—ironically—segregation. What is also true is that Negroes have never been able to utilize the full voting potential of our numbers. Where we can vote, the case has always been that the white political machine stacks and gerrymanders the political subdivisions in Negro neighborhoods, so the true voting strength is never reflected in political strength. Would anyone looking at the distribution of political power in Manhattan ever think that Negroes represented 60 per cent of the population there? . . .

A leadership that is truly "responsible"—not to the white press and power structure, but to the community—must be developed. Such leadership will recognize that its power lies in the unified and collective strength of that community. This will make it difficult for the white leadership group to conduct its dialogue with individuals in terms of patronage and prestige, and will force them to talk to the community's representatives in terms of real power.

The single aspect of the Black Power program that has encountered most criticism is this concept of independent organization. This is presented as third-partyism which has never worked, or a withdrawal into black nationalism and isolationism. If such a program is developed it will not have the effect of isolating the Negro community but the reverse. When the Negro community is able to control local offices, and negotiate with other groups from a position of organized strength, the possibility of meaningful political alliances on specific issues will be increased. That is a rule of politics and there is no reason why it should not operate here. The only difference is that we will have the power to define the terms of these alliances. . . .

The revolution in agricultural technology in the South is displacing the rural Negro community into Northern urban areas. Both Washington, D.C., and Newark have Negro majorities. One-third of Philadelphia's population of two million people is black. "Inner city" in most major urban areas is already predominantly Negro, and with the white rush to suburbia, Negroes will in the next three decades control the heart of our great cities. These areas can become either concentration camps with a bitter and volatile population, whose only power is the power to destroy, or organized and powerful communities able to make constructive contributions to the total society. Without the power to control their lives and their communities, without effective political institutions through which to relate to the total society, these communities will exist in a constant state of insurrection. This is a choice that the country will have to make.

VIEWPOINT 4

"Though it be clarified and clarified again, 'black power' in the quick, uncritical and highly emotional adoption it has received from some segments of a beleaguered people can mean in the end only black death."

Black Power Is a Dangerous Concept

Roy Wilkins (1901–1981)

Roy Wilkins joined the National Association for the Advancement of Colored People in 1931, and was the NAACP's executive director from 1955 to 1977. As director he conferred with presidents, testified before congressional committees, and helped sponsor and shepherd civil rights legislation. Both Wilkins and the organization he led (which was founded in 1909 by whites and blacks to combat racial discrimination) exemplified the legal and reformist approach to civil rights—an approach that some blacks criticized in the 1960s as being outmoded and inadequate.

Wilkins was one of the first critics of the term "black power," which had became popular among many blacks in the 1960s. The following viewpoint is excerpted from an address made to the 1966 annual convention of the NAACP. Wilkins criticizes black power as a form of racism against whites, and reiterates his commitment to the full inclusion of blacks in American society.

In the transition period of the civil rights movement, 1966 is developing into a critical year. The 57th annual convention of our NAACP is thus a gathering of more than ordinary significance.

From Roy Wilkins, keynote address at the NAACP 57th Annual Convention, July 5, 1966.

All about us are alarums and confusions as well as great and challenging developments. Differences of opinion are sharper. For the first time since several organizations began to function where only two had functioned before, there emerges what seems to be a difference in goals.

Heretofore there were some differences in methods and in emphases, but none in ultimate goals. The end was always to be the inclusion of the Negro American, without racial discrimination, as a full-fledged equal in all phases of American citizenship. The targets were whatever barriers, crude or subtle, which blocked the attainment of that goal.

Challenge to Nonviolence

There has now emerged, first, a strident and threatening challenge to a strategy widely employed by civil rights groups, namely, nonviolence. One organization, which has been meeting in Baltimore, has passed a resolution declaring for defense of themselves by Negro citizens if they are attacked.

This position is not new as far as the NAACP is concerned. Historically our Association has defended in court those persons who have defended themselves and their homes with firearms. Extradition cases are not as frequent or as fashionable as they once were, but in past years we have fought the extradition of men who had used firearms to defend themselves when attacked.

We freed seventy-nine Arkansas sharecroppers in a four-year court battle beginning in 1919. They had returned gunfire directed at a meeting they were holding in a church.

We employed the late Clarence Darrow in 1926 to defend a man and his family when a member of a mob threatening his newly-purchased Detroit home was shot and killed. The NAACP has subscribed to nonviolence as a humane as well as a practical necessity in the realities of the American scene, but we have never required this as a deep personal commitment of our members. We never signed a pact either on paper or in our hearts to turn the other cheek forever and ever when we were assaulted.

But neither have we couched a policy of manly resistance in such a way that our members and supporters felt compelled to maintain themselves in an armed state, ready to retaliate instantly and in kind whenever attacked. We venture the observation that such a publicized posture could serve to stir counter-planning, counter-action and possible conflict. If carried out literally as instant retaliation, in cases adjudged by aggrieved persons to have been grossly unjust, this policy could produce—in extreme situations—lynchings, or, in better-sounding phraseology, private, vigilante vengeance.

Moreover, in attempting to substitute for derelict law enforce-

ment machinery, the policy entails the risk of a broader, more indiscriminate crackdown by law officers under the ready-made excuse of restoring law and order.

It seems reasonable to assume that proclaimed protective violence is as likely to encourage counter-violence as it is to discour-
age violent persecution.

"Black Power" and Separatism

But the more serious division in the civil rights movement is the
one posed by a word formulation that implies clearly a difference
in goals.

No matter how endlessly they try to explain it, the term "black
power" means anti-white power. In a racially pluralistic society,
the concept, the formation and the exercise of an ethnically tagged
power means opposition to other ethnic powers, just as the term
"white supremacy" means subjection of all non-white people. In
the black-white relationship, it has to mean that every other ethnic
power is the rival and the antagonist of "black power." It has to
mean "going-it-alone." It has to mean separatism.

Now, separatism, whether on the rarefied debate level of "black
power" or on the wishful level of a secessionist Freedom City in
Watts, offers a disadvantaged minority little except the chance to

shrivel and die.

The only possible dividend of "black power" is embodied in its offer to millions of frustrated and deprived and persecuted black people of a solace, a tremendous psychological lift, quite apart from its political and economic implications.

Ideologically it dictates "up with black and down with white" in precisely the same fashion that South Africa reverses that slogan.

It is a reverse Mississippi, a reverse Hitler, a reverse Ku Klux Klan.

If these were evil in our judgment, what virtue can be claimed for black over white? If, as some proponents claim, this concept instills pride of race, cannot this pride be taught without preaching hatred or supremacy based upon race?

Though it be clarified and clarified again, "black power" in the quick, uncritical and highly emotional adoption it has received from some segments of a beleaguered people can mean in the end only black death. Even if, through some miracle, it should be enthroned briefly in an isolated area, the human spirit, which knows no color or geography or time, would die a little, leaving for wiser and stronger and more compassionate men the painful beating back to the upward trail.

Black Power Is a Product of Despair

In this excerpt from his 1967 book Where Do We Go from Here: Chaos or Community?, *Martin Luther King Jr. presents his own views on the black power slogan.*

The Black Power movement of today, like the Garvey "Back to Africa" movement of the 1920s, represent a dashing of hope, a conviction of the inability of the Negro to win and a belief in the infinitude of the ghetto. While there is much grounding in past experience for all these feelings, a revolution cannot succumb to any of them. Today's despair is a poor chisel to carve out tomorrow's justice.

Black Power is an implicit and often explicit belief in black separatism. Notice that I do not call it black racism. It is inaccurate to refer to Black Power as racism in reverse, as some have recently done. Racism is a doctrine of the congenital inferiority and worthlessness of a people. While a few angry proponents of Black Power have, in moments of bitterness, made wild statements that come close to this kind of racism, the major proponents of Black Power have never contended that the white man is innately worthless.

Yet behind Black Power's legitimate and necessary concern for group unity and black identity lies the belief that there can be a separate black road to power and fulfillment. Few ideas are more unrealistic. There is no salvation for the Negro through isolation.

Race Against Race

We of the NAACP will have none of this. We have fought it too long. It is the ranging of race against race on the irrelevant basis of skin color. It is the father of hatred and the mother of violence.

It is the wicked fanaticism which has swelled our tears, broken our bodies, squeezed our hearts and taken the blood of our black and white loved ones. It shall not now poison our forward march.

We seek, therefore, as we have sought these many years, the inclusion of Negro Americans in the nation's life, not their exclusion. This is our land, as much so as it is any American's—every square foot of every city and town and village. The task of winning our share is not the easy one of disengagement and flight, but the hard one of work, of short as well as long jumps, of disappointments, and of sweet successes. . . .

Our objective is basically as it was laid down in 1909 by the interracial founders of our NAACP. Back there William Lloyd Garrison expressed the strong feeling that the first NAACP conference "will utter no uncertain sound on any point affecting the vital subject. No part of it is too delicate for plain speech. The republican experiment is at stake, every tolerated wrong to the Negro reacting with double force upon white citizens guilty of faithlessness to their brothers."

As it was then, so it is today. The republican experiment is at stake in 1966. More than that, the dream of a brotherhood in equality and justice is imperiled.

Our fraternity tonight, as it was then, is the fraternity of man, not the white, or brown, or yellow, or black man, but man.

CHAPTER 6

Two Historians Examine the Civil Rights Movement

Chapter Preface

Although in some respects the civil rights movement has never "ended" (many civil rights organizations are still operating and America still faces many issues pertaining to racial equality), the year 1968 can be seen as a possible finishing point. That year saw the passage of the last major piece of national legislation inspired by the movement. The Civil Rights Act of 1968 prohibited racial discrimination in the sale or rental of housing, but it also included a statute penalizing people who used interstate commerce to incite or organize a riot, a provision aimed mainly at militant black leaders. That year also saw the release of the report of the National Advisory Commission on Civil Disorders (the Kerner Commission), which warned that despite the passage of civil rights legislation, America was still "moving toward two societies, one black and one white—separate and unequal." The commission, appointed by President Lyndon B. Johnson to examine the wave of urban riots sweeping the nation, recommended broad reforms in welfare, employment, housing, and education—reforms that the United States, bogged down by the Vietnam War and social unrest, largely chose not to enact. Perhaps most significantly, Martin Luther King Jr. was assassinated on April 4, depriving the movement of one of the few people that could inspire and unite its militant and conservative wings and attract widespread interracial support.

The civil rights movement had by then left a significant legacy. It ended most overt forms of racial discrimination and government-supported segregation of public facilities (although de facto segregation persisted in many northern and southern school systems). It brought blacks into the political process in the South and in other areas where they had been excluded, and it largely stopped the system of lynching, violence, and fear that had previously kept blacks in "their place." In addition, the civil rights movement had inspired similar movements by other disaffected groups in American society, including women, Hispanics, American Indians, and gays and lesbians, all of which used protest tactics similar to those employed by the civil rights movement.

Because of its enormous impact on American society, the civil rights movement has been the focus of intense study and reflection by historians, sociologists, journalists, oral historians, and other chroniclers and interpreters of American history. These studies have focused on many different questions surrounding the development of the movement, beyond tallying its achievements and disappointments. Some historians have sought to determine what exactly moved mass numbers of blacks to rise up as they did in the 1950s and 1960s and whether they were simply responding to the charismatic leadership of people such as King or to deeper underlying causes. Others have tried to ascertain to what degree the civil rights movement was the product of local efforts and to what extent it was the achievement of national strategies and groups. The following pair of viewpoints examines the divisions between the major civil rights organizations of the 1960s and focuses on the question of whether such divisions helped or hindered the movement.

VIEWPOINT 1

"The very diversity of leadership that bred competition . . . proved salutary, indeed essential, to the fortunes of the civil rights movement in its direct-action phase."

Divisions Within the Civil Rights Leadership Benefited the Movement

Nancy J. Weiss (b. 1944)

Nancy J. Weiss is a professor of history at Princeton University in New Jersey. Her books include *Farewell to the Party of Lincoln: Black Politics in the Age of FDR* and *Whitney M. Young, Jr., and the Struggle for Civil Rights*. The following viewpoint is taken from a paper presented at a symposium on the civil rights movement held at the University of Mississippi in 1985. In her paper she examines the civil rights movement and its diverse organizations, ranging from the militant students of the Student Nonviolent Coordinating Committee (SNCC) to the more conservative business leaders of the Urban League. She argues that divisions within the national civil rights leadership and between civil rights organizations, while not without negative effects, actually proved essential to the movement's achievements in the decade prior to 1965. The diversity of organizations enabled activists to press for civil rights on several fronts, Weiss contends, including economic pressure, legal action, and political demonstrations. She maintains that in many instances the leaders were able to cooperate on specific projects, such as the 1963 March on Washington. In addition, she argues, leaders of established organizations, such as Roy Wilkins of the National Association for the Advancement of Colored People (NAACP) and Whitney M. Young Jr. of the Urban

Excerpted from Nancy J. Weiss, "Creative Tensions in the Leadership of the Civil Rights Movement," in *The Civil Rights Movement in America*, edited by Charles W. Eagles (Jackson: University Press of Mississippi, 1986). Reprinted by permission.

League, were able to tactically portray themselves as the moderate alternative to black militancy when negotiating with the white power structure. Weiss concludes that as long as most civil rights leaders shared fundamental objectives—which she asserts became less true following 1965—they were able to utilize each other to achieve their goals.

One of the persistent themes in the increasingly rich literature on civil rights leadership is the debilitating effect on the movement of competition among organizations and individuals who sought to lead it. Throughout the direct-action phase of the movement, the Student Nonviolent Coordinating Committee (SNCC), the Congress of Racial Equality (CORE), the Southern Christian Leadership Conference (SCLC), and the National Association for the Advancement of Colored People (NAACP) competed vigorously for publicity and position. The organizations jockeyed for headlines, elbowed one another out of the limelight, moved in on each other's demonstrations, and took issue with each other's tactics. At the same time, individuals coined disparaging labels to describe leaders with whom they disagreed.

What was at stake in this competition and sniping was considerably more than vanity or prestige. Getting the credit for mobilizing demonstrators or negotiating change translated into tangible resources—more adherents, increased financial support, easier access to the white power structure—resources that were essential to a leader's ability to lead and to an organization's ability to survive and flourish.

There is no denying that this kind of competition had negative effects. When name-calling and disputes among the leaders became public knowledge, it proved demeaning and gave the movement's opponents significant political leverage. When, as was frequently the case at the local level, suspicion and conflict between organizations diverted time and energy to one-upping, containing, or negotiating with a rival group, it obviously became more difficult to make headway toward the larger goals of desegregation.

Competition and Cooperation

Still, the very diversity of leadership that bred competition also proved salutary, indeed essential, to the fortunes of the civil rights movement in its direct-action phase. The complexity of the movement's goals; the variety of publics, black and white, that it needed to mobilize; the range of laws, practices, and customs that needed to be altered; and the broad array of strategies and tactics required to accomplish large-scale social change all demanded the simultaneous enlistment of organizations and leaders who could attack the problem from different, sometimes competing perspectives. Thus the models sociologists posit to describe the leadership of social movements—charismatic, enthusiastic, agitational leadership giving way to bureaucratic; or cyclical alternation between mobilizers and articulators—do not accurately capture the essence of the civil rights movement in its direct-action phase. What was distinctive about the civil rights movement up to 1965 was the simultaneous mobilization of diverse leadership working by different means toward a common goal. The movement needed charismatic leaders as well as bureaucrats, mobilizers as well as articulators.

Leaders and organizations in the civil rights movement cooperated at the same time that they competed. Sometimes they did so formally, creating new structures to facilitate their efforts toward common ends. Sometimes the cooperation emerged without advance planning or formal organization, as different organizations contributed in their own ways to the accomplishment of a single, overriding goal. From time to time the virtues of diversity proved themselves not in cooperation, whether conscious or de facto, but in the ability to make creative use of competition, as leaders and organizations played deliberately on the differences among themselves as a tactic to move whites who would otherwise have been less receptive to demands for change.

Organized attempts at cooperation among a diverse group of leaders proved essential to the fortunes of the civil rights movement in local communities in the South. Aldon D. Morris [in *The Origins of the Civil Rights Movement*] has argued for the crucial role of new umbrella organizations (in his terms, "organization[s] of organizations"), embracing black churches, the NAACP, political organizations, and citizens' associations, in initiating and sustaining bus boycotts in Baton Rouge, Montgomery, and Tallahassee in the 1950s, as well as a direct-action protest against discrimination in hiring, bus and train segregation, school segregation, and segregation in places of public accommodation in Birmingham in 1956. These new protest organizations—the United Defense League in Baton Rouge, the Montgomery Improvement Association, the Tallahassee Inter Civic Council, and the Alabama Christian Movement for Human Rights—stimulated the organization of "local movement centers" throughout the South in the late 1950s. In Nashville, Petersburg, Shreveport, and other cities, movement centers, with "interrelated set[s] of protest leaders, organizations, and followers," devised tactics and strategies, trained demonstrators, and launched direct-action protests to attain collectively defined goals. What gave these movement centers their special character and their ability to sustain organized social protest was their incorporation in a common effort of a range of "direct-action organizations of varied complexity."

At the national level, organized attempts at formal cooperation among civil rights leaders and organizations were short-lived and difficult to sustain. They were most effective when they focused on specific short-run goals, as in the case of the planning for the March on Washington. More general attempts at cooperation ultimately proved evanescent, but at least briefly, they accomplished certain goals. The Council for United Civil Rights Leadership (CUCRL) is a case in point.

Bringing Leaders Together

CUCRL emerged out of meetings initiated early in 1962 by the white philanthropist Stephen Currier. Seeking guidance for the Taconic Foundation's grant-making in race relations, Currier brought together the leaders of the NAACP, the National Urban League, SNCC, CORE, SCLC, the National Council of Negro Women, and the NAACP Legal Defense and Educational Fund to discuss the racial situation and advise the Foundation on the most effective way to use its resources. The meetings quickly began to serve a broader purpose. By coming together on a regular basis, the leaders became better acquainted with the purposes and activities of the other organizations. The meetings afforded them a chance for reflection and thoughtful analysis, an opportunity to step back from the day-to-day preoccupations of each one's own organization to look at the broad civil rights picture and to examine aspects of the race problem in greater depth and from new perspectives.

The assassination of Medgar Evers in Jackson, Mississippi, in June, 1963, provided the catalyst that transformed the meetings of the leaders into a formal organization. After consulting with a number of the leaders, Currier invited a large group of corporate and foundation executives to breakfast at the Carlyle Hotel in New York City. He asked each civil rights leader to make a statement about his or her organization and its efforts. While the "basic purpose," in the words of the executive director of the Taconic Foundation, was "to get the ears" of the white establishment so that they could "really understand" what was going on, the point was also to raise money for the civil rights movement. The breakfast meeting resulted in pledges of more than $500,000.

With money coming in, there needed to be some sort of a structure to handle disbursements and serve a coordinating function. Building on the foundation laid by their periodic meetings with Currier, the leaders decided to form a new organization. They called it the Council for United Civil Rights Leadership.

CUCRL served two principal functions: raising money for its constituent organizations and providing a forum for the leaders to share ideas and coordinate strategy. Roy Wilkins, the executive director of the NAACP, called it "a clearing-house to consult, advise and release information about civil rights activities." But there was also a more pointed purpose: to exert a stabilizing (skeptics called it moderating) influence on the movement. As Whitney M. Young, Jr., the executive director of the National Urban League, put it, the idea was "to keep direction of the movement in responsible hands, so it doesn't get 'taken over by some of those fellows waiting in the wings.'"

The promise of "bringing strong, democratic, disciplined and nonviolent leadership" to the civil rights movement proved to be an effective fund-raising device. With $800,000 pledged by mid-July, CUCRL announced a goal of raising $1.5 million by the end of the summer. As the money came in, each organization got its share according to a formula agreed upon by the Council. The emergency funds, which represented a significant addition to the organizations' regular budgets, helped them, a CUCRL spokesman said, to "meet unexpected costs resulting from 'the tremendous increase in civil rights activity across the country'" after those budgets were prepared.

The Council met on a regular basis, at the Carlyle Hotel or at the offices of the Taconic Foundation, the National Urban League, or the Legal Defense Fund. The agendas for the meetings were not in themselves compelling; what was important was that the leaders got together. Fund-raising was a perennial concern, but there was also regular discussion of timely topics—for example, the 1964 Civil Rights Act, other Great Society legislation of special interest to blacks, the Mississippi Summer Project, the Mississippi Challenge. From time to time, the Council spoke as a body to try to influence public policy.

More significant were the opportunities the meetings afforded for sharing information, thinking collectively about the movement, and diminishing tensions among the civil rights organizations. James Farmer, the executive director of CORE, called CUCRL "a talk group." The leaders would discuss what their organizations had been doing, outline plans for the near future, and suggest ways that other organizations might offer help and cooperation. Dorothy Height, who headed the National Council of Negro Women, reflected on the importance to the leaders of regular opportunities for "thinking and sharing and delving and analyzing and studying." "Our lives were such, we were so busy, either keeping the wolf from the door or going out and dealing with issues and problems," that "we didn't have the time to sit and say, 'What does this mean? And why is it important?'"

Just as periodic discussions gave the leaders a chance to think systematically about the direction of the movement, so they also provided some hope for reducing rivalries and tensions among the organizations. Finding some way to "hold . . . together" a group of leaders who were divided by "a lot of natural, very deep rivalry" had been part of Currier's purpose in creating CUCRL. Discussion of "inter-organizational conflicts," "tensions," and "differences" was a regular agenda item when the Council met. Eliminating competition among the organizations would not have been realistic, but the meetings provided a way to keep tempers and jealousies under better control. John Lewis, chairman of SNCC, credited CUCRL with heading off "major disagreements [and] misunderstandings" among the organizations; it "kept us together," he said, and gave the movement "that sense of unity and focus that it needed during that time."

The civil rights movement had a momentum of its own, which the leaders were not able to control. While it was possible to share plans and describe expectations, what actually happened in the streets could not be planned precisely or promised fully in advance. CUCRL gave the leaders a chance to discuss what had happened and explain why and how it had happened. "It meant," Andrew Young, then of SCLC, reflected, "that there was a place where people could talk through events which they were supposed to be in control of but actually weren't." By providing a "forum where they really understood what was going on, where they got to talk it out," Young said, CUCRL made a contribution to the effectiveness of the movement.

As previously stated, one of the characteristics of formal, organized attempts at cooperation among the leadership was that they ultimately proved evanescent. After a time, it became difficult to hold CUCRL together. Despite repeated reaffirmations of the value of regular contact among the leaders, scheduled meetings became less frequent and attendance dwindled. After the fundraising drive of 1963, there were only modest sums to distribute; by mid-decade, the money had virtually run out. Growing tensions within the movement—over black power, over the desirability of commingling the cause of civil rights with the issue of the United States' role in Vietnam—made unity harder and harder to realize. In January, 1967, steps were taken to liquidate the organization.

CUCRL provides an example of a planned attempt at formal cooperation among civil rights organizations and leaders. Cooperation also emerged without planning or organization, as different organizations and leaders contributed in their own ways to the accomplishment of a single, overriding goal.

The Different Roles of Protest Leaders

In developing models to describe the various roles of protest leaders, social scientists typically elaborate functions that are discharged by different leaders at different stages in the development of social movements. Max Weber identified the "charismatic" leader, whom he contrasted with the "bureaucrat." Harold Lasswell distinguished between the "administrator" and the "agitator." John P. Roche and Stephen Sachs used the terms "bureaucrat" and "enthusiast" to make a similar distinction. Joseph R. Gusfield, taking issue with the prevailing assumption that "statesmanlike, bureaucratic administrators" inevitably replace "enthusiastic, agitational leadership" as social movements "become formally organized into stable structures," posited [in *Sociological Quarterly*, Spring 1966] instead a cyclical alternation between what he called "mobilizing and articulating leadership."

Gusfield's categories serve to establish the basic point about the different kinds of functions that leaders of social movements need to discharge. On the one hand, the leader functions as a mobilizer of commitments to the movement, its "soul and conscience," rallying and inspiring adherents through his single-minded dedication to the movement, his intransigence toward groups with different views and interests, and his unwillingness "to temporize with evil, to compromise principle, or to blunt sharp controversy." On the other hand, the leader functions as the articulator of the movement to the larger society, explaining its purposes to an uncommitted or hostile public, acting as "an ambassador . . . between the movement and the society," and using negotiation, bargaining, and compromise to forward the movement's goals.

In the civil rights movement the functions of bureaucrat and enthusiast, administrator and agitator, articulator and mobilizer needed to be discharged simultaneously. Each organization and leader had different approaches, abilities, resources, and contacts to bring to bear on the struggle; the complexity of the goals of the movement demanded that they all be enlisted in order to achieve the desired progress. As Martin Luther King, Jr., put it, "Direct action is not a substitute for work in the courts and the halls of government. Bringing about passage of a new and broad law by a city council, state legislature or the Congress, or pleading cases before the courts of the land, does not eliminate the necessity for bringing about the mass dramatization of injustice in front of a city hall. Indeed, direct action and legal action complement one another; when skillfully employed, each becomes more effective." Or, in the words of Whitney Young, "The day has passed when we could entrust our complete destiny to a single Messianic leader or rely on any monolithic approach. We must think today not in terms of individual leaders or of *the* approach—but of levels of leadership involving many people, with a variety of approaches and tactics. The issue must now become not *which* approach, but how we intelligently deploy our forces and establish roles and division of labor."

Achievements of the Civil Rights Movement

In the following extract from his book The Origins of the Civil Rights Movement, *historian and sociologist Aldon T. Morris summarizes some of the lasting gains of the civil rights movement.*

The Southern civil rights movement had a profound impact on American society. First, it significantly altered the tripartite system of domination, largely dismantling those components which severely restricted the personal freedom of blacks and disfranchised them in the formal political sense. Second, the movement altered and expanded American politics by providing other oppressed groups with organizational and tactical models, allowing them to enter directly into the political arena through the politics of protest.

Prior to the movement the system of segregation forced blacks to live in a separate and limited world characterized by poverty, racial discrimination, powerlessness, symbolic subordination, and imperative acts of deference to white supremacy. The South is a different place today. Most of the "white" schools, washrooms, theaters, swimming pools, parks, bus seats and other facilities are either integrated or at least not segregated by law. This does not mean that the races are thoroughly integrated in the South, because economic and residential segregation, which lead to segregation in other spheres of life, is widespread nationally. Nevertheless, with many symbols of white supremacy dismantled and many facilities formally desegregated, Southern blacks now live in a world where they can function with fewer restrictions and one that does not automatically strip them of human dignity. In a recent speech Stokely Carmichael told a young questioner who doubted that the civil rights movement had made a difference that "blacks in Montgomery will never go to the back of the bus again." That is the essence of the change. The battles of the movement, culminating in the passage of the 1964 Civil Rights Act, made this significant change possible.

Young's analysis of the movement's simultaneous dependence on the energies of "older, established" community leaders ("educators, businessmen and professionals"), "confronters" and "protesters," and "strategist[s]" and "planner[s]" hit right on the mark. None could have functioned effectively without the others. SNCC, CORE, and SCLC supplied the charismatic leadership of the movement, rallied and inspired adherents, and organized them for direct-action protests. The NAACP and the National Urban League supplied bureaucratic stability and professional and technical expertise; their leaders functioned as the ambassadors, negotiators, and bargainers who translated the pressure of direct-action protest into concessions from the white power structure. The dichotomy is not precise, the NAACP also played a mobilizing role in communities in the South, and King, the consummate mobilizer, also functioned in critically important ways to articulate the purposes of the movement to white America.

Distinctive Strengths

Each organization brought the movement its own distinctive strengths and style. SNCC, the most radical of the direct-action groups, focused on the mobilization and empowerment of local blacks to force change in the status quo; initially committed to direct action and voter registration to break the hold of southern racism, it later rejected nonviolence, interracialism, even capitalism, and called for a radical restructuring of society, with racial separatism and the creation of alternative institutions controlled by the poor and powerless. CORE, pacifist in its origins, working in the North as well as the South, started out as a small, interracial band of disciplined activists determined to apply Gandhian techniques of nonviolent direct action to the problem of American race relations; initially committed to staging dramatic demonstrations to make plain the gross injustice of discrimination and provoke changes in the attitudes and behavior of whites, it later lost faith in the vision of integration and, reformist rather than revolutionary, urged the development of black capitalism and of black control over institutions and services in the ghetto. SCLC, led by ministers, powered by Martin Luther King's vision of a "beloved community," and unwaveringly devoted to integration, initially employed a strategy of nonviolent persuasion to dramatize the evils of discrimination and change the hearts and minds of white oppressors; later, it shifted to a strategy of aggressive nonviolent coercion, designed to provoke retaliatory violence, capture the attention of the media, activate national support for the movement, and thus bring pressure for federal intervention, including the passage of civil rights legislation. By contrast, the NAACP, with its lawyers, lobbyists, and publicists, specialized in legal and legislative action to secure black rights; of all the organizations, it had the best connections in Washington. The National Urban League, a professional social work agency, devoted its efforts to improving the economic and social condition of blacks in the cities. Negotiating with the corporate establishment was its particular strength; of all the organizations, it had the best connections with the major foundations.

Sometimes, as with CUCRL, the marshaling of different leaders and organizations under a common banner was cooperative and intentional; sometimes there was no deliberate coordination or planning, and cooperation entailed nothing more than different leaders and organizations chipping away at the problem on the basis of their own particular strengths and resources. In either case, the point still holds: without the simultaneous enlistment of all of these organizations and leaders, civil rights progress would have been much more difficult to come by.

Direct Action and Legal Action

Several examples illustrate the case. The interplay of direct action and legal action is a persistent theme in the history of the movement. In Montgomery, it took a year-long bus boycott, organized by the Montgomery Improvement Association, as well as a suit carried to the United States Federal District Court and later the United States Supreme Court by lawyers from the NAACP Legal Defense Fund, to desegregate the city's buses in 1956. The sit-ins which spread across the South beginning in 1960 brought the arrests of hundreds of demonstrators; while the sit-ins themselves often brought about the desegregation of lunch counters and other public facilities, it took court cases, often argued by Legal Defense Fund lawyers, to overturn the convictions of the protestors. In Birmingham in 1963, as Martin Luther King developed and executed a successful strategy for direct-action protest, he turned repeatedly to the Legal Defense Fund for money and legal advice; when he, Ralph David Abernathy, Wyatt Tee Walker, and Fred Shuttlesworth went on trial for violating a state-court injunction prohibiting them and other movement leaders from conducting demonstrations, they retained attorneys from the Fund.

At so many points, the success of the movement depended directly on the mobilization of the energies and resources of a range of organizations and leaders. In 1961, for instance, when the original group of Freedom Riders assembled by CORE were so badly beaten in Alabama that they were unable to go any further, SNCC sent in new recruits to help continue the Ride. Subsequently, as mob violence against the Freedom Riders became so severe that the Kennedy administration was forced to send federal marshals to Alabama to help protect them, CORE, SCLC, SNCC, and the Nashville Christian Leadership Council set up a Freedom Ride Coordinating Committee, rejected Attorney General Robert F. Kennedy's call for a temporary suspension of the Rides, and sent the Riders on to Mississippi. When they arrived in Jackson, over 300 were arrested and incarcerated in the city and county jails and the state penitentiary. In an effort to bankrupt CORE, the state of Mississippi manipulated trial dates and tripled the bond on each Rider. The NAACP Legal Defense Fund, with $300,000 in bail-bond money in the bank, came to the rescue with a loan. Later, attorneys for CORE and the Legal Defense Fund appealed the convictions to the United States Supreme Court, which found in favor of the Freedom Riders.

In the case of the 1964 Civil Rights Act, SCLC's demonstrations in Birmingham in April and May, 1963, and the retaliatory violence they precipitated, helped to move President Kennedy to submit comprehensive proposals for civil rights legislation to Congress in June. But while direct action may have changed the public mood and softened the President's previous reluctance to take significant action on civil rights, it was not sufficient to lead Congress to enact the legislation. The introduction of the bill by no means spelled the end of intervention by civil rights leaders and organizations. In the long months that the bill languished in Congress, Clarence Mitchell, the NAACP's chief Washington lobbyist, played a continuing role in influencing the framing of its provisions and the prospects for its passage; finally, in the spring of 1964, Whitney Young and Roy Wilkins weighed in in the successful effort to persuade Senate Minority Leader Everett M. Dirksen to support the bill and bring with him enough Republican votes to break the southern filibuster that was holding up its approval.

The problem of employment discrimination similarly illustrates the way in which different civil rights organizations, complementing each other, brought to bear different resources to pursue a common goal. Before the passage of the 1964 Civil Rights Act, whose Title VII mandated equal employment opportunity, direct action demonstrations—sit-ins, picketing, and boycotts, usually organized by CORE, SNCC, and SCLC—were the major resource the civil rights movement used to attack discrimination in employment. After Title VII the focus changed; individuals who were discriminated against had the right to file complaints with the Equal Employment Opportunity Commission and, in the absence of a satisfactory resolution, to press their claims in federal courts. Now what the movement needed were lawyers to assist in filing complaints and to argue employment discrimination cases in court, a resource supplied by the NAACP. At the same time, employers feeling pressure to comply with Title VII needed help in finding qualified blacks, establishing training programs, and easing the transition to an integrated workplace. Here the National Urban League had the contacts, experience, and trained personnel to provide the necessary assistance.

Creative Use of Disunity

From time to time the virtues of diversity also proved themselves not in cooperation, whether conscious or de facto, but in the ability to make creative use of competition and disunity, as leaders and organizations played deliberately on the differences within the movement as a tactic to move whites who would otherwise have been less receptive to demands for change. The movement depended on what James Q. Wilson called "a division of labor between protest leaders and bargainers." Asked about the relationship between demonstration and negotiation, James Farmer answered, "They are not contradictory at all—not mutually exclusive. We find that demonstrations are frequently the catalyst—spur the dialogue. Sometimes demonstrations start the dialogue." To put it simply, agitation on the part of militants served to legitimate the demands and modes of protest of more moderate leaders and to enable those moderates to gain the attention of the white establishment and win concessions from the power structure in ways that would not have been possible without that agitation.

Jack L. Walker's study of the student movement in Atlanta in 1960–61 [published in the *Journal of Negro Education*, Summer 1963] provides an apt illustration of this phenomenon. Responding to the sit-ins that began in Greensboro in February, 1960, Atlanta University students launched demonstrations against segregated lunch counters and businesses that practiced discrimination in hiring. After almost a year of sit-ins, marches, picketing, and boycotts, with repeated but unsuccessful negotiations between students and merchants, the arrest of student demonstrators in February, 1961, and the threat that a planned protest march and rally might result in a riot led student leaders to turn to "one of the oldest, most respected Negro leaders" in Atlanta and ask him "to try to get negotiations started again." Drawing on his friendships with influential whites, he did so, and the resulting negotiations led eventually to a settlement of the controversy.

The division in the black community between the students and their adult supporters, who believed in the efficacy of direct-action protests, and more conservative black leaders, who agreed with the students' goals but disagreed with them over the appropriateness of demonstrations and boycotts as methods to achieve them, proved salutary in accomplishing desegregation. "The students and adult protest leaders," Walker writes,

> by organizing demonstrations and economic boycotts, created a crisis which had to be resolved. . . . But the leaders of the protests did not have the power to resolve the crisis . . . because they had no basis for contact with the dominant white leaders. . . .
>
> The more conservatively inclined leaders, utilizing their reputations and the connections they had built up with the white community through the years, had the function of resolving the crisis situation created by the protest leaders. In this case even the antagonism between the two groups was functional because it

made the conservatives seem more reliable and responsible in the eyes of the whites.

The ability to exploit the disunity of the civil rights movement to accomplish his own ends was part of the stock-in-trade of the National Urban League's Whitney M. Young. As a social worker trained to analyze social processes and to understand and relate to difference, Young was especially well equipped to grasp the value to the civil rights movement of tensions between moderates and militants. Dorothy Height spoke about his ability to recognize the interdependence of different approaches, the value of different roles: "He used to have a way of saying, 'Well, you see, the more they [the militants] pound on the table, then the readier other people are to sit at the table and talk to me.'"

Far from crippling the movement, the creative tension between moderates and militants facilitated the accomplishment of its goals. Without the pressure from direct actionists in the streets, leaders of the white establishment would have been much less ready to negotiate with moderate civil rights leaders. Later, without the rhetoric of black separatism and the resort to violence, the urgency of addressing fundamental issues of civil rights and economic opportunity for blacks would have been much less compelling. Young understood that, and he deliberately used the threat of the militants as a tactic in his dealings with corporate leaders.

John H. Johnson, president of Johnson Publishing Company, remembered with considerable amusement Young's description of his approach. Young told Johnson that he was usually able to gain a hearing from most of the corporate executives he wanted to see. When he had trouble, he would sometimes call Malcolm X and ask *him* to call the executive in question. Suddenly access was no longer a problem; the man always called Young back. "Whitney, what do you think Malcolm wants with me?" he might ask. Young would reply, in effect, "I imagine it would be nice if you were doing something [constructive for blacks] in our community so that you would have an answer to whatever Malcolm has to say."

James Farmer described another variant of Young's technique. Young used "the iron fist of the militants" as "a threatened right cross when his negotiations' left jab failed to produce the desired results," Farmer explained. "'If you don't do what I'm asking you to do,' [Young] would say to corporation heads, 'Jim Farmer and CORE will be coming after you.' The threat usually worked."

In public, it was unseemly to name names, but with the upsurge of separatism and racial violence, it was easy to communicate a similar point. As Young put it in an address to the Conference Board in 1965, "You must either give support to responsible Negro leadership or else irresponsible leadership will take over."

That meant negotiate with the National Urban League, or deal with angry young militants; do something constructive about the race problem, or face the spectre of riots in the streets. With options of that sort, the best choice was clear. In the words of James R. Shepley, the former president of Time, Inc., "I don't think there's any doubt that the average establishmentarian American white would have certainly considered Whitney Young's alternative the best of all possible alternatives that confronted him." As cries of black power grew louder and unrest festered in urban ghettos, businessmen who felt that they had to respond in some way to the race problem looked increasingly to Young and the Urban League for guidance and solutions.

Developments After 1965

After 1965, opportunities for significant cooperation in the civil rights movement became increasingly rare. Before that, no matter how much leaders and organizations may have differed over strategy and tactics, they shared a commitment to common, realizable objectives: desegregation of public facilities, equal access to education and employment opportunity, full and free exercise of the right to vote. Moreover, they could identify the specific actions necessary to realize those objectives—persuasion of public officials and private individuals, passage of new legislation, prosecution of suits in state and federal courts—and they knew how to rally adherents and mobilize resources to accomplish their ends.

After 1965, disagreement over fundamental objectives as well as strategy and tactics split the movement asunder. The controversy over black power, the issue of racial violence, and the argument over linking the movement to opposition to American involvement in Vietnam created irreparable divisions within the movement. What was at issue was not which organization or leader would claim the credit or win the limelight, nor the best strategy for realizing shared goals. Leaders and organizations no longer agreed even on such basic objectives as integration; and while they may still have shared some general, overriding concerns, the very nature of those concerns—for instance, what to do about black unemployment and underemployment, or how to improve the living conditions of blacks in urban ghettos—meant that there was no longer a consensus on what needed to be done, nor, for that matter, an understanding of the probable efficacy of specific strategies or actions. At the same time that the goals of black protest became more diffuse, the targets of protest activity became less clearly identifiable. With the desegregation of lunch counters or the passage of civil rights legislation, it was easy to figure out which individuals and groups had the power to effect change, and to exert pressure accordingly. Objectives such as the improvement of housing or economic conditions in the ghetto were simply less amenable to that kind of analysis and action.

In such circumstances formal cooperation was unthinkable; without clearly defined, realizable objectives, even the unplanned, informal cooperation by which different organizations and leaders brought to bear their own resources and strengths became much less likely to occur. Only the ability to make creative use of competition persisted into the late 1960s, as the threat of black power and racial violence continued to give more moderate leaders the means to make some headway in their dealings with the white establishment.

"A . . . centrally important aspect of the [civil rights] movement's history, and particularly of the interplay amongst those nationally visible organizations, was the extremely debilitating competition that developed between most of those groups."

Divisions Within the Civil Rights Leadership Did Not Benefit the Movement

David J. Garrow (b. 1953)

David J. Garrow won a Pulitzer Prize for his 1986 biography *Bearing the Cross: Martin Luther King Jr. and the Southern Christian Leadership Conference.* His other books include *The FBI and Martin Luther King Jr.* and *Liberty and Sexuality.* He has taught at Duke University in North Carolina and at City College and Cooper Union in New York. The following viewpoint is taken from Garrow's commentary on a paper presented by historian Nancy J. Weiss at a 1985 symposium on the civil rights movement in which Weiss had argued that diversity and division among the national civil rights organizations actually helped the civil rights cause. Garrow responds with two main points. He contends that most of the achievements of the civil rights movement resulted not from the work of nationally recognized organizations and leaders, but from the efforts of relatively forgotten local activists and grassroots organizers such as Charles Sherrod and Amelia P. Boynton. To focus heavily on the national civil rights organizations and

Excerpted from David J. Garrow, "Comment" (on Weiss's article), in *The Civil Rights Movement in America*, edited by Charles W. Eagles (Jackson: University Press of Mississippi, 1986). Reprinted by permission.

their leaders, he maintains, provides a narrow picture of the civil rights movement. Secondly, he argues that both personal and organizational rivalries within the civil rights movement did have serious harmful effects, both in hindering the work of the organizations and local activists, and in damaging relations with potential allies such as white church groups and labor unions.

Too often those who write about the civil rights movement employ too narrow and exclusive a concept of "leadership." Implicitly if not explicitly, they presume that leaders are simply those individuals who are organizational chieftains or spokespersons. They thus restrict our definition of leadership to administrators and articulators, without looking as carefully and as thoughtfully as they should for a more meaningful understanding of "leadership."

A Narrow Conception of Leadership

This overly narrow conception of leadership runs directly parallel to a similar tendency to devote a disproportionate amount of scholarly attention to the national civil rights organizations of the 1950s and 1960s—the National Association for the Advancement of Colored People (NAACP), the Southern Christian Leadership Conference (SCLC), the Student Nonviolent Coordinating Committee (SNCC), the National Urban League (NUL) and the Congress of Racial Equality (CORE). While concentrating studies on those organizations and the individuals who headed them—Roy Wilkins, Martin Luther King, Jr., John Lewis and Stokely Carmichael, Whitney Young, and James Farmer—simultaneously far too little scholarly attention has been devoted to local level civil rights activities and to the grass roots organizers who actually mobilized people to participate actively in the movement.

In the 1950s, the major strategic difference of opinion that existed among black civil rights activists was a division between those who believed that courtroom litigation and judicial decisions were the principal means for advancing black freedom and those who contended that ordinary, grass roots people could take a direct and meaningful hand in pursuing their own freedom. While NAACP Executive Secretary Roy Wilkins and NAACP Legal Defense and Educational Fund director Thurgood Marshall argued that the lawyerly expansion of the principles articulated by the Supreme Court in *Brown v. Board of Education of Topeka* was the surest route to further black gains, Brotherhood of Sleeping Car Porters president A. Philip Randolph and other colleagues maintained that mass action, and not simply elite-sponsored litigation, could bring about substantial racial change.

Those mass action proponents welcomed the Montgomery, Alabama, bus boycott of 1955–1956 as precisely the sort of opening round in a new, mass-based southern freedom struggle they long had hoped for. Similarly, those activists also welcomed the 1957 formation of the ministerially-oriented SCLC and the largely spontaneous black college student sit-in movement that spread like wildfire across the South during the spring and early summer of 1960. On the other hand, NAACP administrators contended that it was only a federal court ruling, not the mass boycott, that actually desegregated Montgomery's buses, and they regretted both the formation of SCLC and the appearance of SNCC, which grew out of the 1960 sit-ins. Within just a few years' time, both SCLC and SNCC, employing different tactical choices, made the mass action strategy the dominant approach of the 1960s black freedom struggle.

That deeply-rooted strategic division is central both to the subsequent history of inter-organizational relations within the movement and to the malapportionment of scholarly attention over the past two decades. Like the one-time chieftains of the elite-oriented civil rights organizations, many scholars have presumed that the policies, statements and actions of the national civil rights organizations are the most important substance of the movement's history. However, a more discerning look at the movement's actual record of achievement in the South, and in the national political arena, reveals, upon careful examination, that the real accomplishments of the black freedom struggle stemmed not so much from the activities of the administrators and articulators as from the efforts of the grass roots organizers who actually built and directed the movement in the South.

Forgotten Leaders

To say that most of the work of the movement was not done by the commonly-identified leaders would seem obvious to all. The basic point, however, is considerably broader than that: what the carefully-scrutinized historical record shows is that the actual human catalysts of the movement, the people who really gave direction to the movement's organizing work, the individuals whose records reflect the greatest substantive accomplishments, were not administrators or spokespersons, and were not those whom most scholarship on the movement identifies as the "leaders." Instead, in any list, long or short, of the activists who had the greatest personal impact upon the course of the southern movement, the vast majority of names will be ones that are unfamiliar to most readers. Allow six brief examples to suffice. In Mississippi, no other individuals did more to give both political direction and emotional sustenance to movement activists than Robert Parris Moses, a SNCC field worker who became the guiding force in COFO, the Council of Federated Organizations, and Fannie Lou Hamer, the relatively unlettered but impressively articulate Sunflower County tenant farmer's wife who in 1964 emerged as an influential grass roots spokeswoman for the thousands of economically poor black citizens who actually comprised the movement's base.

Coping with Divisions

In his account of the civil rights movement Free at Last? *Fred Powledge, a journalist who covered many of the events of the period, tells of interorganizational rifts within the movement.*

It became more apparent, as the Movement passed its formative years and headed toward a sort of maturity, that there were distinct differences among its numerous organizations and personalities. Within the Movement itself, the arguing could be quite forceful, as it would be in any collection of people engaged in a tense, dangerous battle. And, just like military commanders, the leaders of the Movement did not want their arguments reported in public.

One wide-open secret was the fact that Roy Wilkins of the NAACP did not like the way either the Southern Christian Leadership Conference or the Student Nonviolent Coordinating Committee conducted their business. The leaders of these groups tended to classify Wilkins's objections as simple jealousy. While SNCC, which would have felt unfulfilled without criticism, seemed to accept Wilkins's sniping as part of its way of life, Martin Luther King and SCLC tried to make peace and minimize the friction. Said Wyatt Tee Walker in later years: "Dr. King made a summary decision that we wouldn't be a membership organization simply because Roy Wilkins got nervous that if we went to membership, it would cut into their funds. Dr. King always took the back seat." King also went out of his way to help the NAACP and repair interorganizational rifts whenever he could. When the organization held its 1962 convention in Atlanta, King was a speaker. He warned about "outside forces" who might stimulate discord among the rights groups, and added: "The demands of today are too great and the issues are too serious for any of us to be involved in ego-battles and trivial organizational conflicts."

In southwest Georgia, another major scene of movement activism, the guiding spirit of much of the effort there, from the time of his initial arrival in Terrell County as the sole paid field secretary of SNCC to the present day, when he serves on the Albany city council, was Charles Sherrod, a little-heralded organizer who deserves much of the credit for sparking and sustaining the entire southwest Georgia movement. Although Sherrod, like Moses, was an "outside agitator" initially sent in by SNCC, in Selma, Alabama, one of the movement's most famous battlegrounds, the key individual figure was a long-time native, Mrs. Amelia P. Boynton, whose impact there was much like Mrs. Hamer's in Mississippi. A crucial figure in organizing the initial indigenous activism, in first bringing SNCC workers to Selma, and in persuading Dr. King and SCLC to make Selma the focal point of their 1965 voting rights protests, Mrs. Boynton had as substantial an impact on civil rights developments in Alabama as anyone, excepting perhaps only Birmingham's Reverend Fred L. Shuttlesworth, another widely-underestimated and underappreciated grass roots leader.

Lastly, inside of SNCC and SCLC, two individuals who had crucial but often-overlooked roles in repeatedly influencing important movement decisions were Diane Nash and James Bevel, both of whom emerged from the Nashville movement of 1959–1961. Nash played a central part in sustaining the 1961 Freedom Rides when white Alabama violence threatened to halt them, and her April, 1962 memo reprimanding movement activists for not always living up in practice to their much-touted slogan of "jail, no bail" had a significant impact on King and dozens of others. Together with Bevel, Nash in September, 1963, originated one of the most important strategic gameplans of the southern struggle. Four months earlier Bevel, a young SCLC staff aide, had been personally responsible for SCLC's crucial tactical decision to send young children into the streets of Birmingham during the height of the protests there, the crucial turning point in convincing white business leaders to grant the movement's demands and an important influence on President John F. Kennedy's decision to send to Congress the bill that eventually became the 1964 Civil Rights Act. Nash and Bevel, in the immediate aftermath of the Birmingham church bombing that killed four young girls, envisioned a comprehensive mass action campaign to close down the regular functioning of Alabama state government and "GROW"—Get Rid Of [Alabama Governor George C.] Wallace. Though rejected by King and other organization heads at that time, the Nash/Bevel blueprint started King and SCLC on an Alabama Project that eighteen months later, following various changes and refinements, culminated in the landmark Selma-to-Montgomery march and congressional passage of the 1965 Voting Rights Act.

It takes nothing away from King, Wilkins, Whitney Young or James Farmer to acknowledge that Moses, Hamer, Sherrod, Boynton, Nash and Bevel equally merit the designation as civil rights "leaders" if that label is to be applied in its most substantively meaningful way. Indeed, it could be argued further, with considerable justification, that catalytic grass root workers like those six deserve the appellation more than do New York–based bureaucrats such as Wilkins and Young. The real emergence of a sustained and widespread movement in the South can be traced, in many particulars, to the August, 1961, SNCC decision to create a cadre of locally-based, full time grass roots organizers, the first time that indigenous activists in many areas of the rural Deep South had such day-to-day organizational assistance available to them. Those full-time workers, usually affiliated with SNCC, CORE or SCLC, constituted the real backbone of the southern movement during the years of its greatest activism and achievements, 1961–1966. Similarly, the somewhat precipitous decline of the southern freedom struggle between 1966 and 1968 can also largely be traced to the burnout and eventual departure from full time organizing of most of that crucial cadre. Although this is not the place to make the argument in its most extended form, it was the interaction between the existing indigenous activists and these full time field secretaries that generated most of the actual "leadership" of the southern struggle. As many SNCC veterans in particular can well articulate, it was the firsthand experience of working with people, day in, day out, that educated both local activists and field secretaries to the item-by-item, conversation-by-conversation reality of what "leadership" really amounted to in the civil rights movement.

The best of the national organization chieftains and spokespersons, namely King, Lewis and Farmer, all privately appreciated how their heavy responsibilities for making speeches, raising funds, and stimulating organizational publicity oftentimes excessively drew them away from the real, hands on work of the movement. King and Farmer in particular were troubled by how their administrative tasks and the "organization maintenance" needs of SCLC and CORE often took priority over any opportunities for sustained personal involvement in the activities that constituted the real purpose of their organizations. Thus at least these men, if not all of the other administrators and articulators of movement organizations, realized full well that leadership of the freedom struggle lay in many, many hands other than those of the "Big Six" organization heads often singled out by the news media.

Debilitating Competition

A second centrally important aspect of the movement's history, and particularly of the interplay amongst those nationally visible organizations, was the extremely debilitating competition that developed between most of those groups during the 1957–1967 decade. In general, that competition can be divided into two distinct types, organizational and personal. Organizational rivalry was certainly the more powerful and important of the two, centering again and again on two intimately-related maintenance needs of all the national groups: media publicity and the fundraising opportunities that stemmed from such visibility.

Local Protests and National Organizations

William H. Chafe, professor of history at Duke University in North Carolina, argues in The Civil Rights Movement *that local protests, independent of the national organizations, were important in the civil rights movement.*

Careful examinations of local movements . . . challenge the assumption that national leaders, notably Martin Luther King, orchestrated local protest movements in their efforts to alter national public opinion and national policy. There is much to suggest that national civil rights organizations and their leaders played only minor roles in bringing about most local insurgences. It was more often the case that local black movements produced their own distinctive ideas and indigenous leadership rather than that these movements resulted from initiative of national leaders.

The Montgomery bus boycott, for example, began in 1955 as the result of an unplanned act of defiance by Rosa Parks. Martin Luther King, Jr., emerged as a spokesman and as a nationally-known proponent of nonviolent resistance only after Montgomery blacks had launched their movement and formed their own local organization—the Montgomery Improvement Association. King's organization, the Southern Christian Leadership Conference, was formed only after the boycott ended. To be sure, the Montgomery struggle was an extension of previous civil rights reform efforts, but it began as an outgrowth of local institutional networks rather than as a project of any national civil rights organization.

Similarly, no national organization or leader initiated the next major stage of the black struggle, the lunch counter sit-ins of 1960. SCLC, CORE, and the NAACP attempted to provide ideological and tactical guidance for student protesters after the initial sit-in in Greensboro, but student activists insisted on forming their own local groups under student leadership. Even the Student Nonviolent Coordinating Committee, which was founded by student protest leaders, was unable to guide the sit-in movement—a fact that contributed to SNCC's subsequent support for the principle of local autonomy.

In the late 1950s, the primary face-off was between the newly-formed SCLC and the well-entrenched NAACP, eager to guard its southern branches' local predominance despite the legal attacks being mounted against the Association by many southern state governments. Afraid that SCLC, with King's Montgomery success fresh in the minds of millions, might take the lead in the southern struggle, the NAACP's top national bureaucrats instructed their underlings to avoid and oppose SCLC's nascent voter registration efforts. In 1960, when the NAACP worried that the creation of SNCC would badly undercut its own youth council network and shift the movement's initiative to a younger generation with little interest in following the dictates of a national headquarters, SCLC too thought it would be better for the students to operate as an arm of an established organization— namely SCLC—rather than independently. SNCC in turn complained repeatedly that donations intended for the students instead made their way into SCLC's coffers, and when CORE in 1961 initiated the Freedom Ride, the wave of publicity that followed white attacks on the riders led to intense rivalry between CORE, SNCC and SCLC over claiming credit for sustaining the Rides and apportioning the financial costs and benefits stemming from the Rides. Similar disputes over which organization deserved credit, who would pay the bills, and who was reaping the media publicity troubled or followed virtually every other major southern movement effort of the early and mid-1960s.

Unfortunately, organizational competition for publicity and funds was not the only debilitating type of rivalry that troubled the movement. Additionally, and less understandably, there was also, in some instances, intense personal envy and jealousy on the part of some organization heads towards others. Far and away the strongest, most constant and most important example of such petty personal resentment was the intense antipathy that NAACP executive secretary Roy Wilkins developed for SCLC President Martin Luther King, Jr. Already a strong animus as early as 1957–1958, Wilkins' dislike for King and King's public prominence seems to have stemmed principally from a profound unhappiness that someone other than him, the head of the NAACP, would be viewed by almost all Americans as the primary symbol, spokesman and leader of the civil rights struggle and black America.

What most deserves attention is not the often-unpleasant details of these organizational and personal antipathies, but the extremely debilitating effects these rivalries had in and around the movement. These harmful effects can be categorized under three broad headings: the damage that was done among the national organizations themselves, the harm that was done to local allies and activists, and the impairments these tensions caused the movement with actual and potential "external" supporters such as white church groups, labor chieftains and federal government officials. Within the major civil rights groups, a dismaying amount of time, energy and effort was devoted to fanning, parrying or otherwise coping with these internecine conflicts. Although some civil rights staffers, such as Wilkins and Gloster Current of the NAACP, seem—based on their own surviving office files in the NAACP Papers at the Library of Congress—to have positively enjoyed such private verbal attacks on movement colleagues, even for those activists who loathed and avoided such negative jousting, the petty bickering constituted a regular distraction and wasteful diversion.

Often more dismaying and painful was the effect that these interorganizational conflicts had on indigenous local activists who were at first puzzled and then depressed as the reality of national group rivalries became clear to them. In Albany in 1961–1962, in Jackson in 1963, and in many other locales throughout the early and mid-1960s, local black civic activists learned again and again that some of the national civil rights groups, the NAACP in particular, on occasion expended as much energy in competing with other movement organizations as in combatting segregation.

Perhaps most harmfully for the movement, these internal rivalries had a considerable impact—oftentimes an excessive impact—on allied white organizations, which sometimes seem to have cited these internecine problems as grounds—or as an excuse—for moderating the amount of active support they would offer for movement initiatives. Even more notably, the movement's splits also became a prime topic of discussion and analysis within the uppermost reaches of the federal government. Justice Department aides and White House staffers repeatedly pondered how to respond to initiatives from King or Wilkins in such a way as to not offend one or the other; at the height of the Birmingham crisis, as President Kennedy and his top Cabinet officers considered what actions to take, Attorney General Robert Kennedy reminded his brother and the others present that they had to take into account the fact that "Roy Wilkins hates Martin Luther King" (White House Tape #88-4, 5/20/63, JFK Library).

Professor Nancy Weiss is correct to emphasize that the multiplicity of civil rights organizations often worked to the strategic political advantage of the movement; white officials at both the local and federal level often dealt more responsively with some black spokesmen, such as King and Wilkins, simply because they were fearful of otherwise having to cope with more "radical" elements in the movement, particularly SNCC. On one occasion, John Kennedy went so far as to tell a visiting delegation of white Birmingham leaders that they ought to be thankful, rather than upset, at having Martin Luther King and SCLC focusing upon their city; otherwise, Kennedy warned, they would be faced with those "sons of bitches" in SNCC who had "an investment in violence" (White House Tape #112-6, 9/23/63, JFK Library).

Professor Weiss also is correct to focus considerable attention on "CUCRL," the Council for United Civil Rights Leadership, an important movement forum whose role has often been misconstrued when not ignored altogether. Nonetheless, it is essential to appreciate the admixture of motives that lay behind the mid-1963 creation of CUCRL: first, a firm desire on the part of wealthy white movement supporters such as Taconic Foundation President Stephen R. Currier to stabilize if not eliminate the increasingly visible and hostile competition between civil rights groups for contributors' dollars; second, a wish to moderate the southern movement's increasingly aggressive and demanding tone by giving NAACP chief Wilkins and National Urban League head Whitney Young, a good friend of Currier's, a regular and intimate forum for propounding their views to the more direct action-oriented leaders of SNCC, CORE and SCLC; and, third, an intent to exert some amount of control over SNCC's angriest inclinations by centralizing at least a part of movement fundraising and using the resulting allocation process as a carrot-and-stick inducement for SNCC to follow a "responsible" course.

While Professor Weiss may be overestimating the positive value that the CUCRL discussion meetings had for at least a good number of civil rights organization heads, several of whom often sent deputies rather than attend in person, it is more important to recognize and appreciate CUCRL for what it was, a modestly-successful and relatively short-lived response to the centrifugal, competitive tensions within the civil rights movement that even as early as 1963 threatened to rend the black freedom struggle into openly divided camps. Although in large part that public break was postponed until mid-1966, scholars would err if they excessively minimized the deleterious effects that the movement's internal divisions were having even well before that time. Just as they must avoid an overly-narrow conception of leadership and an excessive focus of their research attentions on the nationally-oriented civil rights organizations alone, so must they also, when they do look at those groups and their top executives, do so with an analytically critical eye that allows them to weigh accurately, rather than overstate, the contributions that those organizations made to the black freedom struggle during the 1950s and 1960s.

Appendices

Sites of the
Civil Rights Movement

Acronyms of Organizations

ACMHR Alabama Christian Movement for Human Rights

BPP Black Panther Party

BSCP Brotherhood of Sleeping Car Porters

COHAR Committee on Appeal for Human Rights

COFO Council of Federated Organizations

CORE Congress of Racial Equality

CUCRL Council for United Civil Rights Leadership

MFDP Mississippi Freedom Democratic Party

MIA Montgomery Improvement Association

NAACP National Association for the Advancement of Colored People

SCLC Southern Christian Leadership Conference

SDS Students for a Democratic Society

SNCC Student Nonviolent Coordinating Committee

UNIA Universal Negro Improvement Association

For Discussion

Chapter One

1. Does W.E.B. Du Bois believe that civil rights for blacks are obtainable for the asking? Why or why not? What reasons does he give for his argument that black people should continue to insist on voting power and civil rights?

2. Booker T. Washington secretly worked against Jim Crow laws by quietly financing early court cases against segregation and by protecting blacks from lynch mobs. Does this revelation strengthen the case he makes for accommodation in his Atlanta speech or provide more grounds for Du Bois's criticisms?

3. In what ways do both Marcus Garvey and James Weldon Johnson appeal, directly and indirectly, to black pride? Which author do you find more convincing? Why?

4. Some scholars find great similarities between the arguments of Marcus Garvey and those of Malcolm X (found in chapter 3). Do you agree or disagree that their arguments are alike? Explain your answer.

5. In the 1950s many southerners viewed the NAACP as a dangerous and subversive radical group; some southern states succeeded in outlawing its existence. In the 1960s many black civil rights activists viewed the NAACP as a timid and conservative organization that was too beholden to its white supporters. Could any part of Marshall's speech be cited to make either of these cases? Explain.

6. "Nothing counts but pressure," argues A. Philip Randolph. What kind of pressure is he talking about? Is this a position Thurgood Marshall also takes? Explain your answer.

Chapter Two

1. Some critics of *Brown v. Board of Education* have accused the Supreme Court of substituting sociological concerns for law as the basis for its decision. Is the opinion explaining the reasons for the *Brown* verdict open to such an accusation? Explain your answer.

2. Do the writers and signers of the "Southern Manifesto" endorse outright defiance of *Brown v. Board of Education*? What actions do they propose?

3. What arguments does Herbert Ravenel Sass make about blacks in the South and about segregation? What does he believe whites in other parts of America think about race?

4. What have been the effects of segregation in America, according to Benjamin E. Mays? How, given his arguments presented here, might he respond to the statements made by Sass?

Chapter Three

1. What questions does James Farmer pose to Malcolm X? Does Malcolm X directly and/or successfully answer Farmer's questions? Explain your answer.

2. What criticisms of civil rights organizations and of Farmer himself does Malcolm X make? Do you believe his attacks weaken or strengthen his main points? Explain your answer.

3. What personal experiences of the Freedom Rides does Farmer describe? How do these anecdotes support his arguments?

4. What significance does Malcolm X attach to international events occurring in Africa and elsewhere? How do such events affect what is happening in America, according to him?

5. What objections do the Alabama clergymen make concerning the civil rights demonstrations? What alternatives to demonstrations do they propose?

6. What justification does Martin Luther King Jr. make for breaking the law? What distinction does he make between the actions of civil rights activists and those of people resisting racial integration?

7. Both Martin Luther King Jr. and the Alabama clergymen are speaking as moral leaders making moral arguments. What is the source of their moral authority? What arguments do they make questioning each other's claims to pass moral judgments? Who, in your view, makes a better claim to moral leadership? Explain.

8. What dissatisfaction does Loren Miller express toward liberals? Might this be mitigated by greater participation in the civil rights movement by whites in the South, as Anne Braden suggests? Why or why not?

9. Which of the arguments for and against nonviolence by Martin Luther King Jr., Horace Julian Bond, and Howard Zinn are philosophical? Which are tactical? Explain your answer.

10. Is it accurate or fair to say that Zinn endorses violence in his article? Why or why not?

11. According to Pauli Murray and the people interviewed by Charlayne Hunt, are the struggles for racial and sexual equality necessarily mutually exclusive? Why or why not? Defend your own opinion on this question.

Chapter Four

1. Richard B. Russell described John F. Kennedy's speech as appealing "to the emotions" rather than to reason. Do you agree or disagree? To which emotions is Kennedy appealing? Does Russell himself attempt to appeal to certain emotions as well? Explain.

2. Russell links civil rights legislation with communism. What connections does he draw between the two? How convincing is his argument that this association exists?

3. Lyndon B. Johnson and David Lawrence both appeal to the Constitution to support their positions. Which parts of the Constitution do they emphasize? Can Lawrence's constitutional arguments be characterized as the more legalistic of the two? Why or why not?

Chapter Five

1. Do Bayard Rustin, James Farmer, and the Black Panther Party agree on what problems face blacks in America? How would you summarize their fundamental differences concerning these problems and their possible solutions.

2. Do the views Farmer presents here represent a change of thought from that expressed in his debate with Malcolm X (in chapter 3)? Explain your answer.

3. Is Stokely Carmichael guilty of "reverse racism" in his arguments for black power? Why or why not?

4. What similarities, if any, exist between the opinions found in the viewpoints of this chapter, especially those of Farmer, Carmichael, and the Black Panther Party, with the views of Booker T. Washington and Marcus Garvey in chapter 1?

Chapter Six

1. Why were civil rights organizations unable to cooperate as effectively after 1965 as they had in previous years, according to Nancy J. Weiss?

2. What assertions does David J. Garrow make about the Council for United Civil Rights Leadership (CUCRL)? Do his claims, if true, significantly weaken Weiss's arguments about the organization? Explain.

3. What point is Garrow making when he describes what he calls the "overlooked" heroes of the civil rights movement?

General

1. Were the goals of the civil rights movement fundamentally radical or conservative? Cite viewpoints in support of your answer.

2. What generalizations, if any, can be made concerning the viewpoints of the black authors in this book as compared with those of the white authors? Are such generalizations worth considering? Why or why not?

Chronology

1890	The state of Mississippi adopts poll taxes and literacy tests to disenfranchise black voters.
1895	Booker T. Washington delivers his Atlanta Exposition speech, which accepts segregation of the races.
1896	The Supreme Court rules in *Plessy v. Ferguson* that separate but equal treatment of the races is constitutional.
1900–1915	Over one thousand blacks are lynched in the states of the former Confederacy.
1905	The Niagara Movement is founded by W.E.B. Du Bois and other black leaders to urge more direct action to achieve black civil rights.
1909	The National Association for the Advancement of Colored People (NAACP) is organized.
1910	National Urban League is founded to help the conditions of urban African Americans.
1925	Black nationalist leader Marcus Garvey is convicted of mail fraud.
1928	For the first time in the 20th century an African American is elected to Congress.
1931	Farrad Muhammad establishes in Detroit what will become the Black Muslim Movement.
1933	The NAACP files—and loses—its first suit against segregation and discrimination in education.
1938	The Supreme Court orders the admission of a black applicant to the University of Missouri Law School.
1941	A. Philip Randolph threatens a massive march on Washington unless the Roosevelt administration takes measures to ensure black employment in defense industries; Roosevelt agrees to establish Fair Employment Practices Committee (FEPC).
1942	The Congress of Racial Equality (CORE) is organized in Chicago.
1943	Race riots in Detroit and Harlem cause black leaders to ask their followers to be less demanding in asserting their commitment to civil rights; A. Philip Randolph breaks ranks to call for civil disobedience against Jim Crow schools and railroads.

1946	The Supreme Court, in *Morgan v. The Commonwealth of Virginia*, rules that state laws requiring racial segregation on buses violates the Constitution when applied to interstate passengers.
April 1947	Jackie Robinson breaks the color line in major league baseball.
April 9–23, 1947	Bayard Rustin organizes integrated group trips on trains and buses through Kentucky, Tennessee, North Carolina, and Virginia.
October 29, 1947	*To Secure These Rights*, the report by the President's Committee on Civil Rights, is released; the commission, appointed by President Harry S. Truman, calls for the elimination of racial segregation and recommends government action to secure civil rights for all Americans.
July 26, 1948	President Harry S. Truman issues an executive order desegregating the armed services.
June 1950	The NAACP decides to make its legal strategy a full-scale attack on educational segregation.
May 17, 1954	In *Brown v. Board of Education* the Supreme Court declares separate educational facilities "inherently unequal."
July 11, 1954	First White Citizens Council meeting is held in Mississippi.
September 1954	School year begins with the integration of 150 formerly segregated school districts in eight states; many other school districts remain segregated.
May 31, 1955	The Supreme Court, rejecting the NAACP's plea for complete and total desegregation by September 1955, orders desegregation "with all deliberate speed."
September 23, 1955	An all-white jury finds defendants innocent of murdering black teenager Emmett Till after nationally publicized trial; the defendants later confess to the killing.
November 1955	The Interstate Commerce Commission (ICC) bans racial segregation in all facilities and vehicles engaged in interstate transportation.
December 1, 1955	Rosa Parks is arrested for refusing to give up her bus seat to a white person; the action triggers a bus boycott in Montgomery, Alabama, led by Martin Luther King Jr.
January 30, 1956	The home of Martin Luther King Jr. is bombed.
February 3, 1956	Autherine Lucy wins a federal court order admitting her to the University of Alabama only to have the university permanently "expel" her; the University of Alabama remains segregated for seven more years.

March 12, 1956	101 members of Congress from the South sign the "Southern Manifesto," decrying the *Brown v. Board of Education* decision.
June 1, 1956	Alabama outlaws the NAACP.
December 21, 1956	The Montgomery bus boycott ends after the city receives U.S. Supreme Court order to desegregate city buses.
January 11, 1957	Martin Luther King Jr. and a number of southern black clergymen create the Southern Christian Leadership Conference (SCLC).
August 29, 1957	Congress passes the first civil rights legislation since Reconstruction: The Civil Rights Act of 1957 establishes a civil rights division at the Justice Department and provides penalties for violating the voting rights of a U.S. citizen.
September 4, 1957	On the orders of Arkansas governor Orval Faubus, Arkansas National Guardsmen block nine black students from entering Central High School in Little Rock.
September 24, 1957	President Dwight D. Eisenhower dispatches one thousand paratroopers of the 101st Airborne Division to Little Rock to enforce a federal court order integrating Central High School.
September 29, 1958	The Supreme Court, in *Cooper v. Aaron*, rules that "evasive schemes" cannot be used to circumvent school desegregation.
October 25, 1958	Ten thousand students hold a Youth March for Integrated Schools in Washington, D.C.
1959	Sit-in campaigns by college students desegregate eating facilities in St. Louis, Chicago, and Bloomington, Indiana; the Tennessee Christian Leadership Conference holds brief sit-ins in Nashville department stores.
February 1, 1960	Four black students stage a sit-in at a Woolworth's lunch counter in Greensboro, North Carolina; the sit-in movement to desegregate southern restaurants, hotels, movie theaters, libraries, and parks spreads to other southern states.
April 1960	The Student Nonviolent Coordinating Committee (SNCC) is formed at a student conference in Raleigh, North Carolina.
April 19, 1960	Twenty-five hundred students and community members in Nashville, Tennessee, stage a march on city hall—the first major demonstration of the civil rights movement—following the bombing of the home of a black lawyer.

May 6, 1960	President Eisenhower signs civil rights legislation authorizing federal judges to appoint referees to assist blacks seeking to register and to vote.
June 30, 1960	Zaire becomes the first of eleven African countries to gain independence within one year, inspiring many American blacks.
October 19, 1960	Martin Luther King Jr. is arrested during an Atlanta sit-in; Democratic presidential candidate John F. Kennedy telephones Mrs. King to express concern.
November 8, 1960	John F. Kennedy is elected president by a narrow margin.
December 5, 1960	The Supreme Court rules that discrimination in bus terminal restaurants is a violation of the Interstate Commerce Act.
March 13, 1961	James Farmer, national director of CORE, calls for volunteers to conduct "Freedom Rides" throughout the South.
Spring 1961	Martin Luther King Jr. and President John F. Kennedy hold a secret meeting at which King learns that the new president will not push hard for new civil rights legislation.
May 1961	White and black Freedom Riders are arrested and assaulted in North and South Carolina and Alabama; one bus is burned by a white mob. The CORE-sponsored Freedom Ride disbands and the movement is taken over by SNCC volunteers; the Kennedy administration sends federal marshals to assure the safety of the Freedom Riders.
June 16, 1961	U.S. attorney general Robert Kennedy meets with civil rights leaders and urges them to forgo demonstrations and Freedom Rides and to concentrate on winning the right to vote.
November 1961	Local black organizations in Albany, Georgia, form the Albany Movement to demonstrate for voting rights and desegregation.
December 1961	The SCLC meets with AFL-CIO leaders to strengthen ties between the two organizations.
December 11–14, 1961	Hundreds of demonstrators participate in marches in Albany, Georgia. Martin Luther King Jr. and aides arrive on December 15.
January 1962	FBI director J. Edgar Hoover writes Attorney General Robert Kennedy concerning Martin Luther King Jr.'s alleged ties to the Communist Party.
May 31, 1962	James Meredith files suit claiming racial discrimination after he is denied admission to the University of Mississippi.

August 1962	Albany Movement ends with many of its goals unmet.
August 7, 1962	A SNCC Voter Registration School opens in Pike County, Mississippi, marking the first such effort in the history of the state.
September 1962	Ku Klux Klan dynamite blasts destroy four black churches in Georgia towns.
September 30, 1962	President Kennedy federalizes the National Guard and sends several hundred federal marshals to Mississippi to guarantee James Meredith's admission to the University of Mississippi Law School over the opposition of Governor Ross Barnett and other whites; two persons are killed in a campus riot.
November 20, 1962	President Kennedy signs an executive order barring racial discrimination in federally financed housing.
February 2, 1963	Martin Luther King Jr. and other SCLC leaders arrive in Birmingham, Alabama, to lead a civil rights campaign; Robert Kennedy labels the effort "ill-timed" and urges King to abandon it.
Spring 1963	CORE takes the lead in protesting discrimination in northern cities.
April 1963	Martin Luther King Jr. opens his campaign to desegregate Birmingham and is arrested on April 12; while incarcerated, King composes his "Letter from Birmingham City Jail."
May 3, 1963	Birmingham police chief Eugene "Bull" Connor turns police dogs and fire hoses against nonviolent demonstrators in Birmingham.
May 5, 1963	Three thousand protesters are jailed in Birmingham—the largest number of people imprisoned at any one time in the history of the civil rights movement.
May 10, 1963	An accord is reached in Birmingham; within ninety days lunch counters, rest rooms, and drinking fountains will be desegregated in the city.
June 11, 1963	Black students Vivian Malone and James Hood enter the University of Alabama despite a demonstration of resistance by Governor George Wallace; in a nationally televised speech President John F. Kennedy calls segregation morally wrong.
June 12, 1963	NAACP field secretary Medgar Evers is shot and killed as he enters his home in Jackson, Mississippi.
June 19, 1963	Leaders of nearly one hundred corporations meet in New York City to pledge financial support for the civil rights movement.

July 18–23, 1963	Riots in Harlem follow the shooting of a fifteen-year-old black youth by an off-duty police officer.
August 28, 1963	Over 250,000 Americans gather at the Lincoln Memorial to urge the passage of civil rights legislation and hear Martin Luther King Jr. deliver his "I Have a Dream" speech. Malcolm X dismisses the march as "the Farce on Washington."
September 15, 1963	Four young girls are killed when a bomb explodes at a Baptist church in Birmingham, Alabama.
October 10, 1963	Attorney General Robert Kennedy authorizes the wiretapping of Martin Luther King Jr.'s home phone in Atlanta.
November 22, 1963	President John F. Kennedy is assassinated; Vice President Lyndon B. Johnson assumes the presidency.
January 8, 1964	President Lyndon B. Johnson calls for passage of a civil rights act in his State of the Union address.
April 26, 1964	SNCC workers organize the Mississippi Freedom Democratic Party (MFDP).
Summer 1964	Enlisting the help of white volunteers, SNCC and CORE seek to register black voters across the South in the "Freedom Summer" campaign.
June 21, 1964	Three civil rights workers, Michael Schwerner and Andrew Goodman, both white New Yorkers, and James Chaney, a black student from Meridian, Mississippi, are murdered near Philadelphia, Mississippi.
July 2, 1964	President Lyndon Johnson signs the Civil Rights Act of 1964, which prohibits discrimination in most public accommodations, authorizes the federal government to withhold funds from programs practicing discrimination, and creates the Equal Employment Opportunity Commission.
July 29, 1964	Several national civil rights leaders call for a moratorium on mass marches and demonstrations until after the November 3 presidential election.
August 22–26, 1964	At the Democratic National Convention in Atlantic City, New Jersey, delegates of the Mississippi Freedom Democratic Party ask to be seated as the legitimate Democratic Party of Mississippi; they refuse the compromise offer of two delegate seats.
September 14, 1964	New York City begins a program to end segregation by busing students.
November 3, 1964	Lyndon B. Johnson, with heavy black support, wins the presidential election by a wide margin over Barry Goldwater.
December 10, 1964	Martin Luther King Jr. is awarded the Nobel Peace Prize.

February 18, 1965	Civil rights marcher Jimmie Lee Jackson is shot and killed in Marion, Alabama.
February 21, 1965	Malcolm X is assassinated while addressing a rally of his followers in New York City; three black men are ultimately convicted of the murder.
March 7, 1965	"Bloody Sunday": six hundred marchers outside Selma, Alabama, are attacked by state troopers with nightsticks and tear gas.
March 9, 1965	Martin Luther King Jr. leads a voting rights march in Selma but turns back before a state trooper barricade.
March 11, 1965	The death of white Unitarian minister James J. Reeb following a beating by local whites in Selma triggers demonstrations in many northern cities.
March 15, 1965	President Johnson delivers a televised speech to a joint session of Congress to request passage of a voting rights act.
March 21–25, 1965	Following a federal judge's court order allowing the march, and under federalized protection, Martin Luther King Jr. leads a voting rights march from Selma to Montgomery, Alabama.
August 6, 1965	President Johnson signs the Voting Rights Act of 1965, which outlaws literacy tests and empowers the Justice Department to supervise federal elections in seven southern states.
August 11–16, 1965	Rioting in the black ghetto of Watts in Los Angeles leads to thirty-five deaths, nine hundred injuries, and over thirty-five hundred arrests.
January 1966	Martin Luther King Jr. moves to Chicago to begin his first civil rights campaign in a northern city.
March 25, 1966	The Supreme Court bans poll taxes for all elections.
May 16, 1966	Stokely Carmichael replaces John Lewis as chairman of SNCC.
June 6, 1966	James Meredith is shot by a sniper while on a one-man "march against fear" in Mississippi.
June 7–26, 1966	Other civil rights leaders, including King and Carmichael, complete the "Meredith march"; the slogan "black power" is first used by Carmichael.
July 1966	The CORE national convention adopts a resolution in support of black power; the NAACP convention officially opposes the doctrine.
August 5, 1966	Martin Luther King Jr. leads an integrated march in Chicago and is wounded when whites throw bottles and bricks at demonstrators.
October 1966	The Black Panther Party (BPP) is founded in Oakland, California.

December 1966	SNCC votes to exclude whites from membership.
February 25, 1967	Martin Luther King Jr. delivers his first speech devoted entirely to the war in Vietnam, which he calls "one of history's most cruel and senseless wars"; his position causes estrangement with President Johnson and is criticized by the NAACP.
May 4, 1967	Alabama sheriffs James Clark and Al Lingo are among those who fail to get renominated in Democratic primaries that have significant black participation.
May 10–11, 1967	Rioting at all-black Jackson State College in Mississippi leads to one death and two serious injuries.
June 13, 1967	Thurgood Marshall is the first black to be nominated to serve on the Supreme Court.
June 19, 1967	A federal judge orders Washington, D.C., schools to end de facto school segregation.
July 1967	Rioting in the black ghetto of Newark, New Jersey, leaves 23 dead and 725 injured; rioting in Detroit leave 43 dead and 324 injured; President Johnson appoints Governor Otto Kerner of Illinois to head a commission to investigate recent urban riots.
February 29, 1968	The Kerner Commission issues its report, warning that the nation is "moving toward two societies, one black, one white—separate and unequal."
March 18, 1968	Martin Luther King Jr. travels to Memphis, Tennessee, to help settle a garbage workers strike.
April 4, 1968	Martin Luther King Jr. is assassinated by James Earl Ray in Memphis, Tennessee, precipitating riots in more than one hundred cities.
April 11, 1968	Congress passes civil rights legislation prohibiting racial discrimination in the sale or rental of housing.
May 11, 1968	Ralph Abernathy, Martin Luther King Jr.'s successor as head of the SCLC, leads Poor People's Campaign in Washington, D.C.
October 30, 1969	The Supreme Court replaces its 1954 decision calling for "all deliberate speed" in school desegregation by unanimously ordering that all segregation in schools must end "at once."

Annotated Bibliography

Ralph Abernathy. *And the Walls Came Tumbling Down*. New York: Harper & Row, 1989. The autobiography of a key aide to Martin Luther King Jr. and King's successor as head of the Southern Christian Leadership Conference (SCLC).

Peter J. Albert and Ronald Hoffman, eds. *Martin Luther King Jr. and the Black Freedom Struggle*. New York: Pantheon Books, 1990. A collection of essays assessing the role of King in the civil rights movement.

Harry S. Ashmore. *The Negroes and the Schools*. Chapel Hill: University of North Carolina Press, 1954. A liberal's response to conservative critics of school desegregation.

James D. Bales. *The Martin Luther King Story*. Tulsa, OK: Christian Crusade Publications, 1967. An early derogatory account of the civil rights leader's character and actions.

Numan V. Bartley. *The Rise of Massive Resistance*. Baton Rouge: Louisiana State University Press, 1969. A study of the impact of race on southern politics during the 1950s.

Sally Belfrage. *Freedom Summer*. New York: Viking, 1965. A first-person account of a civil rights worker in Mississippi in the summer of 1964.

Michal R. Belknap. *Federal Law and Southern Order: Racial Violence and Constitutional Conflict in the Post-Brown South*. Athens: University of Georgia Press, 1987. A general study of white opposition to the civil rights movement.

Theodore G. Bilbo. *Take Your Choice: Separation or Mongrelization*. Poplarville, MS: Dream House, 1947. A self-published manifesto by the white supremacist Mississippi senator.

Earl Black. *Southern Governors and Civil Rights*. Cambridge, MA: Harvard University Press, 1976. A study of the impact of segregation on southern gubernatorial races during the 1950s and 1960s.

Albert P. Blaustein and Robert L. Zangrando, eds. *Civil Rights and the American Negro*. New York: Trident Press, 1968. Document collection that includes the texts of civil rights legislative acts and important Supreme Court cases.

Tom P. Brady. *Black Monday*. Winona, MS: Association of Citizens' Councils, 1955. An attack on the *Brown v. Board of Education* decision and a call for white resistance to school integration.

Taylor Branch. *Parting the Waters: America in the King Years, 1954–63*. New York: Simon & Schuster, 1988. A massive social history of the United States and of the civil rights movement from 1954 to the death of President Kennedy.

Carl M. Brauer. *John F. Kennedy and the Second Reconstruction*. New York: Columbia University Press, 1977. A generally favorable portrait of the Kennedy administration and its handling of the civil rights issue.

George Breitman. *The Last Year of Malcolm X*. New York: Pathfinder Press, 1967. An examination of the evolution of Malcolm X's thinking just prior to his assassination.

George Breitman, ed. *By Any Means Necessary*. New York: Pathfinder Press, 1970. Speeches of and interviews with Malcolm X.

Elaine Brown. *A Taste of Power: A Black Woman's Story*. New York: Pantheon Books, 1992. A memoir and history of black women and the Black Panther Party.

Stokely Carmichael and Charles V. Hamilton. *Black Power: The Politics of Liberation in America*. New York: Vintage Books, 1967. Manifesto for black power and black liberation cowritten by the head of the Student Nonviolent Coordinating Committee (SNCC).

Clayborne Carson. *In Struggle: SNCC and the Black Awakening of the 1960s*. Cambridge, MA: Harvard University Press, 1981. A thorough history of the Student Nonviolent Coordinating Committee (SNCC) that examines its creation, evolution, and relationship with other civil rights organizations.

Dan T. Carter. *The Politics of Rage: George Wallace, the Origins of the New Conservatism, and the Transformation of American Politics*. New York: Simon & Schuster, 1995. A critical portrait of the Alabama governor, his use of the race issue, and his impact on national politics.

William H. Chafe. *Civilities and Civil Rights*. New York: Oxford University Press, 1980. A detailed case study of the civil rights issue in Greensboro, North Carolina, and the strategy of the sit-in movement.

Eldridge Cleaver. *Soul on Ice*. New York: McGraw-Hill, 1968. Memoir and manifesto by a noted Black Panther of the 1960s.

E. David Cronon. *Black Moses*. Madison: University of Wisconsin Press, 1968. A biography of black nationalist Marcus Garvey.

Harold Cruse. *The Crisis of the Negro Intellectual*. New York: Morrow, 1967. An examination of the radicalization of the civil rights movement in the 1960s.

John Egerton. *Speak Now Against the Day: The Generation Before the Civil Rights Movement in the South*. New York: Knopf, 1994. A history of the South in the 1930s and 1940s and the people who were active on civil rights issues during this time.

Sara Evans. *Personal Politics: The Roots of Women's Liberation in the Civil Rights Movement and the New Left*. New York: Knopf, 1979. A history of the relationship between the black civil rights movement and the women's liberation movement.

James Farmer. *Lay Bare the Heart: An Autobiography of the Civil Rights Movement*. New York: Arbor House, 1985. The autobiography of civil rights leader and longtime head of the Congress on Racial Equality (CORE).

Herbert Garfinkel. *When Negroes March*. New York: Atheneum, 1969. A study of the March on Washington Movement led by A. Philip Randolph during World War II.

David J. Garrow. *Bearing the Cross*. New York: Morrow, 1986. A thorough account of Martin Luther King Jr. and the organization he led, the Southern Christian Leadership Conference (SCLC).

David J. Garrow. *Protest at Selma*. New Haven, CT: Yale University Press, 1978. An account of the historic 1965 march from Selma to Montgomery and its contribution to the passage of the Voting Rights Act of 1965.

David J. Garrow, ed. *We Shall Overcome: The Civil Rights Movement in the United States in the 1950s and 1960s*. Brooklyn, NY: Carlson Publishing, 1989. A three-volume collection of essays and articles on the civil rights movement.

Peter Goldman. *The Death and Life of Malcolm X*. New York: Harper & Row, 1973. A reevaluation of this controversial figure with special emphasis on his final years and his increasing estrangement from the Nation of Islam.

Roger Goldman with David Gallen. *Thurgood Marshall: Justice for All*. New York: Carroll & Graf, 1992. A collection of essays and recollections of Marshall's career, including an essay on Marshall's jurisprudence while on the Supreme Court.

Lino Graglia. *Disaster by Decree*. Ithaca, NY: Cornell University Press, 1976. A critical look at Supreme Court decisions regarding school desegregation.

Louis R. Harlan. *Booker T. Washington*. 2 vols. New York: Oxford University Press, 1972, 1983. Biography of the influential black leader of the early twentieth century.

Brooks Hays. *A Southern Moderate Speaks*. Chapel Hill: University of North Carolina Press, 1959. An Arkansas politician looks at Little Rock Central High School and its controversial desegregation in 1957.

Langston Hughes. *Fight for Freedom: The Story of the NAACP*. New York: Norton, 1962. A history of the National Association for the Advancement of Colored People by the famous black poet.

James J. Kilpatrick. *The Southern Case for School Segregation*. New York: Crowell, 1962. Defense of the segregated South by a noted southern journalist.

Coretta Scott King. *My Life with Martin Luther King Jr*. New York: Holt, Rinehart & Winston, 1969. The autobiography of the widow of Martin Luther King Jr.

Martin Luther King Jr. *Stride Toward Freedom: The Montgomery Story*. New York: Harper & Row, 1958. A first-person account of the Montgomery bus boycott and a statement of black goals in its aftermath.

Martin Luther King Jr. *Where Do We Go from Here? Chaos or Community?* New York: Harper & Row, 1967. An examination of the state of the civil rights movement in the aftermath of the passage of key civil rights legislation and the urban riots of the mid-1960s.

Martin Luther King Jr. *Why We Can't Wait*. New York: Harper & Row, 1963. A plea for nonviolence and for passage of national civil rights legislation.

Richard Kluger. *Simple Justice*. New York: Knopf, 1975. A detailed history of the NAACP and its court battles for school desegregation culminating in the historic 1954 *Brown v. Board of Education* decision.

Richard Lentz. *Symbols, the News Magazines, and Martin Luther King*. Baton Rouge: Louisiana State University Press, 1990. An examination of the coverage of the civil rights movement by the national news media.

Stephen Lesher. *George Wallace: American Populist*. New York: Addison-Wesley, 1994. A generally sympathetic biography of the southern governor who fought school desegregation.

Peter B. Levy, ed. *Let Freedom Ring: A Documentary History of the Civil Rights Movement*. New York: Praeger, 1992. A collection of primary source documents on the civil rights movement.

David Levering Lewis. *W.E.B. Du Bois: Biography of a Race, 1868–1919*. New York: Holt, 1993. First volume of a two-volume study of the noted black intellectual and civil rights activist.

Manning Marable. *Race, Reform, and Rebellion: The Second Reconstruction in Black America, 1945–1982*. 2nd ed. Jackson: University Press of Mississippi, 1991. A broad survey of the black freedom struggle.

Doug McAdam. *Freedom Summer*. New York: Oxford University Press, 1988. A history of the drive for voting rights in Mississippi during the summer of 1964, based largely on a detailed survey of the participants.

August Meier and Elliott Rudwick. *CORE: A Study in the Civil Rights Movement, 1942–1968*. New York: Oxford University Press, 1973. A comprehensive history of the Congress of Racial Equality.

Kay Mills. *This Little Light of Mine: The Life of Fannie Lou Hamer*. New York: Penguin, 1992. A biography of the sharecropper who led the Mississippi Freedom Democratic Party to the 1964 Democratic National Convention.

Aldon D. Morris. *The Origins of the Civil Rights Movement: Black Communities Organizing for Change*. New York: Free Press, 1984. A history of the civil rights movement that stresses the importance of grassroots activities and leaders.

Victor Navasky. *Kennedy Justice*. New York: Atheneum, 1971. A critical look at the Kennedy administration and its handling of civil rights.

Michael Newton. *Bitter Grain*. Los Angeles: Holloway House, 1991. A biography of Huey Newton and a history of the Black Panther Party he helped found.

Stephen B. Oates. *Let the Trumpet Sound: A Life of Martin Luther King Jr.* New York: HarperPerennial, 1994. A richly detailed biography that concentrates on King's political life after 1955.

Martin Oppenheimer. *The Sit-In Movement of 1960*. Brooklyn NY: Carlson Publishing, 1989. A sociological study of the student-led sit-in movement.

Kenneth O'Reilly. *"Racial Matters": The FBI's Secret File on Black America, 1960–1972*. New York: Free Press, 1989. An account of the activities of the Federal Bureau of Investigation during the civil rights movement and how the agency under director J. Edgar Hoover spent greater energy spying on black leaders than in enforcing federal civil rights laws.

Hugh Pearson. *The Shadow of the Panther*. Reading, MA: Addison-Wesley, 1994. A highly critical history of the Black Panther Party.

Paula F. Pfeffer. *A. Philip Randolph: Pioneer of the Civil Rights Movement*. Baton Rouge: Louisiana State University Press, 1990. A biography and assessment of the labor leader and organizer of the March on Washington Movement.

Fred Powledge. *Free At Last? The Civil Rights Movement and the People Who Made It*. Boston: Little, Brown, 1991. A detailed account of the civil rights movement written by a journalist who covered many of the events.

Howell Raines. *My Soul Is Rested: Movement Days in the Deep South Remembered*. New York: G.P. Putnam's Sons, 1977. An oral history of the civil rights movement from the perspective of those who participated in it.

Armstead Robinson and Patricia Sullivan, eds. *New Directions in Civil Rights Studies*. Charlottesville: University of Virginia Press, 1991. A collection of essays by historians and other scholars on the civil rights movement.

Jo Ann Robinson. *The Montgomery Bus Boycott and the Women Who Started It*. Edited by David J. Garrow. Knoxville: University of Tennessee Press, 1987. A memoir of a participant in this historic boycott that did so much to establish the civil rights movement as a mass-action movement.

Bayard Rustin. *Down the Line*. Chicago: Quadrangle, 1971. The collected writings of a noted civil rights leader and pacifist.

Harvard Sitkoff. *The Struggle for Black Equality*. New York: Hill & Wang, 1981. A brief general history of the modern civil rights movement from the 1954 Supreme Court school desegregation ruling to the onset of the Reagan presidency.

Thomas Sowell. *Civil Rights: Rhetoric or Reality?* New York: Morrow, 1984. A polemical challenge to traditional civil rights thinking and political strategy.

Herman E. Talmadge. *You and Segregation.* Birmingham, AL: Vulcan, 1955. A defense of racial segregation by a prominent Georgia politician.

James M. Washington, ed. *A Testament of Hope.* San Francisco: Harper & Row, 1986. A generous compilation of the important writings of Martin Luther King Jr.

Denton L. Watson. *Lion in the Lobby.* New York: Morrow, 1990. A study of the role of Clarence Mitchell and the NAACP in the passage of civil rights legislation.

Robert Weisbrot. *Freedom Bound: A History of America's Civil Rights Movement.* New York: Norton, 1990. A general survey of the civil rights movement.

Nancy J. Weiss. *Whitney M. Young and the Struggle for Civil Rights.* Princeton, NJ: Princeton University Press, 1989. A biography of the person who led the Urban League from 1961 to 1971.

Charles Whalen and Barbara Whalen. *The Long Debate: A Legislative History of the 1964 Civil Rights Act.* New York: New American Library, 1985. A history of the national legislation that prohibited discrimination in employment and access to public facilities.

Juan Williams. *Eyes on the Prize: America's Civil Rights Years, 1954–1965.* New York: Viking, 1987. The companion volume to the acclaimed PBS television documentary on the civil rights movement.

Robert Williams. *Negroes with Guns.* New York: Marzani & Munsell, 1962. A controversial call for black Americans to reject peaceful integration.

Allan Wolk. *The Presidency and Black Civil Rights.* Rutherford NJ: Fairleigh Dickinson University Press, 1971. An analysis of presidential decision making on civil rights from Eisenhower through Nixon.

C. Vann Woodward. *The Strange Career of Jim Crow.* 3rd ed. New York: Oxford University Press. A masterly description of southern society and race relations prior to the civil rights movement.

William D. Workman Jr. *The Case for the South.* New York: Devon-Adair, 1960. A defense of southern racial practices by a South Carolina editor.

Malcolm X. *The Autobiography of Malcolm X.* With the assistance of Alex Haley. New York: Grove Press, 1965. The autobiography of the Black Muslim leader who was critical of the nonviolent civil rights movement.

Howard Zinn. *The New Abolitionists.* Boston: Beacon Press, 1964. An account of the Student Nonviolent Coordinating Committee by a sympathetic participant in the civil rights movement.

Index